Encyclopaedia
Anatomica

Encyclopaedia Anatomica

A Complete Collection of Anatomical Waxes
Vollständige Sammlung anatomischer Wachse
Collection complète des cires anatomiques

With contributions by | Mit Beiträgen von | Textes de
Monika v. Düring, Georges Didi-Huberman, Marta Poggesi

Photographs by | Fotografien von | Photographies de
Saulo Bambi

*Museo di Storia Naturale dell'Università di Firenze,
sezione di zoologia La Specola*

TASCHEN

KÖLN LONDON MADRID NEW YORK PARIS TOKYO

Contents
Inhalt
Sommaire

The Wax Figure Collection in 'La Specola' in Florence
Marta Poggesi

**The History of
the Collection**

When Peter Leopold of Habsburg-Lotharingen (1747–1792), Grand Duke of Tuscany (ill. p. 7), decided in 1771 to bring together all the 'scientific' collections from the various galleries in the Grand Duchy, the result was an innovation that was unique not only in Europe but anywhere in the world.

Much earlier than other potentates this enlightened ruler – an enthusiastic student of the natural sciences – had understood the importance of the sciences for the cultural advancement of any society. The first thing he did was to examine the various ways in which the findings of science could be made accessible to all those who were interested.

And indeed the Imperial Regio Museo di Fisica e Storia Naturale (The Imperial-Royal Museum for Physics and Natural History, later widely known as 'La Specola', which means 'observatory' in Italian) was the first of its kind, in that from the day of its opening on 21 February 1775 it admitted the general public to its collections. It is true that there were separate opening hours for the upper and the lower classes: the latter – "provided they were cleanly clothed" – were allowed to visit between 8.00 and 10.00 in the morning, which then left enough time before the "intelligent and well-educated people" were admitted at 1.00 in the afternoon. But however discriminatory this distinction may seem to us today, nevertheless one can still sense how innovative it was to open the museum's doors to this broader public.

These collections had originally been started by the Medici family; immensely important as patrons and connoisseurs of the arts they had also done much to promote the sciences. Ample evidence of this may be seen in the Accademia del Cimento (1657–1667) which had amongst its staff such famous scientists as Redi, Magalotti and Galileo's favourite student, Viviani. After the death of Giangastone, the last descendant of the family, the Grand Duchy of Tuscany went to Francis III of Habsburg-Lotharingen, who decided to have an inventory made of all the treasures in his residence. This task was entrusted to the physician and natural historian Giovanni Targioni-Tozzetti (1712–1783), who completed the work in just under a year in 1763/64.

When Peter Leopold succeeded his father to the throne in 1765 –

after the latter had become Emperor of Austria – he therefore found that the groundwork for a re-organisation of the collection had already been done. The work involved in this major undertaking fell to Felice Fontana (1730–1805; ill. p. 29), by profession a teacher of logic at the University of Pisa, but also an anatomist, physicist, chemist and, above all, an internationally renowned physiologist. He devoted himself to restructuring the buildings with such passion that by the end of 1771 the first items could already be moved into the new rooms. As early as 1771 the Grand Duke had already bought the Palace of the Torrigiani in the via Romana, very close to the Palazzo Pitti. He had also bought a number of neighbouring houses and had commissioned the Abbot Felice Fontana of Rovereto to draw up plans for alterations to these buildings in order to create a home for his scientific collections. As director of the new museum, in the early years Fontana travelled throughout Europe acquiring books and collections and establishing contacts in different countries. As a result the museum in Florence became one of the most important museums of its day, not least for its rich scientific library.

Bust of Peter Leopold of Habsburg-Lotharingen

Büste von Peter Leopold von Habsburg-Lothringen

Buste de Pierre Léopold de Habsbourg-Lorraine

Fontana directed the museum until his death. Throughout this time Giovanni Fabbroni was at his side – at first as his assistant (and constant antagonist) and from 1784 onwards as the museum's deputy director, accompanying Fontana on numerous journeys. In 1805 he took over as Director but only for one year.

It is interesting to note that the money to construct the museum for physics and natural history (and many other projects instigated by Peter Leopold) was raised by the sale of valuable objects once owned by the Medici family – despite a testament left by the Palatinate Electress Anna Maria Luisa (1688–1743), Giangastone's sister, which decreed that the estate of the Medici family should in its entirety and irrevocably remain in the ownership of the city of Florence.

The core holdings of the museum, which came principally from the Uffizi, consisted of collections (minerals and shells, for instance), natural history curiosities from the era of the Medici family, Galileo's instruments and equipment from the Accademia del Cimento as well as four wax figures by the Sicilian sculptor Giulio Gaetano Zumbo.

In 1771 a ceroplastic studio was set up together with other workshops essential to the running of the museum (a carpentry shop, a glaziery and a taxidermy studio): these will be discussed in more detail later in this essay. Keen to have astronomy and meteorology included in the museum as well, in 1780 Peter Leopold commissioned the architect Gaspare Paoletti (who had earlier been involved in the restructuring of the palace) to build the Osservatorio Astronomico (the so-called 'little tower'). This was later to be the source of the name 'Specola', which means observatory. The work turned into a major project which led to the building's being much larger than originally planned. In fact many experts had advised against it and had advocated building on the Acetri hills instead. In 1789, the year of the completion, a part of the Boboli Park was incorporated as the museum's Botanic Garden (ill. p. 8).

After the death of his brother Josef in 1790, Peter Leopold became Emperor of Austria and put Tuscany into the hands of his second son Ferdinand III (1769–1824), who had neither his father's vision nor his skill in matters of government. But the times were also against him: Napoleonic expansionism forced the Lotharingians to give up Tuscany which, after various complications, went to the Bourbons of Parma. During this period the museum started to organise the teaching of

'La Specola' seen from the Boboli Garden; engraving from the late 17th century

Die Specola vom Boboli-Garten aus gesehen; Kupferstich vom Ende des 17. Jahrhunderts

La Specola vue du jardin Boboli ; gravure de la fin du XVIIe siècle scientific subjects, which was continued in 1814 after the restoration of the Lotharingians.

Under Ferdinand's rule the museum had to survive a period of unrest and lost a great deal of the scientific importance attached to it in its early years when it enjoyed a reputation as one of the most important centres of learning in Europe according to illustrious foreign authors such as Goethe and Bernouilli. Ferdinand also had major structural alterations made to the palace: in 1820, under the direction of the architect Pasquale Poccianti a corridor was constructed joining the Specola with the *Meridiana* wing of the Palazzo Pitti, so that the Poccianti Corridor now extends the Vasari Corridor – which leads from the Palazzo Vecchio via the Uffizi to the Palazzo Pitti – as far as the Specola.

After his death in 1824 Ferdinand was succeeded by his son Leopold II (1797–1870), affectionately nicknamed 'Canapone' by the Florentines on account of his blond hair. It was thanks to him that the teaching and lectures in the sciences were reinstated, with a particular emphasis on the applied sciences relevant to agriculture and the cultivation of reclaimed land. During his time as regent the Tribuna di Galileo was constructed. Dedicated to the memory of one of the greatest scientists, it was inaugurated in 1841 on the occasion of the third congress of Italian scientists in Florence. The Tribuna is a large room on the first floor of the building and was partially rebuilt by the architect Giuseppe Marelli. Work was started in 1830, the initial plan being simply to add an apse to the existing room, but the scheme was then altered in accordance with the wishes of the Grand Duke: in order to lend more weight to his intended celebration of Galileo and his work, the whole room was to be dedicated to the renowned scientist. As well as a statue, it was to contain all the surviving Galileo memorabilia and the instruments from the Accademia del Cimento. The building of the Tribuna, one of the few examples of late Neo-Classicism in Florence, led to a number of important alterations to the palace, most particularly to the floors below the Tribuna. It also meant that a part of the courtyard was roofed over. The room itself was decorated specifically and exclusively with Tuscan marble and with works by artists – sculptors and painters – who were also exclusively from Tuscany.

After the fall of Leopold II – the last Grand Duke of Tuscany – in 1859 the Istituto di Studi Superiori e di Perfezionamento (Institute of Higher Study and Further Education) was founded. In 1923 this became

Original drawing of a recumbent figure, called *lo spellato* (Room XXVIII, display cabinet no. 740)

Originalzeichnung einer liegenden Figur, genannt *lo spellato* (Saal XXVIII, Vitrine Nr. 740)

Dessin original d'une figure couchée appelée *lo spellato* (salle XXVIII, vitrine n° 740)

the University of Florence. The museum buildings became part of the Institute and now contain the University's Department of Physics and Natural Sciences.

While the founding of the Institute was of inestimable importance it also led to the breaking up of the museum into its various disciplines, which – along with the relevant collections and libraries – had progressively to be relocated at other sites in view of the constantly increasing numbers of students. Even the resistance of many scientists at the time could not hinder this process, with the result that the historical buildings in the via Romana now only contain the zoological collections and the bulk of the anatomical ceroplastics.

The Early Days of Anatomical Wax Models

Wax has been used to make models since time immemorial; it has always been a popular material for artists, both for aesthetic and for technical reasons, because it is easy to work and allows the finished piece to be cast in metal afterwards. It was used widely for religious motifs such as statues of saints or cribs and votive panels. At the time of the Renaissance and throughout 17th century huge numbers of wax figures could be found in churches, particularly in Orsammichele and in Santissima Annunziata. These included limbs, organs or parts of organs as well as portraits, objects and statues – often even life-sized. In the 17th century, wax models were also increasingly used for scientific purposes.

Although the state – and even more so the Church – did its best to prevent corpses being used for anatomical studies and penalised any-one who attempted to do so, by the mid-15th century the first anatomical drawings and treatises were beginning to emerge, generally drawn by great artists and sculptors such as Leonardo da Vinci, Michelangelo, Raphael and Titian, to name but a few. Renowned anatomists such as Fallopio, Cesalpino and Vesalius used drawings by these masters to illus-trate their treatises.

Towards the end of the 17th century Gaetano Giulio Zumbo, working in Bologna where there was a famous school of anatomy, was the first to make anatomical models using coloured waxes. Zumbo came from Syracuse and his works, which are illustrated here, include two male heads (one now in Florence and one in Paris), a female figure (now unfortunately lost) and some other smaller works. Bologna was also the first place to have a proper school of ceroplastics and it was here that the wax modellers working in the museum in Florence during the second half of the 18th century were trained. The painter, sculptor and architect Ercole Lelli (1702–1766) is credited with founding the Bolognese school and, like Zumbo before him, he too made wax models of muscles and inner organs by studying real corpses. He was able to obtain access to the corpses he needed for this work through the support of Cardinal Prospero Lambertini, who became Pope Benedetto XIV in 1740. As an amateur scientist and a man of learning the Cardinal encouraged the study of anatomy at the school in Bologna and bought all the models Lelli made: they are magnificent pieces, now preserved in the Istituto d'Anatomia Umana Normale at the University of Bologna.

Amongst Lelli's assistants were Giovanni Manzolini (1700–1755), who with his wife Anna Morandi (1716–1774) also made numerous models that can likewise still be seen at Bologna University.

At the time, the study of anatomy was progressing throughout Europe but the school of ceroplastics in Florence was in fact a direct offshoot of the school in Bologna. The link was made by the surgeon and child-birth specialist Giuseppe Galletti. Having been much impressed by models made by Lelli and Manzolini, the physician Galetti – together with the wax modeller Giuseppe Ferrini – himself made a number of models in wax and terracotta (now in the Museo di Storia della Scienza in Florence) in order to demonstrate different birth procedures, both normal and with complications.

The Wax Figures in the Specola: The School, Works, Techniques

Although the ceroplastic workshop existed for more or less a century – from 1771 until the mid 19th century – the majority of the wax models in the museum, like the commissioned works for other institutions in Florence and elsewhere, were made during the first 50–60 years of the workshop's activities.

The founding of the school goes back to Felice Fontana. Supported by Grand Duke Peter Leopold, Fontana devoted himself with great energy and determination to setting up a wax workshop, particularly since – as an anatomist and pathologist – he was personally involved in the creation of the models. At first there was just the wax modeller Giuseppe Ferrini working under Fontana's guidance in the workshop, but subsequently the anatomist Antonio Matteucci and the very young

Clemente Susini were also employed. Immensely talented and hugely productive, Susini was later to become the most important and famous of the wax modellers of the Florentine School (ill. p. 47).

We have no precise information today as to where the wax was worked, although it seems most likely that this would have been in studios on the ground floor in the south wing of the palace which is divided into a number of small courtyards and has windows looking out on to the via Romana. Practically none of the original equipment used has survived, but archive records indicate that the following at least were purchased: copper vats in various sizes for melting the wax; modelling tools (ill. p. 33); metal wire in different thicknesses; marble slabs for pressing the wax into thin sheets; scales; tripods for heating substances; slates for making notes and drawings during dissections; crates with handles for transporting the corpses, wooden crates with carrying poles for transporting the wax figures; containers, vases and bottles made from clay or glass for pigments and other substances that were added to the wax. Many of the latter were found with their contents still intact in the museum's store-rooms (ill. p. 32).

Furthermore, it is also clear from the archives how many corpses or parts of a corpse were necessary to make a wax model: astoundingly, over two hundred for a single figure. This startlingly large number is a direct consequence of the fact that there was no way of preserving or freezing the corpses. Consequently there was a constant need for fresh subjects if a dissection were to be accurate and thorough. In order to keep an exact record of all the corpses or parts of corpses – which came from the Santa Maria Nuova hospital about two kilometres away – a register was put up at the door where all corpses being admitted or dispatched to the cemetery were listed: "[...] with regard to the corpses from Santa Maria Nuova, of which it is not known how many there are and because one may not have people die purely for the benefit of the wax collection, a register was put up at the entrance door on which all admissions were noted as well as the number of corpses sent to the cemetery." (from a document written in 1763).

Despite the small number of employees the work progressed very rapidly, when one considers that in 1790 – twenty years after the workshop was set up – the models already filled eight rooms, and this did not even include the models that were made specifically for the hospital in Florence and for other institutions in Italy and abroad (cf. ill. p. 48). Most outstanding amongst the wax figures from the Specola workshop that were soon to be found all over Europe was the collection commissioned in 1781 by the Austrian Emperor Josef, Peter Leopold's older brother, for the military school of medicine in Vienna (called the Josephinum after the Emperor). This collection contains 1200 items made in 1786 and transported to Vienna in two deliveries on the backs of mules. Other models were destined for Pavia, Cagliari, Bologna, Budapest, Paris (today in Montpellier), Uppsala, London, Leiden and elsewhere. These outside commissions occasionally caused problems since the Grand Duke was determined that they should not hold up the production of works for the museum. Thus in the case of such commissions the stipulation was that the modellers and anatomists – Fontana himself worked on the collection for Vienna – were allowed to use the museum's moulds and tools, but that they had to procure the materials themselves and carry out the work with the assistance of craftsmen not in the employ of the museum.

It was Fontana'a ambition to produce as many wax figures as possible in order to create a teaching resource which would in future obviate the need to exhume corpses for the study of the human anatomy. To this end he included in his collections a number of tempera drawings (ill. pp. 10, 11) showing individual parts with numbers around the drawn figure linked by fine lines to the different organs, which could then be identified using these numbers. The relevant written explanations would then be found in a drawer that was part of every wax figure shrine: by this means the user would,

Egisto Tortori:
Small clay bust,
model for a plaster
bust of C. Susini

Kleine Tonbüste,
Modell für eine
Gipsbüste von
C. Susini

Petit buste en argile, modèle d'un
buste en plâtre de
C. Susini

as it were, have access to a complete three-dimensional anatomical treatise (ill. p. 21).

Around 1790 Fontana began another immensely ambitious project which was, however, never realised according to the technical difficulties encountered: the plan was to make a series of painted wooden anatomical models – either life-sized or somewhat larger – which could be taken apart for teaching purposes in order to demonstrate how the organs connect with each other. After a few initial attempts of which only a few examples have survived – one now in the museum, one in Paris and another enormous bust – Fontana had to abandon his plans. Not only was the wood harder to work but it also had a tendency to warp, which meant that all the craftsmen's efforts to make the individual parts fit into each other were rendered useless with time. The only wax model in the museum which has the desired qualities is the so-called 'Venere medicea': a recumbent female figure which can be dismantled from above, layer by layer, eventually revealing a uterus with a small foetus in it. (ill. p. 39)

By this time the museum had increased its personnel to include a graphic artist (Claudio Valvani) and a wood-carver (Luigi Gelati) as well as various anatomists for carrying out the dissections. Amongst the most famous of these was Paolo Mascagni (1755–1815) who left behind extremely beautiful anatomical plates. He specialised in the study of the lymphatic system and it is no coincidence that many of the recumbent statues and the smaller works display this part of the human body in minute detail.

In 1805 Felice Fontana died (ill. pp. 17, 76) but the wax workshop continued with its work, and even after the death of Clemente Susini in 1814 other wax sculptors, such as the Calenzuolis (Francesco Calenzuoli and his son Carlo) and Luigi Calamai (1800–1851) took over. Under Calamai the work was concentrated on comparative anatomical models and botany as well as on pathological models that were made for the Santa Maria Nuova hospital, and which can still be seen today in the Department of Pathological Anatomy in the University. After Calamai's death, Egisto Tortori (1829–1893) took over. Besides making figures of animals and models for the Department of Pathological Anatomy, Tortori also made a bust of Clemente Susini. When Tortori died, however, no-one was appointed to replace him and the workshop was closed down for ever.

Of the wax figures now stored in urns in La Specola, there are 513 of the human anatomy and 65 comparative figures; 5 made by G. G. Zumbo. There are 26 whole figures (including the half-finished figure of a young boy): 13 standing and 13 recumbent, 18 of which are life-sized (6 standing and 12 recumbent) and 8 approximately 60 cm in height (7 standing and 1 recumbent). Almost all are on display: only 14 of the human figures and parts are kept in storage. There are more than 800 framed drawings and almost 900 explanatory notes, and yet it is clear that there must have been more that have gone missing with time. In recent years both the original drawings and the written explanations have been removed from display in order to prevent them suffering further damage through light and humidity. The original frames now contain photocopies so that the collection is as useful as it ever was for teaching purposes and also still constitutes a worthwhile display.

The scientific perfection of these works could hardly be surpassed and although this is mainly appreciated by experts in the field, most visitors are equally impressed by their artistic quality. For however scientifically accurate these exhibits are and whatever their didactic purpose was, they also artworks in their own right. In addition their aesthetic qualities are heightened still further by the beauty of the wooden shrines in which they are kept, despite the fact that many show signs of wear and tear and are badly in need of restoration. The care that originally went into the presentation of this collection is also evident from the equally fragile 18th-century silk drapes and veils – now faded but once bright green.

The importance that was placed on aesthetic appearances may be seen again in the collections of comparative anatomy, of human pathology and above all of botany: small ceramic vases were specially made in the workshop of Ginori von Sesto Fiorentino for the plant models.

We have no detailed knowledge of the technical processes involved in the production of wax figures, and all that is known has had to be deduced from various letters and documents in the state archives and in the archives of the Museum for the History of Science in Florence. Besides this, each wax modeller also had his own technique, and – like any other craftsmen or artists – they were not keen to have their methods spread abroad. However, the following is relatively certain: the dissected item would first of all be copied exactly in chalk or low-grade wax.

Wax death-mask of
Felice Fontana and
plaster relief

Totenmaske aus
Wachs von Felice
Fontana und Gips-
abdruck

Masque mortuaire
en cire de Felice
Fontana et moula-
ge en plâtre

A plaster cast would be taken of this, which could either be very large or made up of a number of sections. It was sometimes possible to make a cast directly from the pieces in question, such as bones for instance. These moulds, which are still stored in the museum (ill. p. 60), subsequently served as a kind of matrix which could also be used repeatedly for making additional casts of the same item. The hardest, most problematical part of the process was, however, the construction of the final model. This required great precision and knowledge of the substances that had to be added to the wax in order to achieve the desired colour and consistency – it was a matter of both skill and experience. The most crucial part of the process was the slow melting of the wax in a water-bath at exactly the right temperature so that it did not discolour. Most commonly the modellers used white wax from Smyrna, Chinese wax or Venetian wax; in order to make it more elastic, turpentine was added as well as paints (thinned with turpentine) and other substances that are recorded in the lists of purchases "needed for the wax models". Before the wax mixture was poured into the mould the latter would be moistened with luke-warm water and rubbed with soft soap to facilitate the removal of the model. Apart from a few which were solid, most of the wax models were hollow and in order to stabilise them they would be stuffed with rags, hemp waste or wood chippings. Figures which were

Pages · Seiten ·
Pages 18–19 :

G. G. Zumbo:
Specimen of a head
(cf. pp. 431, 434)

Präparat eines
Kopfes (vgl.
S. 431, 434)

Préparation anato-
mique d'une tête
(cf. p. 431, 434)

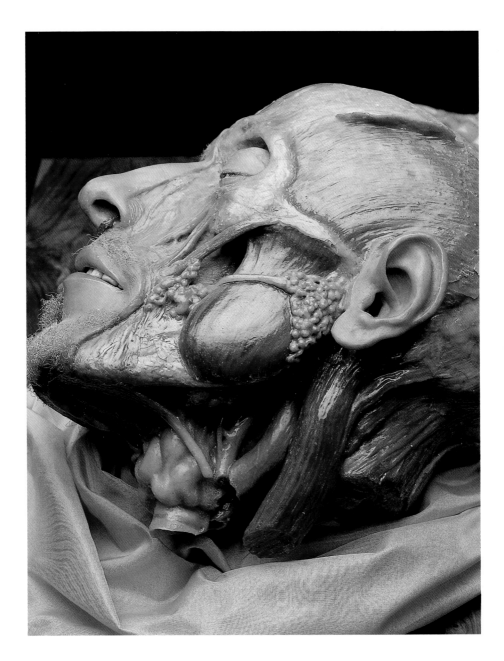

constructed from a number of separate parts generally had a supporting metal frame. After the moulds had been removed, each item would be cleaned and finished, that is to say, equipped with the relevant organs, vessels, nerves and so on until it was complete; a final coating of clear varnish lent the whole a suitably glossy appearance. To ensure that the models were completely accurate each stage had to be supervised by the anatomists who were also responsible for deciding on how to place certain organs so that they might be seen to best advantage.

As has already been mentioned, each wax modeller developed his own technique and equipment, which would become increasingly refined, through the invention of new instruments such as a "drawing iron to turn the wax cylinders" which they used from 1786. Previously this process, which was essential for producing blood vessels, had to be carried out by hand. Towards the close of the century, the wax modellers kept notebooks in which they recorded what they had done each day and which tell us that even in those days it was frequently necessary to carry out restoration work, repairs, improvements and reworkings. In 1793 Susini made a note "about anatomical wax models in need of improvement as a result of flaws that should be treated and which are described in the following by me, Clemente Susini, modeller to the Royal Museum". For instance, on "examination of models of the pharyngeal artery and the jugular vein, leading off from the windpipe one sees two foreign muscles, that is to say, muscles which do not belong in the human form". Having noted further anomalies Susini ends with the comment that "these errors are too grave to be left uncorrected and, for the sake of brevity, I should rather not speak of the many others". Almost all the models have survived in good condition, and only a few have become at all discoloured, although here and there a foetus has darkened in colour and we know that some now greenish veins were once a clear "blue-purple".

The Wax Figures of Gaetano Giulio Zumbo

Gaetano Giulio Zumbo's wax figures deserve a chapter of their own, partly on account of their unusual conception and production but above all because they pre-empted the use of wax for anatomical models by a good century and laid the foundations for everything that was to follow.

Zumbo was born into a noble family in 1656 in Syracuse; the family name was probably Zummo, but this name has now disappeared without trace, and since the debased version 'Zumbo' is much better known and widely used it seems best to use it here. We have little information on his life – and what we have is only fragmentary. It is known that he was educated in the Jesuit Institute in his home town but had to leave following some – otherwise unspecified – "irksome incident". He may well have received his earliest inspiration as an artist from the Classical relics of his homeland, followed later by the pictorial world of Mannerism and the early Baroque. From 1687 to 1691 he lived in Naples and it may well have been there that he created two of the groups still preserved in La Specola: the 'teatrini' with the title *Il Trionfo del tempo* (The Triumph of Time) and *La Peste* (The Plague). According to scholarly experts in the field who have studied Zumbo's work, this may be concluded from the painterly background and the particular arrangement of the figures, both of which point unmistakably to southern Italian precursors. From 1691 to 1694 he worked for Cosimo III de' Medici in Florence, where he created another two 'teatrini': *Il Sepolcro* (or *La Vanità della Gloria Umana*) and *Il Morbo Gallico* (or *Sifilide*) which display many Renaissance features. In 1695 he moved to Genoa where it seems he completed *The Anatomy of a Head* on show in the museum there, and he also made the acquaintance of the French surgeon Guillaume Desnoues. They later worked together on a number of anatomical wax models, including the life-sized figure of a woman giving birth, a smaller model of a woman who has died during child-birth, and the burial of Christ – unfortunately none of which has survived. In 1700 Zumbo and the French physician fell out and Zumbo moved to Marseilles

Explanations of the drawings for *lo spellato* (Room XXVIII, display cabinet no. 740)

Erläuterungen zu den Zeichnungen für *lo spellato* (Saal XXVIII, Vitrine Nr. 740)

Explications des dessins réalisés pour *lo spellato* (salle XXVIII, vitrine n° 740)

where he created a wax head. His last move was to Paris where he entered the service of Louis XIV, and where he died from a brain haemorrhage in 1701. On his death his estate included a beautiful wax head, most probably the very one that is now in the Museum National d'Histoire naturelle. His grave in the L'Eglise de Saint Sulpice was destroyed during the Revolution.

The bulk of this artist's work, largely ignored until fifty years ago, is now in La Specola. The three 'teatrini' which are also known as the *Cera della peste* ('plague figures') and the anatomy of a head were in fact in the Royal gallery (that is to say in the Uffizi) when the Medici were succeeded by the Lotharingians, and were then passed to the Museo de Fisica e Storia Naturale, but never put on display there – perhaps because of the shocking nature of their subject matter. When Peter Leopold set off for Vienna in 1790 he gave the 'plague figures' to the court physician Giovanni Giorgio Asenöhrl, better known as Lagusius. The latter did not even take possession of them but commissioned first Fontana and then Agostino Renzi to sell them for 150 sequins. Renzi was well aware of the importance of these groups and offered them to the new Grand Duke Ferdinand III for the Royal Academy of Fine Arts. When the pieces were rejected as neither "useful nor suitable" he offered them instead to the Duke for the Royal Museum. This proposal was accepted in principle by Giovanni Fabbroni, the deputy director of the museum, and the three works were valued by various experts including Clemente Susini. Since the valuations turned out higher than the price set by Lagusius, the Grand Duke authorised their purchase. Thus Zumbo's works remained in the museum until 1878 when these three dramatic scenes were given for safe-keeping to the museum Nazionale del Bargello. From there they went to the Museo di Storia della Scienza. There they were badly damaged during the torrential rainstorms of 1966 but, on the basis of photographic records, were meticulously and miraculously restored over a period of eighteen months by Guglielmo Galli from the Pietre Dure workshop in Florence. *The Anatomy of a Head*, on the other hand, never left the Specola since it was rightly regarded as an essential component in the scientific collection of the Institute.

The technique used by Zumbo was considerably different from that used later in Florence. *The Anatomy of a Head* was made using a real human skull, which X-ray examination has shown must have belonged to a man of around 25 years old. By contrast, the head now in Paris and

Seconda veduta del secondo pajo dei Nervi del Cervello: detto
Nervo Ottico.

another head (now lost) were made completely from wax, which would seem to indicate advances in the master's technique, perhaps as a result of his collaboration with the French physician Desnoues. The figures in Zumbo's dramatic scenes, executed with the greatest artistry, were almost certainly produced using plaster moulds which in turn had been made from meticulously sculpted clay models. The more or less liquid wax (a mixture of bees' wax, resin, turpentine and pigments) was applied in relatively thin layers in order to achieve the desired consistency and colouration. The scant knowledge we have of Zumbo's technique we owe to the restoration work carried out by Guglielmo Galli after the floods of 1966. This work also revealed evidence of older repairs, for during his work Galli identified pigments that could not have existed in the late 17th century. It also seems that the small self-portrait (ill. p. 55) in the group *Trionfo del Tempo* cannot with any certainty be credited to Zumbo and could well be the work of a contemporary or a later work of Susini's. The *Morbo Gallico*, originally a similar composition, of which now only some fragments remain, was a present from Cosimo III to Filippo Corsini. Unfortunately, this was kept in the cellars of the Palazzo Corsini by the River Arno and was almost completely destroyed during the floods. A few of the figures were found in the gardens, but since there were no

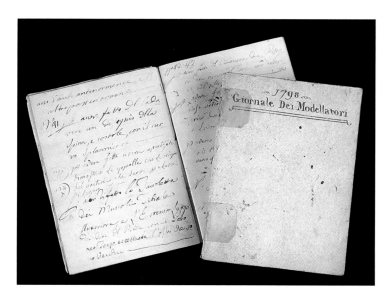

Diary kept by the wax modellers

Tagebuch der Wachsbildner

Cahiers des mode-leurs

photographs of the group it was impossible to reconstruct it. On the occasion of the 200th anniversary of the opening of the museum, which was celebrated with a conference on wax modelling, the Corsini family donated the remains of the work to the museum.

For many years Zumbo's masterpieces were misread as the diseased caprices of an artist revelling in macabre and repellent details. It was not until the mid-20th century that they began to be seen in a more appropriate historical perspective: as realistic documentations of an era when death was omnipresent in the shape of war, famine and major epidemics. This vision of the destruction of human life, of its fragility, of the relentless passage of time, and the constant, specific reminders of death that face us in Zumbo's works are simply typical of the culture and thinking of the 17th century, and put him in the company of other great artists of the time such as Luca Giordano and Mattia Preti.

Pages · Seiten · Pages 26–27:

G. G. Zumbo:
Il Morbo Gallico
(or *Sifilide*)

Syphillis

Die Syphilis

Le Morbo Gallico

Die Wachsfigurensammlung des Museums La Specola in Florenz
Marta Poggesi

Die Geschichte Als Peter Leopold von Habsburg-Lothringen (1747–1792), von 1765 bis 1790 Großherzog von Toskana (Abb. S. 7), 1771 beschloß, alle „wissenschaftlichen" Sammlungen der großherzoglichen Galerien in einem Museum zu vereinigen, führte er eine Neuerung ein, die in Europa und in der Welt ihresgleichen suchte. Viel früher als anderen Herrschern war dem aufgeklärten Landesfürsten, selbst ein begeisterter Student der Naturwissenschaften, deren Bedeutung für die kulturelle Entwicklung der Gesellschaft bewußt geworden. Als erster sann er über Möglichkeiten nach, die Errungenschaften der Naturwissenschaften allen Interessierten zugänglich zu machen.

Und in der Tat war das Imperial Regio Museo di Fisica e Storia Naturale (das Kaiserlich-Königliche Museum für Physik und Naturkunde, das später allgemein „La Specola" – „Sternwarte" im Italienischen – genannt wurde) das weltweit erste seiner Art, das von seiner Eröffnung am 21. Februar 1775 an für das allgemeine Publikum freigegeben wurde. Zwar gab es getrennte Besuchszeiten für Gebildete und für das gemeine Volk; letzteres hatte – „reinliche Bekleidung vorausgesetzt" – von acht bis zehn Uhr morgens Zutritt, um genügend Zeit verstreichen zu lassen bis zum Einlaß „der intelligenten und gelehrten Leute [...] um ein Uhr nachmittags". Auch wenn diese Unterscheidung heute diskriminierend erscheint, kann man doch ermessen, wie innovativ die Öffnung der Bestände für die breite Öffentlichkeit damals gewesen sein muß.

Die Einrichtung der Sammlungen ging auf die Medicis zurück, die sich auch um die Förderung der Wissenschaft verdient gemacht hatten, wie das Beispiel der Accademia del Cimento (1657–1667) zeigt, an der zur Zeit Ferdinando II. de' Medici so bedeutende Wissenschaftler wie Redi, Magalotti und Galileis Lieblingsschüler Viviani lehrten. 1737, nach dem Tod Giangastones, des letzten Abkömmling der Familie, fiel das Großherzogtum Toskana aufgrund der Bestimmungen des Wiener Friedens von 1735 an den späteren Kaiser Franz I. von Habsburg-Lothringen, der eine Aufstellung aller in seiner Residenz enthaltenen Schätze vornehmen ließ. Von 1763 bis 1764 inventarisierte der Arzt und Naturforscher Giovanni Targioni-Tozzetti (1712–1783) die Bestände.

Als Peter Leopold 1765 seinen Vater, der zum Kaiser von Öster-

reich ernannt worden war, als Großherzog der Toskana ablöste, fand er eine gute Arbeitsgrundlage zur
Reorganisation der wissenschaftlichen Sammlungen
vor. Diese Aufgabe sollte dem Abt Felice Fontana
(1730–1805) aus Rovereto (Abb. S. 29) zufallen, seines Zeichens Dozent für Logik an der Universität von
Pisa, aber auch Anatom, Physiker, Chemiker und v. a.
ein international renommierter Physiologe, der sich
der geplanten Neustrukturierung mit solcher Leiden-
schaft widmete, daß bereits Ende 1771 der erste Teil
der Bestände in die neuen Räumlichkeiten verlegt
werden konnte. Bereits 1771 hatte Großherzog Peter
Leopold den Palast der Torrigiani (zuvor im Besitz
der Bini) in der Via Romana in unmittelbarer Nähe

des Palazzo Pitti sowie einige angrenzende Häuser erworben und Fontana mit dem Entwurf des Umbaus der Gebäude beauftragt, um in ihnen
die wissenschaftlichen Sammlungen unterzubringen.

Bust of Felice
Fontana

Büste von Felice
Fontana

Buste de Felice
Fontana

Als Direktor des neuen Museums bereiste Fontana in den ersten
Jahren ganz Europa, um Bücher und Sammlungen zu erwerben und
Kontakte zu Gelehrten in vielen Ländern herzustellen. So wurde das Florentiner Museum zu einem der bedeutendsten seiner Zeit, zumal es
auch über eine reichhaltige wissenschaftliche Bibliothek verfügte. Fontana leitete das Museum bis zu seinem Tod 1805, wobei ihm Giovanni Fabbroni erst als Assistent und ab 1784 als Vize-Direktor (und permanenter
Widersacher) zur Seite stand und ihn auf zahlreichen Reisen begleitete.

Das Geld zur Verwirklichung des Museums für Physik und
Naturkunde (und auch vieler anderer Projekte Peter Leopolds) stammte
aus dem Verkauf wertvoller Gegenstände aus dem Besitz der Medici;
und dies trotz des Testaments der palatinischen Kurfürstin Anna Maria
Luisa (1668–1743), der Schwester Giangastones, in dem das Vermögen
der Medici unwiderruflich an die Stadt Florenz gefallen war. Zum Grund-
bestand des Museums, der vornehmlich aus den Uffizien stammte,
gehörten Sammlungen (etwa von Mineralien und Muscheln), natur-
kundliche Kuriositäten aus der Zeit der Medici, die Instrumente Galileis
und die Gerätschaften der Accademia del Cimento sowie vier Wachsfiguren des sizilianischen Bildhauers G. G. Zumbo.

Um den Bestand des Museums um die Gebiete Meteorologie
und Astronomie zu erweitern, beauftragte Peter Leopold 1780 den Archi-

tekten Gaspare Paoletti (der bereits an der Umstrukturierung des Palastes beteiligt gewesen war) mit dem Bau des Osservatorio Astronomico (dem sog. „Türmchen"), der dem ganzen Komplex später den Namen „Specola" (Sternwarte) geben sollte. Das aufwendige Bauvorhaben, das – trotz der abweichenden Meinung vieler Experten, die einen Neubau auf den Hügeln von Acetri befürwortet hatten – zu einer beträchtlichen Erweiterung des Gebäudes führte, wurde 1789 abgeschlossen. In dasselbe Jahr fällt die Verlegung eines Teils des Boboli-Parks in den Botanischen Garten des Museums (Abb. S. 8).

Nach dem Tod seines Bruders Josef wurde Peter Leopold 1790 Kaiser von Österreich und überließ die Toskana seinem Zweitgeborenen Ferdinand III. (1769–1824), dem die Weitsicht seines Vaters ebenso abging wie dessen Geschick bei den Regierungsgeschäften. Erschwerend kam hinzu, daß die napoleonische Expansion die Lothringer zur Aufgabe der Toskana zwang. 1801 fiel die Toskana schließlich als Königreich Etrurien an Bourbon-Parma. Während dieser Periode richtete das Museum Lehrveranstaltungen in wissenschaftlichen Fächern ein, die auch nach der Restauration der Lothringer 1814 fortgeführt wurden.

Unter Ferdinand III. durchlebte das Museum unruhige Zeiten und verlor seinen Ruf als eines der bedeutendsten Zentren europäischen Wissens, was ihm auch von illustren Besuchern aus dem Ausland wie Goethe und Bernouilli attestiert worden war. Auch Ferdinand III. ließ wichtige Umbauten an dem Palast vornehmen: 1820 wurde unter der Leitung des Architekten Pasquale Poccianti der bereits bestehende Vasari-Korridor, der vom Palazzo Vecchio über die Uffizien zum Palazzo Pitti führt, um den Poccantiani-Korridor bis zur Specola verlängert und so die Specola mit dem Flügel der Meridiana, des Palazzo Pitti, verbunden.

Auf Ferdinand III. folgte 1824 sein Sohn Leopold II. (1797–1870), von den Florentinern seiner blonden Haare wegen wohlwollend „Canapone" genannt. Ihm gebührt das Verdienst, den wissenschaftlichen Studien, insbesondere den anwendungsbezogenen wie etwa der Landwirtschaft, neue Impulse gegeben zu haben. In seine Regentschaft fällt die Realisierung der Tribuna di Galileo, eine Hommage an den großen Forscher, die 1841 anläßlich des dritten Kongresses italienischer Wissenschaftler in Florenz eingeweiht wurde. Bei der Tribuna handelt es sich um einen großen Saal im ersten Stock des Gebäudes, der von dem Architekten Giuseppe Marelli z. T. neu gebaut wurde. Die 1830 begonnenen Arbeiten sahen ursprünglich lediglich eine zusätzliche Apsis in einem bereits existierenden Saal vor. Um jedoch dem Vorhaben, dem berühmten Gelehrten ein würdiges Monument zu errichten, größeren Nachdruck zu verleihen, sollte ihm auf Wunsch des Großherzogs der gesamte Saal gewidmet werden und neben einer Statue alle Andenken Galileis sowie die Instrumente aus der Accademia del Cimento beherbergen. Der Bau der Tribuna, eines der seltenen Beispiele des späten Neoklassizismus in Florenz, führte zu bedeutsamen Änderungen der Palastarchitektur; insbesondere wurden die darunterliegenden Stockwerke umgestaltet und ein Teil des Hofes überdacht. Der Saal wurde mit toskanischem Marmor verkleidet, und für die Ausstattung zeichneten ausschließlich Künstler aus der Toskana – Bildhauer, Maler – verantwortlich.

Nach dem Fall Leopolds II., des letzten Großherzogs der Toskana, wurde 1859 das Istituto di Studi Superiori e di Perfezionamento (Institut für höhere Studien und Weiterbildung) gegründet, aus dem 1923 die königliche Universität von Florenz hervorgehen sollte. Die Gebäude des Museums wurden als Institut für Physik und Naturwissenschaften Teil der Universität.

Trotz der Bedeutung der Einrichtung dieses Instituts, markierte es andererseits für das Museum den Beginn seiner Zergliederung in die verschiedenen Disziplinen, die mit der stetig wachsenden Zahl der Studenten mitsamt der dazugehörigen Sammlungen und Bibliotheken ausgelagert werden mußten. Diesen Prozeß konnte selbst der Widerstand vieler Naturwissenschaftler jener Epoche nicht aufhalten, so daß im historischen Gebäude in der Via Romana letztlich nur die zoologischen Sammlungen und der Großteil der anatomischen Zeroplastiken verblieben.

Die Anfänge der Wachsbildnerei in der Anatomie

Die Verwendung von Wachs zur Modellierung von Figuren geht bis auf die Zeit der Römer zurück. Vor allem in der Kunst war das Material seit jeher sehr beliebt, sowohl aus ästhetischen Gründen als auch aus technischen. Wachs läßt sich einfach verarbeiten und eignet sich hervorragend für die Herstellung von Gußformen, wie etwa für den Bronzeguß. Insbesondere im europäischen Mittelalter wurden Weihgaben oder Heiligenstatuen, Krippen und auch Votivtafeln aus Wachs in großer Stückzahl gefertigt. In der Renaissance und während des gesamten 17. Jahrhunderts konnte man gewaltige Mengen dieser Wachsmodelle in Kirchen, besonders in Orsammichele und in Santissima Annunziata, bewundern, darunter Gliedmaßen, Organe oder Teile davon ebenso wie Porträts, gegenständliche Darstellungen und Statuen, nicht selten sogar lebensgroß. Im 17. Jahrhundert kamen dann in Wachs nachgebildete anatomische Objekte zu wissenschaftlichen Zwecken auf.

Obwohl der Staat und mehr noch die Kirche das Studium der menschlichen Anatomie am Leichnam nach Kräften behinderten und sanktionierten, tauchten Mitte des 15. Jahrhunderts erstmals anatomische Zeichnungen und Traktate auf, in der Regel aus der Feder so berühmter Maler und Bildhauer wie Leonardo da Vinci, Michelangelo, Raffael und Tizian, mit denen bedeutende Anatomie-Forscher wie Falloppio, Cesalpino oder Vesalius ihre Traktate illustrierten.

Gaetano Giulio Zumbo war gegen Ende des 17. Jahrhunderts der erste, der in der berühmten Anatomie-Schule von Bologna für die Modellierung anatomischer Präparate farbige Wachse verwendete. Der aus Syrakus stammende Künstler, dessen Werke im folgenden abgebildet sind, gestaltete zwei Männerköpfe (die sich heute in Florenz bzw. in Paris befinden), eine (leider verlorengegangene) Frauenfigur sowie einige kleinformatige Kompositionen. Ebenfalls in Bologna formierte sich

Pigments and other materials used in the production of wax models in their original containers

Farbstoffe und andere bei der Wachsfigurenherstellung erforderliche Materialien in ihren ursprünglichen Behältern

Colorants et autres matières nécessaires à la création de sculptures en cire dans leurs récipients d'origine die erste Schule der Zeroplastik, aus der in der zweiten Hälfte des 18. Jahrhunderts auch die Wachsbildner des Florentiner Museums hervorgingen. Als Begründer der Bologneser Schule gilt der Maler, Bildhauer und Architekt Ercole Lelli (1702–1766), der – wie schon zuvor Zumbo – die Modellierung wächserner Muskeln und Eingeweide auf der Basis echter Skelette vornahm. Als Kenner und Liebhaber der Naturwissenschaften förderte Kardinal Prospero Lambertini, der 1740 zum Papst Benedikt XIV. ernannt wurde, die anatomischen Studien der Bologneser Schule und kaufte Lellis sämtliche Modelle, die man noch heute im Istituto di Anatomia Umana Normale der Universität Bologna bewundern kann. Von besonderer Bedeutung war auch seine Unterstützung für die Beschaffung der für diese Arbeit notwendigen Leichname. Zu den Assistenten Lellis gehörte außerdem Giovanni Manzolini (1700–1755), der mit Hilfe seiner Frau Anna Morandi (1716–1774) zahlreiche Modelle ausführte, die ebenfalls in der Bologneser Universität aufbewahrt werden.

In jener Zeit wurde das Studium der Anatomie zwar in ganz Europa vorangetrieben, doch die zeroplastische Schule von Florenz stammt direkt von derjenigen Bolognas ab. Die Vermittlung besorgte der Chirurg und Geburtshelfer Giuseppe Galletti, der unter dem Eindruck

Copper vat with modelling tools

Kupferwanne und Modellierbesteck

Bassine en cuivre et instruments à modeler

der Werke von Lelli und Manzolini zusammen mit dem Wachsbildner Giuseppe Ferrini eine Reihe von Modellen aus Wachs und Terracotta anfertigte (die sich zur Zeit im Museo di Storia della Scienza in Florenz befinden), um verschiedene Geburtsvorgänge – normale und dystokische – zu demonstrieren.

Die anatomischen Wachsfiguren der Specola: Schule, Werke, Techniken

Die zeroplastische Werkstatt in Florenz bestand etwa ein Jahrhundert lang – von 1771 bis in die zweite Hälfte des 19. Jahrhunderts hinein –, aber der überwiegende Teil der im Museum aufbewahrten Wachsbildnisse entstand ebenso wie die Auftragsarbeiten für andere Florentiner Institutionen und Auftraggeber in den ersten fünfzig bis sechzig Jahren ihres Bestehens.

Die Gründung der Specola geht auf Felice Fontana zurück, der sich mit voller Unterstützung Großherzog Peter Leopolds deren Ausbau widmete, zumal er sich als Anatom und Pathologe persönlich an der Erstellung der Modelle beteiligte. Anfangs arbeitete lediglich der Wachsbildner Giuseppe Ferrini unter Fontanas Anleitung in der Werkstatt. In der Folge wurden dann der Anatom Antonio Matteucci und der damals noch sehr junge Clemente Susini eingestellt, der aufgrund seines Geschicks und seiner Produktivität zum bedeutendsten und berühmtesten Zeroplastiker der Florentiner Schule avancierte (Abb. S. 47).

Die Wachse wurden vermutlich in den Räumen des Erdgeschosses verarbeitet, deren Fenster zur Via Romana im Südflügel des Palastes mit seinen vielen kleinen Höfen hinausgingen. Von den einstigen Gerätschaften ist kaum etwas erhalten, aber aus Archivunterlagen gehen folgende Ankäufe hervor: Kupferwannen verschiedener Größe, in denen das Wachs geschmolzen wurde; Modellierbesteck (Abb. S. 33); Eisendraht in unterschiedlichen Stärken; Marmorplatten zum Pressen des Wachs; Waagen; Dreifüße zum Erhitzen des Materials; Schiefertafeln für Anmerkungen und Zeichnungen während der Sektionen; Kisten mit Handgriffen zum Transport der Leichen, Holzkisten mit Stangen zum Transport der Wachsfiguren; Behälter, Vasen und Flaschen aus Keramik oder Glas für Farbmittel und andere Substanzen, die dem Wachs beigegeben wurden. Von letzteren wurden in den alten Magazinen des Museums noch etliche mitsamt Inhalt gefunden (Abb. S. 32).

Aus den Archivdokumenten geht ferner hervor, wie viele Leichname oder Leichenteile für die Ausführung eines Modells benötigt wurden:

über zweihundert für eine einzige Figur! Die erstaunlich hohe Zahl erklärt sich aus dem Umstand, daß es keine Konservierungsmöglichkeiten gab, so daß für genaue anatomische Sektionen ständig neue Leichname gebraucht wurden. Um alle Leichen oder Leichenteile, die vom (etwa zwei Kilometer entfernten) Krankenhaus Santa Maria Nuova herbeigeschafft wurden, numerisch genau zu erfassen, war an der Eingangstür eigens ein Register angebracht, auf dem alle Eingänge, aber auch alle für den Friedhof bestimmten Abgänge notiert wurden: „[...] bezüglich der Leichname aus Santa Maria Nuova, von denen man nicht weiß, wie viele anfallen, und weil man die Leute nicht passend für die Wachssammlungen sterben lassen kann: Darum wurde an der Tür des Museums ein Register angebracht, in dem die Leichname, die daselbst gebraucht werden und deren Zahl beträchtlich erscheint, festzuhalten sind und ebenso zu vermerken, wie oft und wie viele zum Friedhof geschickt werden." (aus einem Dokument von 1793).

Ungeachtet der geringen Zahl der Präparatoren gingen die Arbeiten recht schnell voran, wenn man bedenkt, daß um 1790, also zwanzig Jahre nach Beginn, die Modelle bereits acht Säle füllten, nicht gerechnet all jene, die für das Florentiner Krankenhaus und für andere Institutionen in Italien und im Ausland angefertigt worden waren (vgl. Abb. S. 48). Unter den über ganz Europa verstreuten Wachsplastiken aus der Specola-Werkstatt ragen die vom österreichischen Kaiser Josef, dem älteren Bruder von Peter Leopold, für die militärische Medizinschule Wien (das nach ihm benannte Josephinum) 1781 in Auftrag gegebenen hervor. Die Sammlung umfaßt 1 200 Stücke, die 1786 fertiggestellt und in zwei Lieferungen auf dem Rücken von Maultieren nach Wien gebracht wurden. Weitere Plastiken waren für Pavia, Cagliari, Bologna, Budapest, Paris (heute in Montpellier), Uppsala, London, Leiden und andere Städte bestimmt. Diese externen Aufträge warfen gelegentlich Organisationsprobleme auf, da dem Großherzog daran gelegen war, die Herstellung der für das Museum bestimmten Modelle nicht zu verzögern. Darum wurde die Durchführung dieser Aufträge an die Bedingung geknüpft, daß die Plastiker und Anatomen – im Fall der Wiener Sammlung Fontana selbst – zwar museumseigene Abdrücke und Utensilien benutzen durften, das Material aber selbst besorgen und mit Hilfe auswärtiger Handwerker verarbeiten mußten.

Fontana hatte den Ehrgeiz, so viele anatomische Wachsmodelle wie nur irgend möglich zu schaffen, um einen Fundus für didaktische

Zwecke einzurichten, der die direkte Exhumierung von Leichen für das Studium der Anatomie entbehrlich machen sollte. Hierfür stattete er seine Sammlungen mit einer Reihe von Tempera-Zeichnungen aus (Abb. S. 10, 11), auf denen die einzelnen Teile dargestellt werden; von einem Nummernkranz um die gezeichnete Figur ziehen sich dünne gestrichelte Linien zu den verschiedenen Organen, Muskeln, Knochen usw., die anhand der Ziffern identifiziert werden können. Die Blätter mit den entsprechenden Erläuterungen finden sich in einer Schublade, die an jeder Vitrine angebracht wurde: So erhielt man zu jedem Präparat einen regelrechten Anatomie-Traktat (Abb. S. 21).

Um 1790 nahm Fontana ein weiteres ambitioniertes Projekt in Angriff: Es ging um eine Serie anatomischer Teile aus bemaltem Holz, die – im Orignalmaßstab oder in Vergrößerungen – zu didaktischen Zwecken auseinandergenommen werden konnten, um die Beziehungen zwischen den Organen veranschaulichen zu können. Nach einigen Versuchen, von denen nur einige wenige Stücke erhalten sind (Abb. 26), darunter zwei ganze Plastiken (eine im Museum, die andere in Paris) und eine enorme Büste, mußte Fontana das Vorhaben aufgeben, weil das Holz sich nicht nur schwerer bearbeiten läßt, sondern darüber hinaus als organisches Material nicht formbeständig ist, wodurch mit der Zeit die einzelnen Teile ihre Passung zueinander verlieren. Die einzige Wachsplastik des Museums, die die gewünschten Merkmale aufweist, ist die sogenannte „Venere medicea": eine liegende weibliche Figur, von der mehrere Schichten entfernt werden können, bis der Uterus mit einem kleinen Fötus zum Vorschein kommt (Abb. S. 39).

Das Museum hatte mittlerweile seine Mannschaft um einen Zeichner (Claudio Valvani) und einen Holzschnitzer (Luigi Gelati) erweitert und beschäftigte diverse Anatomen für die Sezierung der Leichname. Zu den berühmtesten zählte Paolo Mascagni (1755–1815), der wunderschöne anatomische Tafeln hinterlassen hat und sich auf das Studium des lymphatischen Systems spezialisiert hatte: Nicht zufällig stellen viele liegende Statuen, aber auch kleinere Präparate diesen Apparat des Organismus minutiös dar.

Auch nach dem Tod Felice Fontanas 1805 (Abb. S. 17) setzte die zeroplastische Werkstatt ihre Arbeit fort, und nach dem Tod seines Nachfolgers Clemente Susinis 1814 übenahmen andere Wachsbildner wie die beiden Calenzuoli (Vater Francesco und Sohn Carlo) oder Luigi Calamai (1800–1851) den Betrieb. Unter Calamai konzentrierte sich die

Aktivität auf Modelle der vergleichenden Anatomie und der Botanik sowie auf jene der pathologischen Anatomie, die für das Krankenhaus von Santa Maria Nuova bestimmt waren und heute im Museum für pathologische Anatomie der Universität zu sehen sind. Auf Calamais Stelle rückte nach dessen Tod Egisto Tortori (1829–1893) nach, der neben Tierpräparaten und solchen der anatomischen Pathologie auch eine Büste Clemente Susinis modellierte. Nach Tortoris Tod 1893 löste sich die Werkstatt endgültig auf.

Von den Wachsfiguren, die das Museum La Specola gegenwärtig in Urnen verwahrt, befassen sich 513 mit menschlicher und 65 mit vergleichender Anatomie; 5 Exponate stammen von G. G. Zumbo. Es gibt 26 Figuren (einschließlich eines halbfertigen Jünglings): 13 stehende und 13 liegende Exemplare, davon 18 in Originalgröße (6 stehende und 12 liegende), während acht Figuren etwa 60 cm messen (7 stehende und 1 liegende). Mit Ausnahme von 14 Zeroplastiken zur menschlichen Anatomie, die sich im Magazin befinden, sind alle öffentlich ausgestellt. Hinzu kommen mehr als 800 gerahmte Zeichnungen und annähernd 900 erläuternde Blätter, doch es müssen mehr gewesen sein, da im Laufe der Zeit einiges verlorengegangen ist. In den letzten Jahren wurden die Zeichnungen und die Blätter mit den Erläuterungen entfernt, um sie vor weiteren, durch Licht und Feuchtigkeit bedingte Schäden zu bewahren, und durch Farbkopien ersetzt, so daß die Struktur der Sammlung unter didaktischen Gesichtspunkten wie auch unter solchen einer ausstellungsgerechten Präsentation erhalten blieb (Abb. S. 18).

Während Experten der Materie vor allen Dingen die wissenschaftliche Perfektion der Exponate

Drawing of a head: lateral view, 2nd half of the 18th century (Room XXVIII, display cabinet no. 707)

Zeichnung eines Kopfes: Seitenansicht, 2. Hälfte des 18. Jahrhunderts (Saal XXVIII, Vitrine Nr. 707)

Dessin d'une tête vue latérale, 2e moitié du XVIIIe siècle (salle XXVIII, vitrine n° 707)

beeindrucken werden, steht für die meisten Besucher in erster Linie die künstlerische Leistung im Vordergrund, denn bei aller wissenschaftlichen Strenge und didaktischem Anspruch sind diese Exponate regelrechte Kunstwerke. Ihre ästhetischen Qualitäten unterstreichen überdies die kunstvoll gearbeiteten Holzvitrinen, in denen sie aufbewahrt werden, auch wenn viele zeitbedingte Abnutzungserscheinungen aufweisen und dringend restauriert werden müßten. Welche Sorgfalt bei der Präsentation dieser Sammlung aufgewendet wurde, bezeugen auch die mittlerweile verblaßten, ursprünglich hellgrünen seidenen Draperien und Schleier aus dem 18. Jahrhundert, die sich ebenfalls in einem äußerst prekären Zustand befinden. Welche Aufmerksamkeit der Ästhetik gewidmet wurde, belegen die Sammlungen der vergleichenden Anatomie, der Humanpathologie und v. a. der Botanik, wo für die kleinen Pflanzenmodelle eigens Keramikvasen aus der Werkstatt Ginori von Sesto Fiorentino angefertigt wurden.

Die technischen Verfahren zur Herstellung der Wachsfiguren können nur aus verschiedenen Briefen und Dokumenten aus dem Staatsarchiv und dem des Museums für Wissenschaftsgeschichte in Florenz erschlossen werden. Außerdem hatte jeder Wachsbildner seine eigene Technik, die er – wie alle Handwerker und Künstler – geheimhielt. Von der in der anatomischen Sektion vorbereiteten Vorlage wurde zuerst eine exakte Kopie aus Kreide oder minderwertigem Wachs hergestellt, von der ein Gipsabdruck genommen wurde, der, wenn er sehr groß war, aus verschiedenen Einsatzstücken bestand. Diese Abdrücke, die in einem Depot des Museums aufbewahrt werden, stellten eine Art Matrix dar, die mehrfach für die Reproduktion desselben Modells verwendet werden konnte. Der schwierigste und heikelste Teil war die Konstruktion des definitiven Modells, die große Präzision, Kenntnis der Substanzen, die dem Wachs beigemischt werden mußten, um die gewünschte Farbe und Konsistenz zu erhalten, sowie große Erfahrung und Geschick verlangten. Das Wachs mußte bei der richtigen Temperatur langsam im Wasserbad schmelzen, damit es sich nicht verfärbte. Am häufigsten wurden weißes Wachs aus Smyrna, chinesisches Wachs sowie venezianisches Wachs verwendet. Um das Wachs formbarer zu machen, fügte man Terpentin hinzu, ferner – ebenfalls mit Terpentin verdünnte – Farbstoffe und andere Substanzen, die in den Einkaufslisten als „für die Wachsarbeiten benötigte Sachen" nachgewiesen sind. Damit sich das Modell später leicht aus der Form lösen ließ, wurde die Gußform mit lauwarmem Wasser angefeuchtet und mit weicher Seife eingerieben, bevor man das Wachsgemisch in den Abdruck goß. Abgesehen von einigen Vollwachspräparaten waren die meisten innen hohl und wurden zur Stabilisierung mit Lappen, Werg oder Holzstücken ausgestopft. Figuren, die aus mehreren Teilstücken bestehen, wurden in der Regel durch eine Stützarmatur aus Metall verstärkt. Nach Entfernung des Abdrucks wurde jede Komponente gesäubert und mit entsprechenden Geräten ausgekehlt sowie zur Vervollständigung mit Organen, Gefäßen, Nervensträngen usw. versehen. Eine letzte Schicht durchsichtigen Lacks verlieh dem Ganzen den nötigen Glanz. Um die Originaltreue des Modells sicherzustellen, mußten all diese Arbeitsgänge ständig von den Anatomen überwacht werden, denen auch die Entscheidung über die jeweils günstigste Position zur Hervorhebung bestimmter Organe oblag.

Jeder Wachsbildner verfügte über eine eigene Technik, die mit der Zeit immer mehr verfeinert wurde, u. a. dank neuer Instrumente wie z. B. einem „Zieheisen zum Drehen der Wachszylinder", das ab 1786 den Plastikern zur Verfügung stand. Früher mußte dieser Arbeitsgang, der für die Gestaltung der Blutgefäße unumgänglich war, von Hand bewältigt werden. Um 1790 führten die Wachsbildner einige Jahre lang „Hefte" (Abb. S. 24), in denen sie täglich die ausgeführten Arbeiten eintrugen, und aus denen hervorgeht, daß bereits damals des häufigeren Reparaturen, Verbesserungen und Überarbeitungen anfielen. 1793 legte Susini eine „Notiz [an] über zu korrigierende anatomische Wachspräparate aufgrund im folgenden beschriebener, von mir, Clemente Susini, Modellierer des Königlichen Museums, erkannter Fehler, die es verdienen, behoben zu werden." Zum Beispiel: „Überprüfung des Präparats der Schlundader und der Halsschlagader: Man sieht von der Luftröhre zwei fremde Muskeln abgehen, das heißt solche, die nicht zum menschlichen Körper gehören, und einen, der am Schilddrüsenfortsatz ansetzt, der aber weder der Zungen- noch der Schlund- und schon gar nicht der Schilddrüsengriffel zu sein scheint." Susinis Notiz endet mit der Feststellung: „Diese Fehler sind zu gravierend, um nicht berichtigt zu werden und von den vielen anderen schweige ich lieber, um mich kurz zu fassen." Fast alle Modelle sind gut erhalten, lediglich bei einigen sind Verfärbungen aufgetreten: mancher Fötus ist nachgedunkelt, und von den heute grün schimmernden Venen wissen wir, daß sie einst „blauviolett" waren.

Die Wachsfiguren des Gaetano Giulio Zumbo

Ein besonderes Kapitel gebührt den Wachsfiguren Gaetano Giulio Zumbos, zum einen wegen ihrer ungewöhnlichen Konzeption und Herstellungsmethode, v. a. aber, weil sie der allgemeinen Entwicklung bei der Verwendung von Wachs für anatomische Darstellungen ihrer Zeit um ein Jahrhundert voraus waren.

Zumbo wurde 1656 in Syrakus als Sohn einer alten Adelsfamilie geboren, deren Nachname vermutlich Zummo war und von der es heute keinerlei Spuren mehr gibt; da die entstellende Version „Zumbo" sich allgemein eingebürgert hat, scheint es angebracht, dabei zu bleiben. Von seinem Leben ist wenig überliefert, und auch das nur bruchstückhaft; man weiß, daß er im Jesuiten-Internat seiner Geburtsstadt erzogen wurde und wegen eines nicht näher benannten „lästigen Unfalls" die Schule aufgeben mußte. Die klassischen Zeugnisse seiner Heimat dürften ihm erste künstlerische Anregungen gegeben haben. Später wurde sein künstlerischer Werdegang vom Manierismus und der Frühphase des Barocks beeinflußt. Von 1687 bis 1691 lebte er in Neapel und schuf vermutlich hier zwei der in der Specola aufbewahrten Gruppenszenen, der „teatrini", nämlich *Il Trionfo del tempo* (Der Triumph der Zeit) und *La Peste*. Seine Urheberschaft schließen die Gelehrten, die sich mit Zumbos Werk befaßt haben, aus dem malerischen Hintergrund und der Anordnung der Figuren, die deutlich auf süditalienische Vorbilder verweist.

Von 1691 bis 1694 arbeitete Zumbo für Cosimo III. de' Medici in Florenz, wo er zwei weitere „teatrini" mit Bezügen zur Renaissancekunst fertigstellte: *Il Sepolcro* (oder *La Vanità della Gloria Umana*) und *Il Morbo Gallico* (oder *Sifilide*). 1695 unternahm er einige Reisen nach Bologna, wo er mit großem Interesse die gerade im Aufschwung begriffenen anatomischen Studien verfolgte. Ende 1695 zog er nach Genua, wo er vermutlich die im Museum ausgestellte *Anatomie des Kopfes* vollendete. Hier lernte er den französischen Chirurgen Guillaume Desnoues kennen; auf ihre Zusammenarbeit gehen diverse anatomische Wachsmodelle zurück, darunter die lebensgroße Figur einer Gebärenden, eine bei der Geburt gestorbene Frau in kleinerem Format sowie Geburt und Grablegung Christi – Werke, die leider nicht mehr erhalten sind. 1700 entzweite sich Zumbo mit Desnoues und siedelte zuerst nach Marseille über, wo er einen weiteren Wachskopf anfertigte, und schließlich nach Paris, wo er in die Dienste Ludwigs XIV. trat, bis er 1701 an einer Gehirnblutung verstarb. Unter seinen Sachen fand man einen wunderschönen Wachskopf, der höchstwahrscheinlich mit demjenigen identisch ist, der im Museum National d'Historie Naturelle aufbewahrt wird. Sein Grab, das sich in der Kirche von Saint Sulpice befand, wurde während der Revolution zerstört.

Ein Großteil der Werke dieses bis noch vor einem halben Jahrhundert weitgehend verkannten Künstlers befindet sich im Museum La Specola. Die drei „teatrini", die auch als *Cera della peste* („Pestfiguren") bekannt sind, und die *Anatomie des Kopfes* befanden sich, als die Medici von den Lothringern abgelöst wurden, in der Königlichen Galerie (also in den Uffizien) und wurden anschließend dem Museo di Fisica e Storia Naturale überantwortet, dort aber, vielleicht wegen der Drastik der dargestellten Szenen, nie ausgestellt. Als Peter Leopold 1790 nach Wien aufbrach, schenkte er die „Pestfiguren" dem Hofarzt Giovanni Giorgio Asenöhrl, besser bekannt als Lagusius. Dieser beauftragte erst Fontana und dann Agostino Renzi, Superintendent der Königlichen Apotheke, sie für 150 Zechinen zu verkaufen. Letzterer war sich der Bedeutung der Ensembles durchaus bewußt und bot sie dem neuen Großherzog Ferdinand III. an, erst für die Königliche Akademie der Schönen Künste und daraufhin, da diesem die Stücke weder „nützlich noch angemessen" erschienen, für das Königliche Museum. Dieser Vorschlag wurde vom Vizedirektor des Museums Giovanni Fabbroni befürwortet, und die drei Werke wurden von verschiedenen Experten, darunter Clemente Susini, geschätzt. Da der Schätzwert höher war als der von Lagusius geforderte

View of Room
XXVII

Gesamtansicht des
Saals XXVII

Vue d'ensemble de
la salle XXVII

Preis, autorisierte der Großherzog den Ankauf, und so blieben Zumbos
Werke im Museum, bis die drei Theaterszenen 1878 dem Museum
Nazionale in Bargello zur Aufbewahrung übergeben wurden; von diesem
kamen sie zum Museo di Storia della Scienza, um 1974 schließlich wie-
der zur Specola zurückzukehren. Archivdokumente belegen, daß die
Wachsfiguren verschiedentlich restauriert wurden, u. a. von Susini und
Tortori. Die Pestdarstellungen, die sich im Museo di Storia della Scienza
befanden, wurden während der sintflutartigen Regenfälle im Jahre 1966
schwer beschädigt. In über 18monatiger Kleinarbeit gelang es Guglielmo
Galli aus der Werkstatt der Pietre Dure in Florenz, sie nach vorhandenen
Fotografien wiederherzustellen. Die *Anatomie des Kopfes* hingegen hat
die Specola nie verlassen, da sie zu Recht als einschlägig für die wissenschaftliche Sammlung des Instituts betrachtet wurde.

Die von Zumbo angewandte Technik unterscheidet sich stark
von jener der späteren Florentiner Schule. Die *Anatomie des Kopfes* wurde an einem echten Schädel ausgeführt, der nach dem Befund der Rönt-
genaufnahmen einem etwa 25jährigen Mann gehört haben muß. Der in
Paris befindliche Kopf und ein weiteres, verschollenes Exemplar sind
hingegen ganz aus Wachs modelliert, was auf eine Fortentwicklung seiner Verarbeitungstechnik schließen läßt, die möglicherweise auf die

Zusammenarbeit Zumbos mit Desnoues zurückgeht. Die Figuren der „teatrini", deren Gestaltung bis in die kleinsten Details von großer Kunstfertigkeit zeugt, wurden mit an Sicherheit grenzender Wahrscheinlichkeit von Gipsabdrücken hergestellt, denen ihrerseits sorgfältig geformte Tonmodelle zugrunde lagen. Das mehr oder weniger flüssige Wachs (ein Gemisch aus Bienenwachs, Kolophonium, Terpentin und Farbstoffen) wurde in dünnen Schichten aufgetragen, um die jeweils gewünschte Konsistenz und Farbigkeit zu erhalten. Die wenigen überlieferten Notizen über Zumbos Technik verdanken wir den von Guglielmo Galli nach den Wasserschäden von 1966 durchgeführten Restaurierungen, die zudem auch Spuren älterer Reparaturen anhand des Nachweises von Farbstoffen, die es Ende des 17. Jahrhunderts noch nicht gab, zutage förderten. Auch das kleine Selbstporträt (Abb. S. 55) aus dem Ensemble *Il Trionfo del Tempo* kann nicht mit Bestimmtheit Zumbo zugeschrieben werden, es könnte das Werk eines Zeitgenossen oder des späten Susini sein. Der *Morbo Gallico*, von der Anlage her eine vergleichbare Komposition, von der nur noch wenige Bruchstücke existieren, war ein Geschenk Cosimos III. an Filippo Corsini, das in den Kellern des Palazzo Corsini am Arno aufbewahrt wurde und von der Überschwemmung praktisch vollständig zerstört wurde; man fand ein paar Figuren im Garten wieder, aber da es keine Fotografien des Ensembles gab, war eine Rekonstruktion nicht möglich. Anläßlich des 200jährigen Jubiläums der Museumseröffnung, das mit einem Kongreß über Wachsplastik zelebriert wurde, übergab die Familie Corsini die Reste dieses Werks dem Museum.

Lange Zeit hindurch wurden Zumbos Meisterwerke als krankhafte Kaprizen eines sich an der Darstellung makabrer und abscheulicher Details ergötzenden Künstlers erachtet. Erst Mitte dieses Jahrhunderts ging man dazu über, sie in ihrer historischen Perspektive wahrzunehmen: als realistische Dokumente einer Epoche, in der der Tod mit Kriegen, Hungersnöten und großen Epidemien allgegenwärtig war. Diese Vision der Zerstörung, der Hinfälligkeit menschlichen Lebens, des unerbittlichen Vergehens der Zeit, dieses beständige Memento mori, mit dem uns Zumbos Werke in einer Fülle von Details konfrontieren, ist ein typisches Beispiel für die Kultur des 17. Jahrhunderts, wie sie uns auch von anderen großen Künstlern jener Zeit, etwa von Luca Giordano oder Mattia Preti, überliefert wird.

Pages · Seiten · Pages 44–45:

G. G. Zumbo: Il Sepolcro

The burial

Das Begräbnis

L'Enterrement

La collection de figures de cire du musée La Specola à Florence
Marta Poggesi

Le musée et son histoire

Lorsqu'en 1771 Pierre Léopold de Habsbourg-Lorraine (1747–1792), grand-duc de Toscane de 1765 à 1790 (ill. p. 7), décida de réunir en un seul musée toutes les collections « scientifiques » des galeries grand-ducales, il entreprenait quelque chose d'absolument inédit en Europe et dans le monde entier. Homme éclairé, bien en avance sur les autres souverains de son époque, le prince était passionné de sciences naturelles, conscient de leur importance pour le développement culturel de la société. C'est lui qui songea le premier à rendre accessibles à tous les découvertes réalisées dans ce domaine.

Appelé plus tard « La Specola », observatoire en italien, le « Imperial Regio Museo di Fisica e Storia Naturale » (Musée impérial royal de physique et d'histoire naturelle) ouvrit ses portes le 21 février 1775, au grand public, ce qui le rendit unique en son genre dans le monde entier. Certes, les heures d'ouverture étaient différentes pour les hommes cultivés et le commun des mortels : ces derniers dont on exigeait une « tenue propre » ne pouvaient visiter le musée que de huit heures à dix heures du matin afin de laisser suffisamment de temps entre leur passage et l'arrivée « des personnes intelligentes et savantes […] à une heure de l'après-midi ». Mais même si cette distinction nous paraît discriminatoire de nos jours, on peut se figurer que l'accès des collections au grand public représentait jadis une incroyable innovation.

La création de ces collections remontait aux Médicis, grands mécènes et amateurs d'art, qui encouragèrent également les sciences avec la fondation, par exemple, de l'Accademia del Cimento (1657–1667) où enseignaient, à l'époque de Ferdinand II de Médicis, d'illustres savants comme Redi, Magalotti et Viviani, l'élève favori de Galilée. Après la mort de Jean Gaston, le dernier rejeton de la famille en 1737, le grand-duché de Toscane passa, conformément au traité de Vienne, aux mains du futur empereur François Ier de Habsbourg-Lorraine (1745–1765) qui fit dresser la liste des trésors de sa nouvelle résidence. En un peu moins d'un an, de 1763 à 1764, le médecin et naturaliste Giovanni Targioni-Tozzetti (1712–1783) parvint à faire l'inventaire des collections.

Lorsqu'en 1765 Pierre Léopold succéda à son père devenu empereur d'Autriche, il s'aperçut qu'en raison du travail déjà effectué il pouvait aisément entreprendre la réorganisation des collections scientifiques. Cette tâche devait revenir à l'abbé Felice Fontana (1730–1805), originaire de Rovereto (ill. p. 29). Professeur de logique à l'université de Pise, il était également anatomiste, physicien, chimiste et surtout physiologiste de réputation internationale. L'abbé se lança dans cette entreprise avec tant d'ardeur qu'à la fin de 1771, on pouvait déjà transporter la première partie des collections dans les nouvelles salles. La même année, le grand-duc Pierre Léopold avait fait l'acquisition du palais des Torrigiani (qui appartenait auparavant à la famille Bini), situé dans la via Romana à deux pas du palais Pitti, ainsi que de quelques maisons avoisinantes. Il chargea ensuite Fontana de transformer les bâtiments afin qu'ils puissent abriter les collections scientifiques. Nommé par ailleurs directeur du nouveau musée, l'abbé sillonna l'Europe durant les premières années pour acheter des livres et des collections et nouer des contacts avec les savants d'autres pays. C'est ainsi que le musée florentin devint l'un des plus importants de son époque d'autant plus qu'il possédait une vaste bibliothèque scientifique.

Egisto Tortori : Coloured plaster relief of Clemente Susini

Gipsbüste von Clemente Susini, farbig gefaßt

Buste en plâtre polychrome de Clemente Susini

Fontana dirigea le musée jusqu'à sa mort en 1805. Il fut secondé dans son travail par Giovanni Fabbroni qui l'accompagna dans ses nombreux voyages et devint son adversaire permanent en accédant au poste de directeur adjoint en 1784.

L'argent pour la réalisation du Musée de physique et d'histoire naturelle (et de beaucoup d'autres projets de Pierre Léopold) fut obtenu en vendant des objets précieux appartenant aux Médicis et ce, malgré le testament de la princesse palatine Anna Maria Luisa (1668–1743), la sœur de Jean Gaston, qui avait légué d'une façon irrévocable toute la fortune des Médicis à la Ville de Florence.

Les fonds du musée, provenant essentiellement des Offices, comprenaient des collections diverses (minéraux, coquillages …), des curiosités de sciences naturelles de l'époque des Médicis, les instruments de Galilée, les appareils de l'Accademia del Cimento et quatre figures de cire du sculpteur Giulio Gaetano Zumbo.

Voulant élargir le musée aux domaines de l'astronomie et de la météorologie, Pierre Léopold demanda en 1780 à l'architecte Gaspare

Paoletti (qui avait déjà participé à la transformation du palais) de construire l'Osservatorio Astronomico (la « petite tour ») qui devait donner plus tard à l'ensemble du complexe le nom de « Specola » (observatoire). Il s'agissait d'un projet ambitieux qui agrandissait considérablement le bâtiment et fut achevé en 1789, malgré les avis divergents de nombreux experts, lesquels auraient préféré bâtir une nouvelle construction sur les collines de l'Acetri. La même année, une partie du parc Boboli fut intégrée au jardin botanique du musée (ill. p. 8).

A la mort de son frère Joseph, Pierre Léopold lui succéda à la tête de l'Empire en 1790 et céda la Toscane à son fils cadet Ferdinand III (1769–1824) qui était bien loin de posséder la largeur d'esprit de son père et son habileté à gouverner. Pour couronner le tout, la Toscane fut prise par les Français en 1799. Après maintes complications, elle devint en 1801 le royaume d'Etrurie et fut remise aux Bourbon-Parme. Durant ces années, le musée organisa des cours dans les disciplines scientifiques, qui se poursuivirent après la restauration des Lorrains en 1814.

Le musée vécut une période mouvementée sous Ferdinand III. Il perdit son importance scientifique qui l'avait caractérisé à ses débuts, époque où il était considéré comme l'un des plus grands centres du savoir européen, ce qu'attestaient d'ailleurs des visiteurs étrangers aussi illustres que Goethe et Bernouilli. A l'instar de son père, Ferdinand III entreprit des transformations importantes dans le palais : en 1820, un

1793 catalogue of the wax models

Katalog der Wachspräparate von 1793

Catalogue des préparations en cire de 1793

corridor reliant la Specola à l'aile de la Méridienne, un pavillon du palais Pitti, fut construit sous la direction de l'architecte Pasquale Poccianti. Ce nouveau passage prolongeait jusqu'à la Specola le corridor Vasari existant qui conduisait du palais Vecchio au palais Pitti en passant par les Offices.

A la mort de Ferdinand III en 1824, le grand-duché passa aux mains de son fils Léopold II (1797–1870), surnommé gentiment « Canapone » par les Florentins en raison de ses cheveux blonds. C'est à lui que revient le mérite d'avoir donné un nouvel élan aux études scientifiques, en particulier à celles que l'on pouvait appliquer concrètement comme dans l'agriculture par exemple. C'est également sous sa régence que fut construite la Tribuna di Galileo, hommage au grand chercheur, qui fut inaugurée à Florence, en 1841, à l'occasion du troisième congrès des scientifiques italiens. La Tribuna est une grande salle au premier étage du bâtiment en partie reconstruit par l'architecte Giuseppe Marelli. Les travaux commencés en 1830 ne prévoyaient à l'origine qu'une abside supplémentaire dans une salle déjà existante, mais les plans furent modifiés à la demande du grand-duc. Voulant honorer avec grandeur la mémoire de l'illustre savant, il décida de lui consacrer la salle entière qui abriterait, outre une statue de Galilée, tous les objets que l'on avait conservés de lui ainsi que ses instruments se trouvant à l'Accademia del Cimento. La construction de la Tribuna, l'un des rares témoignages du néoclassicis-

A page of the register recording receipts for corpses from the hospital

Registerseite mit Vermerk der Eingänge der Leichname aus dem Krankenhaus

Page du registre avec les indications des arrivées des cadavres provenant des hospices

49

me à Florence, entraîna d'importantes modifications dans l'architecture du palais : les étages inférieurs furent transformés et la cour fut en partie couverte. On fit venir des peintres et des sculpteurs de la région pour décorer la salle recouverte entièrement de marbre de Toscane.

L'Istituto di Studi Superiori e di Perfezionamento (institut d'études supérieures et de perfectionnement), transformé en 1923 en université royale, fut fondé en 1859 après la chute de Léopold II, le dernier grand-duc de Toscane. Evénement déjà important en soi, la fondation de l'Institut a marqué par ailleurs pour le musée le début de son démembrement en différents départements qui, en raison du nombre toujours croissant des étudiants, durent s'installer en d'autres lieux avec leurs collections et leurs bibliothèques. Seul le département de physique et de sciences naturelles du musée demeura au siège de l'Institut. Malgré l'opposition de nombreux scientifiques de l'époque, le bâtiment historique de la via Romana n'abrita plus finalement que les collections zoologiques et la plus grande partie de la céroplastie anatomique.

Les débuts de la céroplastie dans l'anatomie

L'utilisation de la cire pour modeler des figures remonte à l'époque des Romains. De tout temps, la cire fut un matériau très apprécié, dans l'art en particulier, pour des raisons esthétiques et techniques. La cire se laisse aisément travailler, elle est idéale comme moule pour couler le bronze par exemple. C'est surtout dans l'Europe du Moyen Age que l'on fabriqua en cire un grand nombre d'offrandes, de statues de saints, de crèches et d'ex-voto. A la Renaissance et durant tout le XVIIᵉ siècle, on pouvait admirer d'innombrables modèles en cire dans les églises italiennes, en particulier dans l'Orsammichele et la Santissima Annunziata. Ces modèles étaient des membres et des organes humains, mais aussi des portraits et des statues bien souvent grandeur nature. Au XVIIᵉ siècle apparurent ensuite des modèles anatomiques reproduits pour les besoins de la science.

Bien que l'Etat et encore plus l'Eglise eussent interdit et puni l'étude du corps humain sur les cadavres, les premiers dessins anatomiques firent leur apparition au milieu du XVᵉ siècle. Ils furent réalisés en général par des grands peintres et sculpteurs comme Léonard de Vinci, Michel-Ange, Raphaël et Titien, pour ne citer que les plus célèbres. D'illustres chercheurs, tels Falloppio, Cesalpino ou Vesalius, utilisèrent les dessins de ces artistes pour illustrer leurs traités d'anatomie.

A la fin du XVIIe siècle, Gaetano Giulio Zumbo fut le premier à se servir dans la célèbre école d'anatomie de Bologne de cire colorée pour modeler des préparations en cire. Originaire de Syracuse, l'artiste dont les œuvres sont reproduites plus loin, réalisa deux têtes d'homme (l'une conservée à Florence, l'autre à Paris), une figure féminine (malheureusement disparue) et quelques petites compositions. C'est à Bologne également que fut fondée la première école de céroplastie dont sortirent, durant la seconde moitié du XVIIIe siècle, les sculpteurs du musée florentin. Considéré comme le fondateur de l'école de Bologne, le peintre, sculpteur et architecte Ercole Lelli (1702–1766) modela, comme Zumbo avant lui, des muscles et des viscères en cire sur de vrais squelettes. Amateur de sciences naturelles, le cardinal Prospero Lambertini, élu pape en 1740 sous le nom de Benoît XIV, encouragea les études anatomiques de l'école de Bologne et acheta tous les modèles de Lelli, de magnifiques exemplaires que l'on peut admirer aujourd'hui encore à l'Istituto di Anatomia Umana Normale de l'université de Bologne. Enfin, et ceci est d'une grande importance, il apporta son soutien aux chercheurs devant se procurer des cadavres pour leurs travaux. Parmi les assistants de Lelli, signalons Giovanni Manzolini (1700–1755) qui, avec l'aide de sa femme Anna Morandi (1716–1774), réalisa de nombreux modèles conservés également à l'université de Bologne.

A cette époque, l'étude de l'anatomie était en plein essor dans toute l'Europe. L'école céroplastique de Florence fut fondée sur le modèle de l'école de Bologne à l'instigation de Giuseppe Galletti. Chirurgien et accoucheur, il s'inspira des œuvres de Lelli et de Manzolini pour créer avec le sculpteur Giuseppe Ferrini toute une série de modèles en cire et en terre cuite (elles se trovent actuellement au Museo di Storia della Scienza de Florence) devant illustrer différents types d'accouchements, normaux et dystociques.

L'atelier de céroplastie à Florence fut actif pendant un siècle environ, de 1771 à la seconde moitié du XIXe siècle, mais la majeure partie des objets en cire conservés au musée, de même que les travaux réalisés pour les institutions florentines et d'autres commanditaires, furent effectués durant les soixante premières années de son existence (ill. p. 42).

La fondation de la Specola remonte à Felice Fontana qui, pleinement soutenu par le grand-duc Pierre Léopold, s'y consacra avec une

Les figures en cire de la Specola : l'école, les œuvres, les techniques

énergie d'autant plus grande qu'il participait lui-même à la création des modèles en tant qu'anatomiste et pathologiste. Au début, le sculpteur Giuseppe Ferrini travailla seul à l'atelier sous la direction de Fontana. Plus tard, on engagea l'anatomiste Antonio Matteucci ainsi que Clemente Susini, un tout jeune homme à l'époque, qui se révéla si habile et si productif qu'il ne tarda pas à devenir le plus célèbre céroplasticien de l'école florentine (ill. p. 47).

On ignore aujourd'hui où on travaillait la cire, probablement dans les salles du rez-de-chaussée dont les fenêtres donnent sur la Via Romana. Ces salles sont situées dans l'aile sud du palais, qui est pourvue de nombreuses courettes. La plupart des appareils d'origine ont disparu, mais leur acquisition figure encore dans les archives : bassines en cuivre de plusieurs tailles dans lesquelles on faisait fondre la cire ; instruments à modeler (ill. p. 33) ; fils de fer de grosseur différente ; plaques de marbre servant à presser la cire en fines couches ; balances ; trépieds pour chauffer le matériau ; ardoises pour les notes et les dessins réalisés pendant les dissections ; caisses munies de poignées pour le transport des cadavres, caisses en bois munies de tiges pour le transport des figures de cire ; récipients, vases et bouteilles en céramique ou en verre pour les couleurs et autres substances ajoutées à la cire. On retrouva dans les anciens entrepôts du musée un grand nombre de ces récipients avec leur contenu (ill. p. 32).

Les archives nous indiquent par ailleurs qu'il fallait réunir plus de deux cents cadavres ou parties de cadavres pour fabriquer une seule figure. Ce nombre incroyablement élevé s'explique pour la bonne raison que le formol et la réfrigération étant inconnus, il fallait constamment recourir à des cadavres frais pour les dissections. Afin de recenser exactement les cadavres provenant des hospices de Santa Maria Nuova à deux kilomètres de là, on tenait un registre dans lequel étaient notées toutes les arrivées, mais aussi tous les départs pour le cimetière : « [...] à propos des cadavres de Santa Maria Nuova dont on ignore le nombre et parce qu'on ne peut pas faire mourir les gens pour les besoins des collections de cire, il a été décidé de placer un registre à la porte du musée afin de consigner les cadavres utilisés en ce lieu, dont le nombre semble considérable, et afin de noter la fréquence des envois au cimetière. » (extrait d'un document de 1793).

Malgré le petit nombre de préparateurs, les travaux allaient bon train si l'on considère qu'aux environ de 1790, soit vingt ans après leur commencement, les modèles remplissaient déjà huit salles, sans compter ceux que l'on avait fabriqués pour les hospices de Florence et d'autres institutions en Italie et à l'étranger (cf. ill. p. 48). De toutes les sculptures en cire qui sortirent de l'atelier de la Specola pour être envoyées aux quatre coins de l'Europe, les plus remarquables sont celles effectuées pour l'école militaire de médecine à Vienne. Commandée en 1781 par l'empereur d'Autriche Joseph II, le frère aîné de Pierre Léopold, la collection fut achevée en 1786. Elle comprenait 1200 pièces qui furent acheminées à dos d'âne jusqu'à Vienne et nécessitèrent deux voyages. D'autres sculptures prirent la route de Pavie, de Cagliari, de Bologne, de Budapest, de Paris (elles se trouvent aujourd'hui à Montpellier), d'Uppsala, de Londres, de Leyde et de bien d'autres villes encore. Ces commandes de l'extérieur soulevaient parfois des problèmes d'organisation car le grand-duc ne tolérait aucun retard dans la fabrication de certains modèles pour le musée. On décida donc que pour ces commandes, les sculpteurs et les anatomistes – Fontana lui-même dans le cas de la collection viennoise – pouvaient certes utiliser les moulages et les instruments du musée, mais qu'ils devaient se procurer eux-mêmes le matériel et se faire assister d'artisans étrangers au musée.

Si Fontana tenait absolument à créer le plus grand nombre possible de modèles anatomiques en cire, c'est parce qu'il voulait constituer une réserve qui rendrait superflue l'exhumation de cadavres pour les cours d'anatomie. C'est également dans ce but qu'il réalisa toute une série de dessins (ill. p. 10, 11) illustrant les différentes parties du corps : les organes, les muscles, les os, etc., étaient reliés par des lignes discontinues à des chiffres qui permettaient leur identification. Les dessins et les explications étaient conservés dans un tiroir du coffre où se trouvait la figure de cire correspondante. Chaque préparation était ainsi accompagnée d'un véritable traité d'anatomie (ill. p. 21).

Vers 1790, Fontana se lança dans un projet encore plus ambitieux qu'il ne put mener à bien à cause des difficultés qu'il rencontra. Il s'agissait d'une série de pièces d'anatomie en bois peint – de taille réelle ou agrandies – que l'on aurait pu démonter afin de montrer les liens entre les différents organes. Après quelques tentatives dont on a gardé seulement un petit nombre d'exemplaires, à savoir deux sculptures entières (une au musée, l'autre à Paris) et un buste gigantesque, Fontana dut abandonner son projet. Non seulement le bois se laissait difficilement travailler, mais étant un matériau organique, il se déformait avec le temps et les différentes pièces ne s'adaptaient plus. La seule sculpture du musée présentant les caractéristiques souhaitées fut fabriquée en cire. Il s'agit de la « Venere medicea », une figure féminine allongée dont on peut retirer les éléments superposés jusqu'à l'apparition de l'utérus et d'un petit fœtus (ill. p. 39).

Le musée avait entre-temps agrandi son équipe. Il avait engagé le dessinateur Claudio Valvani, le sculpteur sur bois Luigi Galati ainsi que plusieurs anatomistes pour la dissection des cadavres. L'un des plus célèbre fut Paolo Mascagni (1755–1815) qui laissa à la postérité de magnifiques planches anatomiques. Il s'était spécialisé dans l'étude du système lymphatique, ce n'est donc pas un hasard si à la Specola cette partie de l'organisme est représentée avec une grande minutie sur de nombreuses statues, mais aussi sur des préparations plus petites.

La mort de Felice Fontana (ill. p. 17) en 1805 n'empêcha pas l'atelier de poursuivre son travail, et à la mort de son successeur Clemente Susini, en 1814, ce furent d'autres sculpteurs, comme les Calenzuoli (le père Francesco et le fils Carlo) ou Luigi Calamai (1800–1851), qui se chargèrent de la direction. Sous Calamai, les activités se concentrèrent sur des modèles d'anatomie comparative et de botanique ainsi que sur les modèles d'anatomie pathologique qui étaient destinés aux hospices de Santa Maria Nuova et que l'on peut voir aujourd'hui au musée d'anatomie pathologique de l'université. Après sa mort, Calamai fut remplacé par Egisto Tortori (1829–1893) qui, à côté de préparations d'animaux et d'anatomie pathologique, modela également un buste de Clemente Susini. A la mort de Tortori, en 1893, l'atelier cessa définitivement ses activités.

De nos jours, le musée La Specola abrite 513 modèles en cire d'anatomie humaine, soixante-cinq d'anatomie comparative et cinq réalisés par G. G. Zumbo. Il possède aussi vingt-six figures (dont un tronc de jeune garçon) : treize debout et treize couchées, dont dix-huit grandeur nature (six debout et douze couchées) et huit mesurant soixante centimètres environ (sept debout et une allongée). A l'exception de quatorze sculptures sur l'anatomie humaine se trouvant dans les entrepôts, toutes sont exposées au public. Il faut également ajouter plus de huit cents dessins encadrés et près de neuf cents feuillets explicatifs dont le nombre était jadis certainement supérieur, mais qui ont été égarés au cours des siècles. Ces dernières années, on a retiré des salles d'exposition les dessins et les feuilles explicatives pour les préserver des dommages causés par la lumière et l'humidité. Ils ont été remplacés par des photocopies en couleur de sorte que la structure de la collection a pu être conservée aussi bien du point de vue de la présentation que du point de vue didactique.

Tandis que les experts en la matière sont impressionnés par la perfection scientifique des objets exposés, la plupart des visiteurs s'intéressent surtout à leur côté artistique, car ils sont malgré toute leur rigueur scientifique et leur vocation didactique, de véritables œuvres d'art. La beauté de ces objets est mise en valeur par les coffres en bois très travaillés, dans lesquels ils sont conservés. Malheureusement beaucoup de ces coffres se sont abîmés

avec le temps et auraient grand besoin d'être restaurés. Datant du XVIIᵉ siècle, les draperies et voiles en soie, à l'origine vert clair, et se trouvant eux aussi dans un bien triste état, montrent quel soin fut toujours apporté à la présentation de la collection.

G. G. Zumbo: Self-portrait (detail from *The Triumph of Time*)

Selbstporträt (Ausschnitt aus *Der Triumph der Zeit*)

Autoportrait (détail de *Le Triomphe du Temps*)

Ce souci d'esthétique se constate par ailleurs dans les collections d'anatomie comparative, d'anatomie pathologique et en particulier dans les collections de botanique où des vases en céramique furent réalisés spécialement pour les petits modèles de plantes par l'atelier Gionori de Sesto Fiorentino.

Comme les procédés techniques pour la fabrication des figures en cire ne nous ont pas été transmis de façon explicite, nous ne pouvons les reconstituer qu'à partir des diverses lettres et documents des archives nationales et du Musée des sciences de Florence. Pour compliquer le tout, chaque sculpteur avait sa propre technique qu'il se gardait bien de divulguer. Une chose est sûre cependant : une fois les parties du corps disséquées, on en faisait une copie exacte en craie ou en cire de qualité inférieure dont on tirait un moulage en plâtre qui, s'il s'avérait de grande taille, pouvait être constitué de plusieurs pièces. Pour certains organes, comme les os, on pouvait faire directement un moulage en plâtre (ill. p. 60). Ces moulages conservés aujourd'hui encore dans les entrepôts du musée constituaient une sorte de matrice que l'on pouvait utiliser plusieurs fois pour reproduire le même modèle. L'étape la plus complexe et la plus délicate était la construction du modèle définitif. Elle exigeait une grande précision, une connaissance approfondie des sub-

stances qu'il fallait mélanger à la cire pour obtenir la couleur et la consistance souhaitées, ainsi que beaucoup d'expérience et de savoir-faire. La
cire devait fondre lentement au bain-marie pour que sa couleur ne soit
pas altérée. On utilisait le plus souvent de la cire blanche de Smyrne, de
la cire chinoise et de la cire de Venise. Pour la rendre plus malléable, on y
ajoutait de la térébenthine ainsi que des colorants, dilués eux aussi dans
de la térébenthine, et d'autres substances apparaissant sur les listes
d'achat sous la mention « matières nécessaires pour les travaux en
cire ». Afin que plus tard, le modèle se détache facilement du moule,
celui-ci était humidifié à l'eau tiède et frotté avec un savon doux avant
que l'on y coule le mélange de cire. Mis à part quelques préparations
complètement en cire, la plupart étaient creuses à l'intérieur et remplies
de chiffons, d'étoupe ou de morceaux de bois pour une plus grande stabilité. Les statues constituées de plusieurs pièces assemblées les unes
aux autres étaient en général renforcées par une armature métallique.
Une fois le moule ôté, la figure était soigneusement nettoyée, puis can-
nelée avec les outils appropriés et, finalement, dotée de ses organes,
vaisseaux, nerfs, etc. Une dernière couche de vernis transparent lui
conférait le brillant nécessaire. Afin d'être sûr que le modèle soit confor-
me à l'original, toutes les étapes étaient constamment surveillées par les
anatomistes qui décidaient également de la meilleure position pour
mettre en valeur tel ou tel organe.

Comme nous l'avons déjà dit, chaque sculpteur possédait sa
propre technique et ses méthodes particulières qu'il perfectionnait avec
le temps en utilisant de nouveaux instruments, comme par exemple cette « filière à tirer les cylindres en cire » mise à leur disposition dès 1786.
Avant, cette opération permettant de modeler les veines et les artères
devait être faite à la main. Autour de 1790, les sculpteurs tinrent pendant
quelques années des « cahiers » (ill. p. 43) dans lesquels ils notaient
quotidiennement les travaux effectués, et qui nous permettent de
constater qu'à l'époque déjà ils devaient entreprendre des restaurations,
des réparations, des améliorations et des corrections. En 1793, Susini
rédigea une « [...] note sur les préparations anatomiques en cire à corri-
ger en raison des erreurs constatées par moi, Clemente Susini, mode-
leur du musée royal, erreurs qui méritent d'être réparées. » Par exemple :
« Vérification de la préparation de l'artère pharyngée et de la carotide :
on peut voir partant de la trachée-artère deux muscles étrangers n'appartenant pas au corps humain et un muscle rattaché au prolongement de

la thyroïde, mais qui ne semble être ni le muscle de la langue, ni du pharynx et encore moins de la thyroïde. » La note de Susini se termine avec la constatation suivante : « Ces erreurs sont trop graves pour ne pas être corrigées. Je passe toutes les autres sous silence car je désire être bref. » Presque tous les modèles se trouvent en bon état de conservation, quelques-uns seulement ont changé de couleur : certains fœtus sont devenus foncés et les veines qui présentent aujourd'hui une teinte verte étaient jadis ‹ bleu violet ›.

Les figures en cire de Gaetano Giulio Zumbo

Les sculptures en cire de Gaetano Giulio Zumbo méritent qu'on leur consacre un chapitre à part, non seulement en raison de leur conception et de leur méthode de fabrication inhabituelles, mais surtout parce qu'étant en avance d'un siècle sur les autres représentations anatomiques en cire, elles constituent la base de toutes celles qui suivront.

Né en 1656 à Syracuse, Zumbo est issu d'une famille de la vieille noblesse qui s'appelait probablement Zummo et dont il ne reste plus aucune trace aujourd'hui. Comme le nom de « Zumbo » est plus connu et est passé dans l'usage, il nous semble opportun de le garder. Nous savons peu de choses sur sa vie, quelques fragments tout au plus. Elevé chez les Jésuites dans sa ville natale, il dut quitter le collège à cause d'un « incident ennuyeux » qui n'est pas précisé. Les œuvres classiques qu'il put voir dans sa patrie ont certainement eu au début une influence sur sa formation artistique et culturelle. Plus tard, ce furent les thèmes et les sujets du maniérisme et du baroque qui exercèrent un ascendant sur lui. Il vécut à Naples de 1687 à 1691 où il réalisa probablement deux des groupes allégoriques appartenant à la Specola, les « teatrini », à savoir *Il Trionfo del Tempo* (Le Triomphe du Temps) et *La Peste*. Les spécialistes qui se sont penchés sur l'œuvre de Zumbo affirment que le fonds pittoresque et l'agencement des figures trahissant l'influence des maîtres d'Italie du Sud sont le signe de sa paternité. De 1691 à 1694, Zumbo travailla à Florence pour Cosme III de Médicis et acheva d'autres « teatrini » : *Il Sepolcro* (ou *La Vanità della Gloria Umana*) et *Il Morbo Gallico* (ou *Sifilide*) qui se réfèrent à l'art de la Renaissance. En 1695, il entreprit quelques voyages pour Bologne où il manifesta beaucoup d'intérêt pour les études anatomiques alors en plein essor. A la fin de 1695, il s'installa à Gênes. C'est là probablement qu'il acheva *L'anatomie de la tête* exposée à la Specola. C'est là aussi qu'il rencontra le chirurgien français

Guillaume Desnoues avec lequel il collabora pour des modèles anatomiques en cire comprenant, entre autres, une parturiente grandeur nature, une femme morte en couches de format plus petit ainsi que la naissance et la mise au tombeau du Christ. Malheureusement, ces œuvres
n'ont pas été conservées. En 1700, Zumbo se brouilla avec le médecin
français et partit pour Marseille où il effectua une tête en cire, puis pour
Paris où il entra au service de Louis XIV. Il demeura dans cette ville jusqu'à sa mort, en 1701, emporté par une hémorragie cérébrale. Parmi ses
affaires, on trouva une magnifique tête en cire qui est, selon toute proba-
bilité, celle conservée de nos jours au Musée national d'histoire naturelle. Enterré en l'église de Saint-Sulpice, sa tombe fut détruite pendant la
Révolution.

Une grande partie des œuvres de cet artiste encore largement
méconnu il y a un demi-siècle est conservée au musée La Specola. Les
trois « teatrini », connus également sous le nom de *Cera della peste*
(figures de la peste), et l'anatomie de la tête se trouvaient à la Galerie
royale (c'est-à-dire aux Offices) lorsque les Lorrains succédèrent aux
Médicis. Ils furent ensuite envoyés au Museo di Fisica e Storia Naturale
où ils ne furent jamais exposés, peut-être à cause du réalisme brutal des
scènes. Lorsque Pierre Léopold partit pour Vienne en 1790, il offrit les
« figures de la peste » au médecin de la cour, Giovanni Giorgio Asenöhrl,
plus connu sous le nom de Lagusius. Celui-ci ne les garda pas mais
chargea Fontana et, plus tard, Agostino Renzi, surintendant de la Phar-
macie royale, de les vendre pour 150 sequins. Conscient de leur valeur,
le surintendant les proposa au nouveau grand-duc Ferdinand III, d'abord
pour l'Académie royale des beaux-arts où l'on jugea ces figures « ni
utiles ni appropriées », puis pour le Musée royal. Cette proposition fut
appuyée par Giovanni Fabbroni, directeur adjoint du musée, et les trois
œuvres furent estimées par différents experts dont Clemente Susini.
Comme les estimations dépassaient le prix réclamé par Lagusius, le
grand-duc consentit à leur acquisition. Les « teatrini » restèrent au
musée jusqu'en 1978, date à laquelle ils furent remis au Museo Nazionale de Bargello. Après avoir été cédés au Museo di Storia della Scienza, ils
revinrent finalement à la Specola en 1974. Comme le prouvent les
archives, les sculptures en cire furent plusieurs fois restaurées dans le
passé, entre autres par Susini et Tortori. Se trouvant au Museo di Storia
della Scienza, celles « de la peste » furent gravement endommagées par
les pluies diluviennes de 1966. Très méticuleusement, Guglielmo Galli

Page · Seite · Page 59:

Detail from pages
92–93

Detail der Seiten
92–93

Détail des pages
92–93

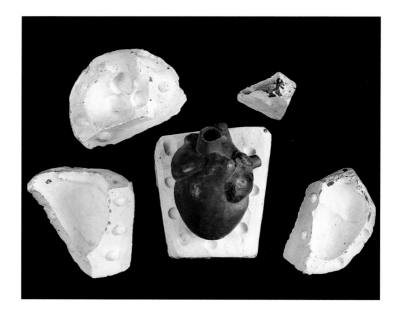

de l'atelier de Pietre Dure à Florence parvint au bout de dix-huit mois à les remettre en état en s'aidant de photographies. *L'anatomie de la tête* en revanche n'a jamais quitté la Specola puisqu'elle était à juste titre considérée comme présentant intérêt particulier pour la collection scientifique de l'institut.

La technique employée par Zumbo se distingue fortement de celle de l'école florentine à venir. *L'anatomie de la tête* fut exécutée sur un vrai crâne ayant appartenu, si l'on en croit les radios, à un homme âgé de vingt-cinq ans. En revanche, la tête conservée à Paris et une autre disparue aujourd'hui ont été fabriquées entièrement en cire, ce qui permet de conclure à une évolution de sa technique, due probablement à la coopération du céroplasticien sicilien avec Desnoues. Les figures des « teatrini » exécutées avec une grande habileté dans les moindres détails, ont été très probablement obtenues à partir de moulages de pièces qui, à leur tour, se basaient très soigneusement sur des modèles en argile. La cire plus ou moins liquide (un mélange de cire d'abeille, de colophane, de térébenthine et de colorants) était appliquée en couches de diverses épaisseurs suivant la consistance et la coloration souhaitées. Si l'on possède aujourd'hui quelques précisions sur la technique de

Zumbo, c'est grâce aux travaux de restauration de Guglielmo Galli entrepris après les inondations de 1966, qui révélèrent par ailleurs les traces de réparations plus anciennes du fait de la présence de colorants n'existant pas encore à la fin du XVIIᵉ siècle. Le petit autoportrait (ill. p. 55) du groupe *Il Trionfo del Tempo* ne peut pas être attribué à Zumbo avec certitude, il pourrait être l'œuvre d'un contemporain ou de Susini plus tard. Celui intitulé *Il Morbo Gallico*, à l'origine une composition du même type et dont il n'existe plus que quelques fragments, fut offert à Filippo Corsini par Cosme III. Conservé en permanence dans les caves du palais Corsini sur l'Arno, il fut pratiquement détruit par les inondations. On retrouva quelques figures dans les jardins mais, n'ayant pas de photographie de l'ensemble, une reconstruction s'avéra impossible. A l'occasion du bicentenaire de l'ouverture du musée, qui fut célébrée avec un congrès sur la céroplastie, la famille Corsini fit don au musée des restes de cette œuvre.

Pendant longtemps, les chefs-d'œuvre de Zumbo furent considérés comme les caprices malsains d'un artiste se plaisant à reproduire des détails macabres et repoussants. Ce n'est qu'au milieu de notre siècle qu'on les considéra dans leur véritable perspective historique, comme des documents réalistes d'une époque où les guerres, les famines et les grandes épidémies étaient le lot quotidien des hommes. Cette vision de la destruction, de la précarité de l'existence humaine, de la fuite inexorable du temps, ce « memento mori » continuel auquel les œuvres de Zumbo nous confrontent avec une foule de détails, est un exemple typique de la culture du XVIIᵉ siècle, telle qu'elle nous a été également transmise par d'autres grands artistes de l'époque, comme Luca Giordano ou Mattia Preti.

Pages · Seiten ·
Pages 62–63:

G. G. Zumbo:
La Peste

The plague

Die Pest

La peste

Wax Flesh, Vicious Circles
Georges Didi-Huberman

Wax Flesh

Wax is the material of all resemblances. Its figurative virtues are so remarkable that it was often considered a prodigious, magical material, almost alive – and disquieting for that very reason. Even if we leave aside Pharaonic Egypt and its spellbinding texts, Pliny the Elder's *Natural History* already catalogues, in the Roman period, the entire technical-mythical repertory of the medical, cosmetic, industrial, and religious properties of wax. Closer to our time, a Sicilian wax-worker, a modest supplier of exvotos and crèche figurines, expressed some fifteen years ago his wonder at the strange powers of this material, nonetheless so familiar to him: "It is marvelous. You can do anything with it [...]. It moves." (R. Cedrini, 1991).

Yes, wax "moves." To say that it is a *plastic* material is above all to say that it gives way almost without resistance before every technique, before every formative process that one would impose on it. It goes exactly where you ask: it can be cut like butter with the sculptor's chisel, or warmed up and easily modeled with the fingers; it flows effortlessly into molds whose volume and texture it adopts with astounding precision. Wax also "moves" in the sense that it permits the inscription, the duplication, the temporal as well as spatial displacement of the forms which impress themselves into it, transforming, effacing, and reforming themselves infinitely. Which is why, from Aristotle to Freud, this material has provided the privileged metaphor of the work of memory, and even of sensorial operations in general.

But still more, wax "moves" in the sense that it "upsets." The *unstable* material par excellence – if stability is understood as the fixed character of qualities – wax presents a disconcerting multiplicity of physical properties. It seems to be a substance unconcerned by the contradiction of material qualities: it is solid, but easily liquefied; impermeable, yet readily soluble in water; it can be opaque or transparent, matte or polished, slippery or sticky, brittle or malleable; its consistency can be endlessly modified through the addition of a wide range of resins. It is a fragile and temporary material, but is most often used for objects destined to endure. It is untouched by the traditional distinction and hierarchy of the plastic arts, for it can be sculpted, modeled, and molded. To

G. G. Zumbo:
Il Morbo Gallico
(or *Sifilide*)

Syphillis (detail)

Die Syphilis
(Detail)

Le Morbo Gallico
(détail)

Florence, Museo
de la Specola

be sure, this paradox of consistency is a paradox of transitory physical states. It is a name for the fundamental *passivity* – malleability – and *fragility* of wax, which would thus be to the notion of material (conceived as stable) what the butterfly is to the notion of the image (conceived as fixed). Not only is the state of each always consequent on some kind of metamorphosis, splendid as it is fragile – but the candle's wavering flame is equally dangerous for both.

Wax "moves": it warms up in my hand, it assumes the temperature of my body, and at that moment becomes capable of involuting before the detail of my fingers, taking my prints, transiting softly, as though biologically, from one form to another. Thus this vegetal material that bees have "digested" in their bodies and in a sense rendered organic, this material nestled against my flesh, becomes *like flesh*. This is its subtlety, but also its sovereign *power*: everything in it – plasticity, instability, fragility, sensitivity to heat, and so on – suggests the feeling or fantasy of flesh. Let one not be misled by this fundamental *anthropomorphism*: it is not simply a matter of seeing wax as a material particularly apt to reproduce the forms of the human body (if only by molding them); it is above all a matter of inquiring into a more subtle, more anthropological, yet also more textural connivance between this material and the simulacra of the flesh.

The response to this question is not to be found only in the history of the specific uses of wax – a history of which I can only offer the barest outlines here – but even more in the phenomenology of its optical and tactile qualities: there probably exists no other substance that can imitate with such polyvalence both the *external flesh*, the skin, and all the *internal flesh*, the muscles and viscera which are also our flesh, but which in general are felt, seen, and touched as though they were violently heterogeneous to the integuments or the more civilized surfaces of our bodies. As shown, for example, in the celebrated Freudian dream of "Irma's injection," the vision of the internal flesh often appears as an anxious insight, the inverse of human form, the formless itself. This is the direction taken by Lacan's interpretation (which comes very close to Bataille), in *Le Séminiare, II: Le moi dans la théorie de Freud et dans la technique de la psychanalyse* (J. Lacan, 1980). Now, it is precisely through such *reversibility* that the material virtues of wax become marvelous: even in its ever-to-be-expected indecision between form and the formless, wax remains, historically and phenomenologically, the incomparable material of *organic resemblances*. This, no doubt, is the principle reason for the intense fascination that this material has exerted over the long time-span of its history.

**Believers,
Artists,
Scientists**

Fascination – the power of empathy – is often accompanied in the order of discourse by something like *malaise*. Now, all malaise calls up resistance, avoidance, even censorship. We can observe, for example, that the attention brought to the history of wax sculpture has had the effect of destabilizing the conventional categories of art history, revealing something like a methodological gap at the very heart of the discipline.

In a well-known article entitled "Artist, Scientist, Genius," Erwin Panofsky quite rightly insisted on the epistemological "decompartmentalization" initiated by the Renaissance: it was at this point, he says, that "those particular branches of natural science which can be called sciences of observation or description (zoology, botany, paleontology, physics in many respects, anatomy above all) began a rapid development directly linked to the development of the techniques of representation." It was also at this point that theory rejoined practice in "the suppression of the barriers that had separated the 'liberal arts' from the 'mechanical arts' in the Middle Ages – separating theoretical knowledge, considered as the work of pure intellect, from the plastic activities in which the figurative arts were involved." (E. Panofsky, 1952).

However, the "history of art as a humanistic discipline," from Vasari to the adepts of Panofsky's iconology, has reinstated other compartments – whose elaboration was in fact begun by the 16th-century academies. Among them are the aesthetic and social distinction between artist and artisan. Now, wax seems to partake more of artisanal technique than of artistic *disegno*: it does not belong among the "noble" materials of sculpture, it only enters humanist aesthetics at the bottom rungs of the ladder, linked as it can be – like plaster, for instance – to the "intermediary" or "humble" procedures of artistic creation. Thus on the subject of the simultaneous rise of anatomical science and the "techniques of representation," one finds infinite glosses on the anatomist Leonardo da Vinci, while the wax oeuvre of Gaetano Giulio Zumbo – masterful in its artistry and invention, in addition to its achievements in anatomy and description – is with rare exceptions still confined to the carefully quarantined domain of curiosities or to the history of the sciences, and presented within the strict context of the anatomical exhibition (in Florence, Leonardo is in the Uffizi, while Zumbo is in the Specola, on the other side of the Arno).

This caesura – this censorship – is, I repeat, simply the other side of the malaise and the *non-aesthetic* feeling procured by the excessive resemblance of objects in wax. As Ernst Gombrich said outright: "[before] the proverbial resemblance of wax images [...] we feel a certain

Michelangelo: Wax model of slave, 16th century

Michelangelo: Sklavenmodell, Wachs, 16. Jahrhundert

Michel-Ange: Modèle d'esclave en cire, XVIe siècle

London, Victoria and Albert Museum

unease, due to the fact that it is situated outside the limits of symbolization." (E. H. Gombrich, 1959, p. 53). In short, wax would always seem to go too far: the resemblance it produces is so radical, so unmediated, that the "real" of the image obfuscates everything else, pushing the "symbol" (the value of signification, the iconological content) into the background. Horst Janson went even further, excluding from any veritable history the crass, trivial productions – always out of line, *mauvais genre* – of a material which, in his eyes, was so given to crude realism that it became inapt for style, and thus, for art itself. (H. W. Janson, 1988) Curiously, then, the history of art will have aesthetically recompartmentalized that which it had recognized as epistemologically decompartmentalized. One could say, in a word, that Panofsky's iconology surreptitiously closed down everything that Warburg's iconology had attempted to open up a generation before, by means of its "methodological enlargement of the frontiers" of the discipline. (A. Warburg, 1990, p. 215). Today the disturbing, unaesthetic production of wax objects is primarily studied by anthropologists or historians of culture. But it is hardly surprising that Warburg – the inventor of an art history conceived as a veritable *Kulturgeschichte*, that is, implying a veritable anthropology of images – should have been a pioneer in restoring wax to its fundamental role in the visual culture of the Renaissance, by establishing the close relation between the high art of the Florentine portrait in the Quat-

Wax mask from Cumae, c. 1st century BC (left)

Wachsmaske aus Cumae, ca. 1. Jahrhundert v. Chr. (links)

Masque de cire de Cumes, vers le Ier siècle avant J.-C. (à gauche)

Naples, Museo Archeologico Nazionale

trocento and the votive production of wax effigies for the Santissima Annunziata (A. Warburg, 1902).

Julius von Schlosser was – from the viewpoint which interests us here, that of the material – the first to draw the consequences from this lesson in method. The author of a 1911 monograph entitled *The History of the Wax Portrait*, he dared to take the full *anthropological* measure of the phenomenon, approaching the diversity of its functions (funerary, votive, artistic, and scientific, without forgetting its uses in freak-shows) as an astonishing survival of forms across the long time-span of Western history, from the Roman funerary masks to the advent of photography (J. von Schlosser, 1993). The approach was courageous, not only for the type of erudition it entailed, but even more so because it forced the art historian to question his "classical" concept of art and his habitual practice of history.

It seems possible to approach the "surviving" or transhistorical character of these images (one can consider, for example, the effigy of Marat in the Musée Grévin as a survival of the one which, in the first century before Christ, portrayed Caesar with his twenty-three wounds) by reflecting on the *originary* nature of the figurative practices linked to wax. After all, the Roman meaning of the word *imago* implies the impression of a face and the confection of a positive in wax, which, as Pliny explains in his *Natural History, XXXV*, was then colored and attained a state of "extreme resemblance." The "origin," of course, is not taken here as a supposedly initial source in this complex history, not does it designate a state of quintessence or simplicity. It merely speaks of the repetitive and *anachronistic* character of images in wax, whose "evolutionary law" escapes any clearly oriented pattern of explanation. For example, the Roman mask discovered in Cumae, with its glass eyes and what certain authors identify as traces of artificial hair (ill. p. 68, left), is formally closer to Madame Tussaud's effigies than to a Renaissance funerary mask like that of Fra Angelico in Rome (ill. p. 68, right).

Wax is also, as we know, the privileged material of seals (ill. p. 90), where it legitimates the existence of a symbolic power: royal authority, a juridical contract, the authentication of a relic, and so on. Unlike a simple mimetic or metaphorical representation, the wax imprint, we may say, *incarnates the symbolic power*. Operating not by optical imitation but by direct duplication, by contact with the ductile material, it produces images which are corporeally *engendered* – and not ideally invented – by the *matrix* or negative of the seal. The analogy with the flesh (the womb) is so strong that numerous medieval authors, among them Saint Francis of Assisi, used the biblical image of the wax seal to evoke the stigmatizing mark of divine power in the hearts of the faithful. Such as the famous expressions of Psalms, 67:5 (*sicut cera fluxerunt ... a facie Domini*) or 12:5 (*et factum est cor meum tamquam cera liquescens*), which St. Francis takes up in his hymn books.

This "incarnate power" of wax does not only form a metaphor in the discourse of the great mystical authors. It is everyday "flesh" for the believer – *liturgical flesh*. It is handled and kissed during mass, as the *Agnus Dei*; it burns and is infinitely exchanged in the form of candles (from humble votive candles to the massive plague candles fashioned along the ramparts of the city, in order to obtain divine protection); it is modeled and exhibited in the form of all kinds of holy dolls or crèche figurines. In the form of the funerary effigy, it shares in the transmission of power and in the ideology of the "king's two bodies." Its textural analogy with flesh (density, grain, color, brilliance . . .) is so great that it ends up serving as an organic relic, like the pink wax tongue exhibited alongside an *Agnus Dei* in a reliquary in the Schnütgen Museum in Cologne (ill. p. 80).

Omnipresent in these inexhaustible liturgical stagings, wax thus becomes an artifact of the flesh, an artifact whose symbolic power is precisely that of making people believe in the resurrection of the flesh. This is why the ex-voto in wax predominates throughout all of Mediterranean civilization: it offers a veritable encyclopedia of organic resemblances, external or internal, an encyclopedia where the description of the organs is woven of all possible fantasies, as in the "popular anatomy" described by Freud with respect to the hysterical body (ills. pp. 86, 97). This is also why, in so many churches, the *wax faces* of saints stand for the *waxen faces* of real cadavers, seen as miraculously uncorrupted. Finally, this is the reason why the bourgeois Florentines of the Renaissance, still steeped in a profound Christian religiosity – but already readers of Pliny, who described the wax *imago* as a distinctive sign of civic *dignitas* – gave themselves over to the extreme, hyperrealist game of wax ex-votos molded directly on their face and hands.

This votive practice would be no more than a "curiosity" of local history – as it has generally been considered, in fact – if it had not had certain decisive consequences on all the visual and artistic culture of the

Renaissance, as Warburg, the first, intuitively grasped. This is indeed "decompartmentalization" at work, a decompartmentalization due largely to the plastic and technical potential of wax itself: for the Florentine *fallimagini* – that is, votive "image makers," active since the 14th century, perhaps since the end of the 13th – would ultimately pass on their technical mastery of *realism by contact* (casting, pouring of wax, coloration of the material) to the great artists of the Quattrocento.

In short, the material of wax, this "believers' flesh," was slowly to become something like "artists' flesh." It is fascinating to see how the latter were able to expand the technical stereotypes of religious craft to the level of a veritable *heuristics*, that is, an experimentation open to all its stylistic consequences. Donatello, for example, offered a striking counterpoint to the classical face of his *Judith* by creating the veil covering her head with a procedure that only the plasticity of the material made possible: he dipped a real cloth in hot wax and tossed it onto a cardboard or wooden mannequin, so that it would form the most natural, least "stylized" folds; he then had the hardened object directly cast in bronze.

We know that most of the innumerable bronze objects of the Renaissance first existed as *modelli* in wax – the "lost wax" that gives its name to the most common technique of casting. It was only from the 16th century onwards, with the development of the aesthetic taste for the sketch, that the sculptors' *modelli* and *bozetti* would be saved from destruction by the use of more complex technical procedures. Thus we can still admire the extraordinary wax models attributed to Michelangelo and his workshop, preserved at the Victoria and Albert Museum in London in particular (ill. p. 73).

It is striking to see in three dimensions what the anatomical studies of Leonardo da Vinci offered in two. Namely, "a composition of the surfaces" of the human body, to use Alberti's phrase – a body now conceived the basis of the *écorché*. As Goethe would later say: "What is the outside of an organic nature, if not the eternally changing appearance of the inside?"

Thus we are led back to the terrain of the human anatomy (ill. p. 74), as though the figurative uses of wax described an *anthropological circle* where everything, in one way or the other, must ultimately have to do with the theater of the human body. Did the "believers' flesh" of the votive waxes not manifest, above all, the organic unease of the donors?

Did the "artists' flesh" of the *modelli* not manifest, above all, their visual curiosity for the relation between the surfaces and the depths of the human body? And it is from these two precedents that the "scientists' flesh" of the 18th-century anatomical waxes can be historically and technically inferred: beyond the fact that the Florentine artists traditionally belonged to the guild of doctors and apothecaries (*Arte dei medici e speziali*), beyond the fact that the first anatomical écorché in wax was fashioned by the artist Cigoli (whose échorché dating from 1600 is today preserved at the museo nationale del Bargello in Florence), the capital point here lies in the tradition of technical know-how linked to a privileged material (wax) and a privileged figurative challenge (the flesh).

Thus it is no accident that the first great school of medical ceroplastics was born in Florence, at the very heart of humanism and of the "decompartmentalization" of the different branches of knowledge in the Renaissance. The great modelers of the Specola – Susini, Calami, Calenzuoli, Tortori – inherited, perhaps without their full awareness, knowledge and know-how from the long distant past times and cultural regions far removed from any "scientific" attitude. For in the exact anatomical description of a leg by Clemente Susini (ill. p. 74) there survives the religious framing of a votive leg (ill. p. 86) as well as the artistic concerns of a leg modeled in the studio of Michelangelo (ill. p. 73).

Vicious Circles   It is astonishing to observe that this "anthropological circle" was rounded in its entirety by a single man – the same man who gave wax sculpture its most extreme and disquieting masterpieces. I am speaking of Gaetano Giulio Zumbo (ill. p. 55). His whole life seems to have been a long voyage from his native Sicily to the north, and from "believers' flesh" (the world of religious figurines) to "scientists' flesh" (the hospital morgues where, from Bologna to Genoa and Paris, he carried out extraordinary anatomical models). Between the two, Zumbo discovered the Roman baroque; and then in Florence, for the Medici court, he fashioned four celebrated allegorical groups where the study of different states of the decomposition of flesh is pushed so far that it is alternately fascinating and revolting.

Exact putrescence and baroque mortality: Zumbo produces artifacts of a raw, non-transposed anatomy, endlessly observed on real cadavers – and yet also subtly staged works of art, diverted and endlessly reinvented from the models provided by Bernini, or indeed Poussin. The conjunction of these two effects gives rise to a supplement of malaise, the very malaise which no doubt kept the four allegorical groups out of the Uffizi. Beyond realism, and even beyond style: Zumbo's oeuvre has always been considered from the angle of perversity, indeed of perversion. Here the "anthropological circle" is so radically shut upon itself that it becomes like a "vicious circle." This work casts us into the element of resemblance, as though into a region of infernal disquiet. It is the unease of organic resemblances, where nothing – above all not the "idealization" of an academic style – can preserve us from the formless.

The first author of stature to have recognized the overwhelming grip of this "vicious circle" was none other than the Marquis de Sade. His account of the sexual abominations and murders of Juliette and her companions in the city of Florence in *Histoire de Juliette* is studded with texts from the *Voyage in Italy* he had written some twenty-three years earlier: Sade's description of Zumbo's works – their "fearful truth," he writes – is deployed in a context that mingles desire, cruelty, and death. Thus the Sicilian master of the wax anatomical sculpture is at the origin of two cultures which are generally considered contradictory: on the one hand, *black romanticism* and its popular destiny, incarnated by the wax museums of Curtius, Madame Tussaud, or Grévin; and on the other hand, *positivism* and its popular destiny, incarnated by the 19th-century anatomical museums – part science exhibits and part freak shows,

Flayed leg, formerly attributed to Michelangelo, 16th century

Bein (Muskelmodell), ehemals Michelangelo zugeschrieben, 16. Jahrhundert

Jambe d'écorché, autrefois attribué à Michel-Ange, XVIe siècle

London, Victoria and Albert Museum

which exhibited the consequences of vice in the form of terrifying pathological models (ill. p. 89).

One certainly ought not to see this "popular destiny" of wax
sculpture – even in its farcical aspect, even in its predilection for the twin
themes of sexual vice and bloody crime – as a simple vulgarization of a
malaise already present in certain votive or funerary effigies. When Julius
von Schlosser evokes the *déclassement* of wax sculpture in the 19th century, he does not forget to convoke Warburg's notion of survival, and he
does not forget, consequently, to revoke "all teleological pretensions and
judgments of value" (J. von Schlosser, 1910/11, p. 120). Georges Bataille,
for his part, made such *déclassement* a characteristic operation of the
formless. How can one not see, in this very movement, a radical ques-
tioning of classical aesthetics? How can one not see – Schlosser made it
the entire conclusion of his book – that the very existence of the wax
objects displaces any classical reference to the notion of beauty?

Here indeed is a *displacement* that contemporary aesthetics has
taken up and radicalized: there is no longer any need to conceive, with
Vasari, of any kind of "biological" progress in the arts; to that, Nietzsche
opposed the eternal return – a vicious circle – and the mingling of the
Dionysian in the Apollonian. There is no longer any reason to aspire to
ideals hewn in marble; to that, Freud opposed the tragic play of desire
and mourning, the vicious circle of *Unheimlichkeit*. Once again, wax

Anatomical leg,
18th century

Bein, anatomi-
sches Modell,
18. Jahrhundert

Jambe, modèle
anatomique, XVIIIe
siècle

Florence, Museo
de la Specola

would be a material for all this
uneasy flesh, for all these vicious
circles. A *trap-material* to catch
our fantasies. A *flight-material*
where resemblance is plastically
exchanged for dissemblance,
appearance for disappearance
(indeed, Medardo Rosso probably
used wax for exactly that, see ill.
p. 99). A material where the compact mass of flesh is exchanged
for the "indistinct breath of the
image."

Fleisch aus Wachs: Circuli vitiosi
Georges Didi-Huberman

Wachs ist der Stoff aller Ähnlichkeiten. Seine figuratven Eigenschaften
sind so bemerkenswert, daß es in Geschichtsdarstellungen oft als ein
wunderhaftes, magisches, ja fast belebtes und eben deshalb beunruhi-
gendes Material betrachtet wurde. Von den Schriften über die Hexenkün-
ste im Ägypten der Pharaonen einmal ganz abgesehen, hat im römischen Zeitalter bereits Plinius der Ältere in seiner *Naturkunde* das
gesamte technisch-mythische Repertoire der medizinischen, künstlerischen, kosmetischen, industriellen und religiösen Verwendungen des
Wachses beschrieben. Aber auch noch vor etwa fünfzehn Jahren begei-
sterte sich ein sizilianischer Wachsbildner, ein bescheidener Lieferant
von Exvotos und Krippenfiguren, über die seltsame Macht, die dieser
ihm doch so vertraute Werkstoff in seinen Augen birgt: „Wachs ist wun-
dervoll. Man kann alles mit ihm machen. [...] Es bewegt sich." (R. Cedrini, 1991)

Ja, Wachs „bewegt sich": Wenn man Wachs als einen *plastischen*
Werkstoff bezeichnet, so bedeutet dies vor allem, daß es sich jeder technischen Bearbeitung und jeder Formgebung, die man ihm angedeihen
lassen möchte, nahezu widerstandslos fügt. Es „geht" genau dahin, wo
man es von ihm verlangt: Es läßt sich vom Meißel des Bildhauers wie
Butter schneiden, es läßt sich erwärmen und ist leicht mit den Fingern
zu modellieren, es kann in Formen gegossen werden, deren Volumen
und Textur es mit verblüffender Präzision annimmt. Wachs „bewegt
sich" auch in dem Sinne, daß es die Eingravierung, Duplizierung und –
zeitliche wie räumliche – Verschiebung der Formen erlaubt, die in ihm
immer wieder neu eingeprägt, gewandelt und umgebildet werden können. Im Denken der Philosophen von Aristoteles bis Freud wurde Wachs
bevorzugt als Metapher für die Arbeit des Gedächtnisses, ja für die der
Sinneswahrnehmungen überhaupt herangezogen.

Wachs „bewegt sich" aber auch im Sinne eines „Wandelns". Als
instabiler Stoff schlechthin – vorausgesetzt, man versteht unter Stabilität
die Beständigkeit seiner Qualitäten – weist Wachs eine verwirrende Vielfalt physikalischer Eigenschaften auf. Es scheint, als sei es eine Substanz, die keinen Widerspruch stofflicher Qualitäten kennt: Es ist fest,
aber leicht zu verflüssigen; undurchlässig, aber problemlos in Wasser zu

lösen; es kann opak sein oder durchsichtig, matt oder poliert, glatt oder griffig, brüchig oder geschmeidig; seine Konsistenz kann durch den Zusatz verschiedenster Harze unbegrenzt verändert werden. Obwohl es ein anfälliges und vergängliches Material ist, wird es meist für Gegenstände verwendet, die überdauern sollen. In der traditionellen Untergliederung und Hierarchie der bildenden Künste hat das Wachs keinen festen Platz, da es sowohl behauen, modelliert als auch gegossen werden kann. Bei diesem Paradox der Konsistenz handelt es sich um ein Paradox vorübergehender physikalischer Zustände, das die grundsätzliche *Passivität* – Formgeschmeidigkeit – und *Anfälligkeit* des Wachses bezeichnet.

Zu der Vorstellung, die man sich von einem Werkstoff macht (dem man Stabilität unterstellt), verhält Wachs sich sozusagen so wie ein Schmetterling zum Bild (das als beständig gilt): Nicht nur folgt beider Zustand stets aus einer Metamorphose, die prächtig und anfällig zugleich ist, auch sind beide von der Flamme einer Kerze gleichermaßen gefährdet.

Wachs „bewegt sich": Es erwärmt sich in der Hand, nimmt die Körpertemperatur an und kann sich nun ins Detail meiner Finger schmiegen und deren Abdrücke aufnehmen, auf sanfte, ja gleichsam biologische Weise von einer Form in eine andere übergehen. Von den Bienen in ihrem Körper „verdaut" und dadurch gewissermaßen organisch geworden, wird dieser pflanzliche Stoff, wenn er sich an mein Fleisch schmiegt, selbst *zu Fleisch*. Gerade darin liegt seine subtile und doch souveräne *Macht*: Seine Plastizität, Instabilität, Anfälligkeit und Wärmeempfindlichkeit suggerieren das Gefühl oder die Vorstellung von Fleisch.

Diese grundlegend *anthropomorphische* Qualität darf nicht ver-
kannt werden, denn es geht nicht allein darum, im Wachs einen Werkstoff zu erkennen, der in besonderem Maße zur Nachbildung menschlicher Körperformen geeignet ist (und sei es nur durch deren Abgießen).
Vielmehr kommt es darauf an, einer subtileren, anthropologischeren,
auch textürlicheren Übereinstimmung zwischen diesem Stoff und den
Trugbildern des Fleisches nachzuspüren.

Die Antwort hierauf findet sich nicht nur in der Geschichte der
spezifischen Anwendungen des Wachses (die hier nur schematisch
angerissen werden kann), sondern auch in der Phänomenologie seiner
optischen und haptischen Qualitäten selbst: Es gibt wohl keine Substanz, die mit derartiger Vielseitigkeit das *äußere Fleisch*, die Haut, und
zugleich all das *innere Fleisch* nachahmt, alle jene Muskeln und Eingeweide, die zwar ebenfalls unser Fleisch sind, die wir jedoch im allgemeinen
gegenüber der Haut oder den zivilisierteren Oberflächen unseres Körpers als ungeheuer fremdartig empfinden. Wie beispielsweise Freuds
berühmter Traum von Irmas Injektion zeigt, tritt die Vision des inneren
Fleisches zumeist als eine Angstvision, als die Kehrseite des menschlichen Gesichts, als das Unförmige schlechthin auf. In diesem Sinne ver-
fährt insbesondere auch Lacans – übrigens sehr Bataillesche – Deutung
in *Das Ich in der Theorie Freuds und in der Technik der Psychonalyse*
(J. Lacan, 1980). Gerade in einer solchen *Umkehrbarkeit* wirken nun die
materiellen Tugenden des Wachses Wunder. Bis hin zum stets erfahrba-
ren Wechsel von der Form zum Unförmigen bleibt Wachs historisch und
phänomenologisch der Werkstoff aller *organischen Ähnlichkeiten* par
excellence. Das ist der Hauptgrund für die lebhafte Faszination, die
dieser Werkstoff über den langen Zeitraum seiner Geschichte hinweg
ausgeübt hat.

Die Faszination – die Kraft der Empathie – geht in der Ordnung des Dis-
kurses oft mit so etwas wie einem *Unbehagen* einher. Nun ruft aber jede
Form von Unbehagen nach Widerstand, Vermeidung, ja Zensur. Sobald
sich die Kunstgeschichte mit der Geschichte des Wachsbildnisses
beschäftigt, wird im Kern dieser Disziplin so etwas wie eine methodolo-
gische Verwerfung sichtbar.

Erwin Panofsky sprach in seinem berühmten Aufsatz „Artist,
Scientist, Genious" mit vollem Recht von der „Entgrenzung" der Wis-

**Gläubige,
Künstler,
Gelehrte**

sensgebiete, die in der Renaissance stattfand: Zu jener Zeit, sagte er, nahmen die „Einzelzweige der Naturwissenschaften, die man Beobachtungs- oder Beschreibungswissenschaften nennen kann (die Zoologie, Botanik, Paläontologie und in vielerlei Hinsicht die Physik, insbesondere aber die Anatomie), einen Aufschwung, der unmittelbar mit dem Aufschwung der Darstellungstechniken zusammenhing". Und zu jenem Zeitpunkt vereinigten sich auch Theorie und Praxis in der „Aufhebung der Schranken, die im Mittelalter die ‚freien Künste' von den ‚mechanischen Künsten' getrennt hatten, d. h. die Schranken zwischen der theoretischen Erkenntnis, die als reines Verstandeswerk betrachtet wurde, und den gestalterischen Tätigkeiten, zu denen die bildenden Künste zählten." (E. Panofsky, 1952)

Seit Vasari bis zu den heutigen in der Nachfolge Panofskys stehenden Ikonologen hat die „Kunstgeschichte als humanistische Disziplin" durchaus manche Grenzen neu gezogen, und zwar exakt diejenigen, die die Akademien des 16. Jahrhunderts zu errichten begonnen hatten – so etwa die ästhetische und soziale Unterscheidung zwischen Künstler und Kunsthandwerker. Nun scheint die Wachsbildnerei eher dem Kunsthandwerk anzugehören als den bildenden Künsten im engeren Sinne: Wachs zählt nicht zu den „edlen" Werkstoffen der Bildhauerei, in der humanistischen Ästhetik steht es auf den unteren Sprossen der Stufenleiter, mit ihm verbindet man – ebenso wie mit Gips – eher die „Zwischenschritte" oder „anspruchslosen Verfahren" der künstlerischen Schöpfung.

Deshalb finden sich bezüglich des gemeinsamen Aufschwungs der anatomischen Wissenschaft und der „Darstellungstechniken" in der historischen Literatur Erörterungen über den Anatom Leonardo da Vinci in Fülle, während die sowohl auf künstlerisch-innovativer als auch auf anatomisch-beschreibender Ebene meisterhaften Wachsarbeiten Gaetano Guilio Zumbos bis auf wenige Ausnahmen ganz dem Bereich der Kuriosa oder der Geschichte der Wissenschaften zugerechnet werden. So finden sich denn auch in Florenz die Werke Leonardos in den Uffizien und die Zumbos in der Specola, am anderen Ufer des Arno.

Diese Zäsur – diese Zensur – ist, dies sei nochmals betont, nur die andere Seite des Unbehagens und des nichtästhetischen Empfindens, die von der ungeheuren Ähnlichkeit der Wachsgegenstände ausgelöst werden. Ernst Gombrich spricht ohne Umschweife von „jenen oft zitierten Wachsfiguren, die uns so unheimlich sind, weil sie tatsächlich jene Grenze zwischen Symbol und Wirklichkeit überschreiten" (E. H. Gombrich, 1967, S. 82).

Kurz, Wachs tue des Guten stets zuviel: Die erzeugte Ähnlichkeit sei so radikal, so unvermittelt, daß die „Wirklichkeit" des Bildes alles andere überblende und das „Symbol" (den Bedeutungswert, den ikonologischen Gehalt) in den Hintergrund dränge. Horst Janson ging noch weiter und verwies aus der Geschichte der Skulptur jene trivialen, grellen, stets ins *mauvais genre* fallenden Erzeugnisse eines Werkstoffs, der nach seiner Auffassung dem rohen Realismus derart Vorschub leiste, daß er zur Ausprägung eines Stils und deshalb auch zur Kunst untauglich sei (H. W. Janson, 1982).

Merkwürdigerweise hätte also die Kunstgeschichte auf der ästhetischen Ebene gerade das wieder eingegrenzt, dessen Entgrenzung sie doch auf der epistemologischen Ebene anerkannt hatte. In groben Zügen zusammengefaßt, könnte man sagen, daß die Panofskysche Ikonologie heimlich wieder schloß, was die Warburgsche Ikonologie eine Generation zuvor mittels einer „methodischen Grenzerweiterung der Kunstwissenschaft" zu öffnen versucht hatte (A. Warburg, 1992, S. 185).

Heute sind es vor allem die Ethnologen oder die Kulturhistoriker, die die Nicht-Ästhetik, die verstörende Produktion von Wachsobjekten erforschen. Doch es ist nicht verwunderlich, daß Warburg, der Erfinder einer als Kulturgeschichte gedachten – und somit eine regelrechte Anthropologie der Bilder voraussetzenden – Kunstgeschichte in bahnbrechender Weise dem Wachs seine fundamentale Rolle in der visuellen Kultur der Renaissance zurückgab, indem er die enge Verbindung zwischen der großen florentinischen Porträtkunst des Quattrocento zu den Votivbildnissen aus Wachs in der Santissima Annunziata nachwies (A. Warburg, 1902).

Unter dem Gesichtspunkt des Werkstoffs, hat Julius von Schlosser als erster die Konsequenzen aus dieser Methodenlehre gezogen. Als er 1911 seine *Geschichte der Porträtbildnerei in Wachs* verfaßte, wagte er sich daran, die ganze anthropologische Dimension dieses Phänomens auszuloten, wobei er sowohl auf die Vielfalt der Funktionen (Begräbnisse, Votivbildnisse, Kunst, Wissenschaft und Jahrmarkt) einging als auch auf das erstaunliche Überdauern dieser Kunstform in der abendländischen Tradition (von den römischen Totenmasken bis zur Entstehung der Fotografie). Diese Herangehensweise war nicht nur der von ihr erforderten Gelehrsamkeit halber mutig, sondern darüber hinaus auch des-wegen, weil sie die Kunsthistoriker zwang, ihre „klassische" Auffassung der Kunst ebenso wie ihre gängige Praxis der Geschichtsschreibung in Frage zu stellen.

Das „Fortdauern" oder Transhistorische dieser Darstellungen (so ließe sich beispielsweise das Bildnis Marats im Musée Grévin als ein Fortdauern desjenigen betrachten, das im 1. Jahrhundert v. Chr. Cäsar mit seinen 23 Wunden darstellt) wird vielleicht deutlich, wenn man an den *ursprünglichen* Charakter der wachsbildnerischen Praktiken zurückdenkt. Schließlich meint die lateinische Bedeutung des Wortes *imago* den Abdruck des Gesichts und die Anfertigung eines Wachspositivs, über das es bei Plinius dem Älteren in der *Naturkunde XXXV* heißt, daß es farbig und „so ähnlich wie möglich" war.

Der Begriff „Ursprung" zielt hier selbstverständlich nicht auf eine vorgeblich erste Quelle in dieser komplexen Geschichte, auch nicht auf einen quintessentiellen oder einfachen Zustand. Er besagt lediglich den repetitiven und *anachronistischen* Charakter der Wachsbilder, deren „Entwicklungsgesetz" sich jedem eindeutigen Schema entzieht: So ist die in Cumae gefundene römische Maske mit ihren Glasaugen dem, was nach Auffassung einiger Autoren Spuren eines Haarschmucks sind (Abb. S. 68, links), in formaler Hinsicht einem Bildnis von Madame Tussaud näher als einer Totenmaske der Renaissance wie der des Fra Angelico in Rom (Abb. S. 68, rechts).

Wachs war bekanntlich auch das Siegelmaterial schlechthin (Abb. S. 90). Es legitimierte das Bestehen

Reliquary-altar with Agnus Dei, 18th century

Reliquienaltar mit Agnus Dei, 18. Jahrhundert

Autel-reliquaire avec Agnus Dei, XVIIIe siècle

Cologne, Schnütgen Museum

einer symbolischen Macht: Es beglaubigte die königliche Autorität, den juristischen Vertrag, die Echtheit einer Reliquie usw. Im Unterschied zu einer bloßen mimetischen oder metaphorischen Repräsentation inkarniert der Wachsabdruck diese Macht; da es sich nicht um eine optische Imitation handelt, sondern um eine direkte Duplizierung des Siegels, wird ein Abbild erzeugt, das der *Matrix* oder dem Negativ des Siegels körperlich entspricht und nicht ideell erfunden wurde. Die Analogie zum Fleisch ist so stark, daß zahlreiche Autoren des Mittelalters das biblische Bild vom Siegel im Fleische wieder aufgegriffen haben, um die stigmatisierende Einprägung der göttlichen Macht in die frommen Herzen zu veranschaulichen. So etwa der berühmte Wortlaut der Psalmen, XCVII, 5 (*sicut cera fluxerunt ... a facie Domini*) oder XII, 5 (*et factum est cor meum tamquam cera liquescens*), die Franz von Assisi in seinen Antiphonien aufgriff.

Diese „leibhaftige Macht" des Wachses wirkt nicht nur in den Diskursen der großen mystischen Autoren als Metapher. Es ist das tägliche „Fleisch" für die Gläubigen – ein *liturgischer Leib*. Bei der Messe wird es in Gestalt des *Agnus Dei* berührt und geküßt; in Gestalt der Kerzen – von der allerbescheidensten bis hin zu den riesigen gedrehten Wachsstöcken, die zu Pestzeiten entlang der Stadtmauern aufgestellt wurden, um so die Stadt unter Gottes Schutz zu stellen – brennt es und wird unendlich. Es wird modelliert und ausgestellt in all den verschiedenen Arten von Andachtspuppen oder Krippenfigürchen. In seiner Gestalt als Grabkerze hat es teil an der Machtübertragung und der Ideologie der „zwei Körper des Königs". Seine textürliche Analogie zum Fleisch (Dichte, Beschaffenheit, Farbe, Glanz ...) ist so groß, daß es schließlich als organische Reliquie dient, wie jene rosafarbene Wachszunge, die in einem Reliquienkästchen im Kölner Schnütgenmuseum neben einem *Agnus Dei* ausgestellt ist (Abb. S. 80).

In diesen unerschöpflichen liturgischen Inszenierungen wird das allgegenwärtige Wachs somit zu einem Artefakt des Fleisches, ein Artefakt, dessen symbolische Macht die Auferstehung des Fleisches glaubhaft machen soll. Aus diesem Grund überwiegt das Wachs-Exvoto in der gesamten Mittelmeerkultur: Es bietet eine regelrechte Enzyklopädie äußerer oder innerer organischer Ähnlichkeiten, eine Enzyklopädie, in der die Beschreibung der Organe sich mit allen möglichen Phantasmen zu jener „volkstümlichen Anatomie" verwebt, von der Freud bezüglich des hysterischen Körpers sprach (Abb. S. 86, 97). Aus demselben Grund stehen in so vielen Kirchen die *Wachsantlitze* der Heiligenbilder für die *wächsernen Antlitze* wirklicher Leichname, die als auf wundersame Weise unverwest erscheinen sollen. Die Florentiner Bürger der Renaissance schließlich, die bereits Plinius lasen, bei dem die *imago* aus Wachs als vornehmer Ausdruck ziviler *dignitas* beschrieben steht und die noch von tiefer christlicher Religiosität geprägt waren, ließen sich wiederum aus diesem Grund auf jenes äußerste, hyperrealistische Spiel der unmittelbar von ihrem Gesicht und ihren Händen abgeformten Wachs-Exvotos ein.

Dieser Votivbrauch wäre nur ein örtliches historisches „Kuriosum" – so wurde er im übrigen meistens eingeschätzt –, wenn er nicht, wie Warburg erstmals einsichtig entwickelte, einige entscheidende Auswirkungen auf die visuelle und künstlerische Kultur der Renaissance gehabt hätte. Und gerade dies ist die „Entgrenzung", die stattgefunden hat – eine Entgrenzung, die größenteils dem plastischen und technischen Potential des Wachses zu verdanken ist: Die florentinischen *fallimagini*, die „(Votiv-)Bildmacher", die seit dem 14., möglicherweise sogar bereits seit dem 13. Jahrhundert tätig waren, müssen ihr technisches Können eines „Realismus durch Kontakt" (Wachsabdruck oder -abguß, Einfärbung des Materials) den großen Künstlern des Quattrocento mitgeteilt haben.

Kurzum, Wachs, dieses „Fleisch für Gläubige", wird nach und nach zu so etwas wie „Fleisch für Künstler" geworden sein. Es ist faszinierend zu sehen, wie es letzteren gelungen ist, die technischen Stereotypen des religiösen Kunsthandwerks in den Rang einer regelrechten *Heuristik*, das heißt eines allen stilistischen Konsequenzen aufgeschlossenen Experimentierens, zu erheben. Donatello zum Beispiel hat dem klassischen Antlitz seiner *Judith* einen packenden Kontrapunkt entgegengestellt, indem er den ihr Haupt bedeckenden Schleier nach einem Verfahren schuf, das allein die Geschmeidigkeit des Werkstoffs zuließ: Er tauchte ein Stück Tuch in heißes Wachs und warf es auf eine Schneiderpuppe aus Pappe oder Holz, damit es sich auf die spontanste, natürlichste, am wenigsten „stilisierte" Weise falte; dann ließ er das erhärtete Gebilde direkt in Bronze gießen.

Wir wissen, daß die meisten der unzähligen Bronzeobjekte der Renaissance zunächst *modelli* aus Wachs waren, gemäß dem Wachsausschmelzverfahren, der damals geläufigsten Gußtechnik. Erst seit dem 16. Jahrhundert, als sich der ästhetische Geschmack an der Skizze entwickelte, wurden die *modelli* und *bozzetti* der Bildhauer mit Hilfe komplexerer Verfahren vor der Zerstörung bewahrt. So können wir noch heute die außergewöhnlichen Wachsmodelle Michelangelos und seiner Werkstatt bewundern, insbesondere die im Londoner Victoria and Albert Museum (Abb. S. 73): Wir sind verblüfft, dort dreidimensional zu erblicken, was die anatomische Studie bei Leonardo da Vinci zweidimensional darbot: eine „Komposition der Oberflächen" – der Ausdruck stammt von Alberti – des menschlichen Körpers, die nunmehr von der Frage des bloßgelegten Inneren her gedacht ist. Oder wie Goethe es später in *Diderots Versuch über die Malerei* ausdrücken sollte: „Was ist das Äußere einer organischen Natur anders, als die ewig veränderte Erscheinung des Innern?"

Damit befinden wir uns also wieder auf dem Gebiet der menschlichen Anatomie (Abb. S. 74), ganz so, als ob die figurativen Verwendungen des Wachses einen *anthropologischen Zirkel* beschreiben würden, in dem alles auf die eine oder andere Art das Theater des menschlichen Körpers beträfe. Bekundet das „Fleisch für Gläubige" der Votivwachse nicht vor allem die organische Beunruhigung der Stifter? Bekundet das „Fleisch für Künstler" der *modelli* nicht vor allem die visuelle Wißbegierde auf die Beziehung zwischen der Oberfläche und den Tiefen des menschlichen Körpers?

Historisch wie technisch ist aus diesen beiden Vorläufern das „Fleisch für Gelehrte" in Form der anatomischen Wachsdarstellungen des 18. Jahrhunderts hervorgegangen. Abgesehen davon, daß die Florentiner Künstler traditionsgemäß der Zunft der Ärzte und Apotheker (*Arte dei medici e speziali*) angehörten und daß der allererste anatomische Körperaufriß aus Wachs von dem Künstler Cigoli stammt, dessen anatomischer Aufriß von 1600 heute im Museo nazionale del Bargello in Florenz aufbewahrt wird, liegt der entscheidende Punkt in der Vermittlung der Fertigkeiten, die mit einem bevorzugten Werkstoff (dem Wachs) und einer bevorzugten figurativen Herausforderung (dem Fleisch) verbunden sind.

Es ist also kein Zufall, daß die erste große Schule der medizinischen Wachsbildnerei in Florenz entstand, dem Zentrum des Humanismus und der „Entgrenzung" des Wissens in der Renaissance. Die großen Präparatoren der Specola – Susini, Calenzuoli oder Tortori – haben, vielleicht ohne sich dessen bewußt zu sein, Wissensinhalte und Fertigkeiten beerbt, die aus Zeiträumen weit vor und aus Kulturräumen fern aller „Wissenschaftlichkeit" stammten. In Clemente Susinis exakter anatomischer Beschreibung eines Beins (Abb. S. 74) lebt sowohl das religiöse Umfeld des Bein-Exvotos (Abb. 86) fort als auch die künstlerische Bemühung, die das in der Werkstatt Michelangelos modellierte Bein (Abb. 73) erkennen läßt.

Circuli vitiosi Dieser „anthropologische Zirkel" wurde zur Gänze von einem einzigen Mann durchlaufen – eben dem Mann, der die Wachsplastik um die extremsten und beunruhigendsten Meisterwerke bereichert hat. Die Rede ist von Gaetano Giulio Zumbo (Abb. S. 55). Sein ganzes Leben war, so scheint es, eine einzige lange Reise aus dem heimatlichen Sizilien gen Norden und vom „Fleisch für Gläubige" (der Welt der Votivfigurinen) zum „Fleisch für Gelehrte" (den Leichenhallen in den Hospitälern, in denen er, von Bologna über Genua bis Paris, außerordentliche anatomische Modelle anfertigte). Zwischen diesen beiden Stationen entdeckte Zumbo das römische Barock und modellierte in Florenz für den Hof der Medici vier berühmte allegorische Gruppen, in denen die Erforschung der verschiedenen Verwesungsstadien des Fleisches so weit vorangetrieben ist, daß sie wechselweise abstoßen und faszinieren.

Exakter Zerfall und barocker Tod: Zumbo produzierte Artefakte einer brutalen, nicht bildlich-übertragenen, unzählige Male anhand wirklicher Leichname beobachteten Anatomie – und zugleich subtil entrückt inszenierte, unzählige Male aus den bei Bernini, ja Poussin gegebenen Formen neuentwickelte Kunstwerke. Die Verbindung dieser beiden Wirkungen erzeugt ein zusätzliches Unbehagen, das dafür sorgte, daß die vier allegorischen Gruppen keinen Eingang in die Uffizien fanden. Zumbos Werk wurde, jenseits seines Realismus und auch jenseits seines Stils überhaupt, stets unter dem Gesichtspunkt der Verderbtheit, ja der Perversion gesehen. Der „anthropologische Zirkel" ist bei ihm so radikal geschlossen, daß er zu so etwas wie einem Circulus vitiosus wird. Tatsächlich befinden wir uns vor diesem Werk im Element der Ähnlichkeit wie in einem Höllenkreis der Beunruhigung. Es ist die Beunruhigung durch die organischen Ähnlichkeiten, in der nichts – und schon gar nicht die „Idealisierung" eines akademischen Stils – uns vor dem Unförmigen retten wird.

Der erste Schriftsteller von Gewicht, der die Macht dieses Circulus vitiosus erkannte, war kein anderer als der Marquis de Sade. Seine Erzählung von den sexuellen Ruchlosigkeiten und Mordtaten Juliettes und ihrer Spießgesellen in *Histoire de Juliette* sind durchwirkt von den Texten aus *Voyage d'Italie*, die Sade etwa zwanzig Jahre zuvor auf einer

Italienreise verfaßt hatte: Die Beschreibung der Werke Zumbos – und ihrer, wie er schreibt, „erschreckenden Wahrheit" – ist also in einen Kontext gerückt, in dem sich Begehren, Grausamkeit und Tod vermengen. So steht der sizilianische Meister der anatomischen Wachsplastik fortan am Ursprung zweier Kulturen, die im allgemeinen als Gegensätze aufgefaßt werden: einerseits die *schwarze Romantik* und ihr populäres Fortwirken, inkarniert in den Wachsfigurenkabinetten des Dr. Philipp N. Curtius, der Madame Tussaud oder des Musée Grévin; andererseits der *Positivismus* und sein populäres Fortwirken, inkarniert in den halb wissenschaftlichen, halb schaubudenhaften anatomischen Museen, die im 19. Jahrhundert alle Folgen des Lasters in Gestalt abschreckender pathologischer Modelle vorführten (Abb. S. 89).

In diesem „volkstümlichen Fortwirken" der Wachsskulptur – bis hin zu ihren farcenhaften Aspekten und der Vorliebe für das Themengespann von sexuellem Laster und blutigem Verbrechen – darf man sicherlich keine bloße Vulgarisierung oder Beunruhigung sehen, die bereits in bestimmten Votiv- oder Totenbildnissen vorhanden waren. Wenn Julius von Schlosser von der *Ächtung* der Wachsskulptur im 19. Jahrhundert spricht, vergißt er dabei nicht, den Warburgschen Begriff des Fortdauerns heranzuziehen, und vergißt dementsprechend ebensowenig, „allen teleologisch intendierten Ansprüchen und Wertungen" eine Absage zu erteilen (J. von Schlossser, 1910/11, S. 120). Georges Bataille wiederum hat die Ächtung zu einer charakteristischen Operation des *Unförmigen* erklärt. Ist in dieser Entwicklung die Infragestellung der klassischen Ästhetik nicht unübersehbar? Ist nicht unübersehbar – Julius von Schlosser hat daraus die gesamte Schlußfolgerung seiner Darlegung gezogen –, daß durch die schiere Existenz der Wachsobjekte jede klassische Berufung auf den Begriff der Schönheit verschoben ist?

Gerade dieser *Verschiebung* hat sich die zeitgenössische Ästhetik angenommen und hat sie radikalisiert: Es gibt keinen Grund mehr, einen „biologischen" Fortschritt der Künste zu entwerfen, wie Vasari es wollte; dem setzt Nietzsche die ewige Wiederkehr – ein Circulus vitiosus – und die Einmischung des Dionysischen ins Appolinische entgegen. Es gibt keinen Grund mehr, marmorne Ideale anzustreben; dem setzt Freud das tragische Spiel von Begehren und Trauer entgegen, den Circulus vitiosus der *Unheimlichkeit*. Einmal mehr wäre Wachs der Stoff für all dieses beunruhigte Fleisch, für alle diese Circuli vitiosi. Ein verfänglicher Stoff, an den sich unsere Phantasmen heften. Ein flüchtiger Stoff, bei dem

Ähnlichkeit und Unähnlichkeit, Erscheinen und Verschwinden plastisch ineinander übergehen – genau zu diesem Zweck hat Medardo Rosso wahrscheinlich Wachs verwendet (Abb. S. 99) –, bei dem die dichte Masse des Fleisches plastisch übergeht in den „undeutlichen Atem des Bildes".

Chairs de cire, cercles vicieux
Georges Didi-Huberman

La cire est le matériau de toutes les ressemblances. Sa vertu figurative est si remarquable qu'elle fut souvent considérée comme une matière prodigieuse, magique, presque animée – inquiétante à ce titre même. Sans parler de l'Egypte pharaonique et de ses textes d'envoûtement, l'*Histoire naturelle* de Pline l'Ancien déclinait déjà, à l'époque romaine, tout le répertoire technico-mythique des propriétés médicales, artistiques, cosmétiques, industrielles ou religieuses, de la cire. Plus près de nous, un artisan cirier de Sicile, modeste fournisseur d'ex-voto et de figurines pour la crèche, s'émerveillait encore, il y a une quinzaine d'années, de l'étrange pouvoir que cette matière – à lui si familière, pourtant – recelait à ses yeux : « Elle est merveilleuse. On peut tout faire avec. [...] Elle bouge. » (R. Cedrini, 1991).

Oui, la cire « bouge » : dire qu'elle est un matériau *plastique*, c'est dire avant tout qu'elle s'involue, presque sans résister, dans chaque geste technique, dans chaque mise en forme qu'on veut lui imposer. Elle va exactement là où on le lui demande : elle se laisser découper comme du beurre par le ciseau du sculpteur, elle se laisse réchauffer et facilement modeler par les doigts, elle se laisse couler dans des moules dont elle prend le volume et la texture avec une précision stupéfiante. La cire « bouge » aussi en ce sens qu'elle permet l'inscription, la duplication et le déplacement – temporel autant que spatial – des formes qui, en elle, s'impriment, se transforment, s'effacent ou se reforment à l'infini. Voilà pourquoi ce matériau a offert, depuis Aristote jusqu'à Freud, la métaphore privilégiée du travail de la mémoire et, même, de l'opération sensorielle en général.

Mais la cire « bouge » également en ce sens qu'elle « remue », si j'ose dire. Matériau *instable* par excellence – à condition d'entendre par stabilité le caractère fixe de ses qualités –, la cire présente une multiplicité déconcertante de propriétés physiques. On dirait une substance qui ignore la contradiction des qualités matérielles : elle est solide, mais aisément liquéfiable ; imperméable, mais aisément soluble dans l'eau ; elle peut être opaque ou transparente, mate ou polie, lisse ou adhérente, cassable ou malléable ; elle peut être indéfiniment modifiée dans sa consistance par l'adjonction des résines les plus diverses. Elle est un matériau fragile et temporaire, mais utilisé le plus souvent pour des objets destinés à durer. Elle ignore la distinction et la hiérarchie traditionnelles des arts plastiques, puisqu'elle peut être tout à la fois sculptée, modelée ou moulée. Ce paradoxe de la consistance est un paradoxe d'états physiques transitoires, bien sûr. Il nomme une *passivité* – une malléabilité – et une *fragilité* fondamentales de la cire, qui serait pour ainsi dire à la notion de matériau (supposé stable) ce que le papillon est à la notion d'image (supposée fixe) : non seulement l'état de l'un ou de l'autre est toujours consécutif à quelque métamorphose, splendide autant que fragile, mais encore la flamme de la bougie est aussi dangereuse pour l'un que pour l'autre.

La cire « bouge » : elle s'échauffe dans ma main, elle prend la température de mon corps, et à ce moment même devient capable de s'involuer dans le détail de mes doigts, de recueillir mes empreintes, de passer doucement, comme biologiquement, d'une forme à une autre. Alors, ce matériau végétal que les abeilles ont « digéré » dans leur corps et, donc, en un sens, ont rendu organique, ce matériau contre ma chair devient *comme une chair*. Telle est bien sa subtile, mais souveraine *puissance* : tout en elle – plasticité, instabilité, fragilité, sensibilité à la chaleur ... – impose le sentiment ou le fantasme de la chair. Qu'on ne se méprenne pas sur cet *anthropomorphisme* fondamental : il ne s'agit pas seulement de voir dans la cire un matériau particulièrement apte à reproduire les formes du corps humain (ne serait-ce qu'en les moulant) ; il s'agit surtout de s'interroger sur une connivence plus subtile, plus anthropologique, plus texturale aussi, entre ce matériau et les simulacres de la chair.

La réponse à une telle question se trouve non seulement dans l'histoire des usages spécifiques de la cire – histoire dont je ne peux ici proposer qu'un schéma bien sommaire –, mais encore dans la phénoménologie même de ses qualités optiques et tactiles : il n'existe probablement pas de substance qui imite avec autant de polyvalence la *chair externe*, la peau, et toutes les *chairs internes*, c'est-à-dire les muscles et viscères qui sont notre chair aussi, mais sont en général ressenties par nous – vues et touchées – comme violemment hétérogènes aux téguments ou aux surfaces plus civilisées de notre corps. Ainsi que le montre, par exemple, le célèbre rêve freudien de « L'injection d'Irma », la vision des chairs internes se donne le plus souvent comme une vision d'angoisse, l'envers de la forme humaine, l'informe même. C'est en ce sens que va notamment l'interprétation – très bataillienne, au demeurant – de J. Lacan, *Le Séminaire, II. Le moi dans la théorie de Freud et dans la technique de la psychanalyse* (J. Lacan, 1980). Or, c'est précisément dans une telle *réversibilité* que les vertus matérielles de la cire font merveille : jusque dans son va-et-vient toujours probable de la forme à l'informe, la cire demeure, historiquement et phénoménologiquement, le matériau par excellence de toutes les *ressemblances organiques*. Telle est, sans doute, la raison principale de l'intense fascination exercée par ce matériau dans la longue durée de son histoire.

La fascination – puissance d'empathie – s'accompagne souvent, dans l'ordre du discours, de quelque chose comme un *malaise*. Or, tout malaise appelle résistance, évitement, voire censure. On s'aperçoit, en fait, que l'attention portée à l'histoire de la sculpture en cire a pour effet de déstabiliser les catégories usuelles de l'histoire de l'art, révélant au cœur de cette discipline quelque chose comme une faille méthodologique.

Croyants, artistes, savants

Dans un article célèbre intitulé « Artiste, savant, génie », Erwin Panofsky a bien eu raison d'insister sur le « décloisonnement » épistémologique instauré à la Renaissance : c'est à ce moment, dit-il, que « les branches particulières des sciences naturelles qu'on peut appeler sciences d'observation, ou de description (zoologie, botanique, paléontologie, physique à plusieurs égards, anatomie avant tout), prirent un essor directement lié à l'essor des techniques de représentation ». C'est à ce moment aussi que se réunirent théorie et pratique dans « la suppression de ces barrières qui au Moyen Age avaient séparé les ‹ arts libéraux › des ‹ arts mécaniques › – séparé la connaissance théorique, considérée comme l'œuvre du pur intellect, et les activités plastiques dont relevaient les arts figuratifs. » (E. Panofsky, 1952). L'« histoire de l'art comme discipline humaniste », depuis Vasari jusqu'aux iconologues d'aujourd'hui disciples de Panofsky, a cependant bien réinstauré d'autres cloisons – celles-là mêmes que les académies du XVIe siècle avaient commencé de construire : telle la distinction, esthétique et sociale, de l'artiste et de l'artisan. Or, la cire semble relever de la technique et de l'artisanat plutôt que du *disegno* artistique en tant que tel : elle n'appartient pas aux matériaux « nobles » de la sculpture, elle n'entre dans l'esthétique humaniste que par le bas de l'échelle, liée qu'elle peut être – comme le plâtre, notamment – aux procédures « intermédiaires » ou « modestes » de la création artistique. Voilà pourquoi, concernant l'essor conjoint de la science anatomique et des « techniques de représentation », on pourra trouver dans la littérature historique une infinité de gloses sur Léonard de Vinci anatomiste, quand l'œuvre en cire – œuvre magistrale, tant sur le plan artistique et inventif que sur le plan anatomique et descriptif – de Gaetano Giulio Zumbo reste, à de rares exceptions près, confinée au strict domaine de la curiosité ou de l'histoire des sciences, ainsi qu'au strict contexte de l'exposition anatomique (à Florence, Léonard est aux Offices et Zumbo à la Specola, de l'autre côté de l'Arno).

Cette césure – cette censure – n'est, je le répète, que l'autre face du malaise et du sentiment *non esthétique* que procure l'excessive ressemblance des objets en cire. Ernst Gombrich le disait sans ambages : « [devant] la ressemblance proverbiale des images de cire [...] nous éprouvons un certain malaise, du fait qu'elle se situe en dehors des limites de la symbolisation. » (E. H. Gombrich, 1971, p. 86). Bref, la cire en ferait toujours trop : la ressemblance produite serait si radicale, si peu médiatisée, que le « réel » de l'image y viendrait tout offusquer, et repousser le « symbole » (la valeur de signification, la teneur iconologique) à l'arrière-plan. Horst Janson renchérissait en excluant de toute véritable histoire de la sculpture les productions triviales, criardes, toujours *mauvais genre,* d'un matériau selon lui si propice au réalisme brut qu'il en devenait inapte au style, donc à l'art lui-même (H. W. Janson 1982).

Curieusement, donc, l'histoire de l'art aura recloisonné sur le plan esthétique ce dont elle avait pourtant reconnu le décloisonnement sur le plan épistémologique. On pourrait, résumant à grands traits, dire que l'iconologie selon Panofsky a subrepticement refermé tout ce que l'iconologie selon Warburg avait tenté, une génération plus tôt, d'ouvrir par un « élargissement méthodique des frontières » de la discipline (A. Warburg, 1990, p. 215). Aujourd'hui, ce sont surtout les ethnologues ou les historiens de la culture qui étudient l'inesthétique, la gênante production des objets en cire. Mais on ne saurait s'étonner que Warburg, inventeur d'une histoire de l'art pensée comme *Kulturgeschichte* – c'est-à-dire supposant une véritable anthropologie des images – ait, de façon pionnière, restitué à la cire son rôle fondamental dans la culture visuelle de la Renaissance, en établissant le rapport étroit qui lie le grand art florentin du portrait, au Quattrocento, avec la production votive des effigies en cire de la Santissima Annunziata (A. Warburg, 1902)

Julius von Schlosser fut – du point de vue qui nous intéresse ici, à savoir le point de vue du matériau – le premier à tirer toutes les conséquences de cette leçon de méthode : auteur en 1911 d'une monographie sur l'*Histoire du portrait en cire,* il osa prendre toute la mesure *anthropologique* du phénomène, en abordant la diversité des fonctions (funéraire, votive, artistique, scientifique et foraine) comme l'étonnante *survivance* des formes dans la longue durée de notre tradition occidentale (depuis les masques funéraires romains jusqu'à l'avènement de la photographie). L'approche était courageuse, non seulement pour le type d'érudi-

Pages · Seiten · Pages 92–93:

G. G. Zumbo: *Il Trionfo del Tempo*

The Triumph of Time

Der Triumph der Zeit

Le Triomphe du Temps

tion qu'elle demandait, mais encore parce que l'historien de l'art y voyait mis en question son concept « classique » de l'art comme sa pratique usuelle de l'histoire.

Il semble possible d'aborder le caractère « survivant » ou trans-historique de ces images – on peut considérer, par exemple, l'effigie de Marat au musée Grévin comme une survivance de celle qui, au Ier siècle avant J.-C., représenta César avec ses vingt-trois blessures – en réfléchissant sur le caractère *originaire* des pratiques figuratives liées à la cire. Après tout, le sens romain du mot *imago* suppose l'empreinte du visage et la confection d'un positif en cire, dont Pline nous précise bien dans son *Histoire naturelle*, XXXV, qu'elle était colorée et atteignait à une « ressemblance extrême ». L'« origine », bien sûr, ne vise pas ici une source supposée première dans cette histoire complexe, pas plus qu'elle ne désigne un état de quintessence ou de simplicité. Elle dit simplement le caractère répétitif et *anachronique* des images en cire, dont la « loi d'évolution » échappe à tout schéma orienté : ainsi, le masque romain découvert à Cumes, avec ses yeux de verre et – selon certains auteurs – ses traces de cheveux postiches (ill. p. 68, à gauche) est-il plus proche formellement d'une effigie de Madame Tussaud que d'un masque funéraire de la Renaissance tel que celui de Fra Angelico à Rome (ill. p. 68, à droite).

La cire est aussi, nous le savons, la matière par excellence des sceaux (ill. p. 90). Elle légitime l'existence d'un pouvoir symbolique : autorité royale, contrat juridique, authentification d'une relique, etc. A la différence d'une simple représentation mimétique ou métaphorique, l'empreinte de cire, pourrait-on dire, *incarne ce pouvoir* : opérant par duplication directe – et non par imitation optique –, par contact dans le matériau ductile, elle produit des images corporellement *engendrées* – et non idéellement inventées – par la *matrice* ou le négatif du sceau. L'analogie charnelle est si forte que nombre d'auteurs médiévaux, saint François d'Assise notamment, auront repris l'image biblique du sceau dans la cire pour évoquer la marque stigmatisante du pouvoir divin dans les cœurs dévots. Telles, les expressions fameuses de *Psaumes,* XCVII, 5 (*sicut cera fluxerunt ... a facie Domini*) ou XII, 5 (*et factum est cor meum tamquam cera liquescens*), qui seront reprises par saint François d'Assise dans ses *Antiphonaires*.

Cette « puissance incarnée » de la cire ne fait pas seulement métaphore dans le discours des grands auteurs mystiques. Elle est une

« chair » quotidienne pour le croyant – une *chair liturgique*. Elle se manipule et s'embrasse à la messe sous la forme de l'*Agnus Dei* ; elle s'échange à l'infini et s'embrase sous la forme de cierges – depuis la modeste chandelle jusqu'au gigantesque cierge « filé » que l'on confectionne, en temps de peste, à la longueur des remparts de la ville, aux fins de mettre celle-ci sous protection divine – ; elle se modèle et s'expose sous toutes les formes de poupées dévotes ou de figurines pour la crèche. Elle participe, dans sa forme d'effigie funéraire, à la transmission du pouvoir et à l'idéologie des « deux corps du roi ». Son analogie texturale avec la chair (compacité, grain, couleur, brillance ...) est si grande qu'elle finit par faire office de relique organique, telle cette langue de cire rose, exhibée aux côtés d'un *Agnus Dei* dans un reliquaire du Schnütgen-Museum de Cologne (ill. p. 80).

Dans ces inépuisables mises en scène liturgiques, la cire, omniprésente, devient donc un artefact de la chair, artefact dont le pouvoir symbolique serait précisément de faire croire à la résurrection de la chair. Voilà pourquoi l'ex-voto de cire prédomine dans toute la civilisation méditerranéenne : il offre une véritable encyclopédie des ressemblances organiques, externes ou internes, une encyclopédie où la description des organes se tisse de tous les fantasmes possibles, cette « anatomie populaire » dont Freud parlait à propos du corps hystérique (ill. p. 86, 97). Voilà aussi pourquoi, dans tant d'églises, les *visages de cire* des effigies de saints valent pour les *visages cireux* de cadavres réels qui seraient miraculeusement incorrompus. Voilà enfin pourquoi les bourgeois florentins de la Renaissance, déjà lecteurs de Pline – chez qui l'*imago* de cire est décrite comme un signe distinctif de *dignitas* civique – et encore pétris d'une profonde religiosité chrétienne, se sont prêtés au jeu extrême, hyperréaliste, des ex-voto en cire directement moulés sur leur visage et sur leurs mains.

Cette pratique votive ne serait qu'une « curiosité » historique locale – ainsi qu'on l'a généralement considérée, du reste – si elle n'avait eu, comme Warburg en développa l'intuition première, quelques conséquences décisives sur toute la culture visuelle et artistique de la Renaissance. Tel est bien le « décloisonnement » à l'œuvre, un décloisonnement dû en grande partie aux potentialités plastiques et techniques de la cire elle-même : les *fallimagini* florentins – c'est-à-dire les « faiseurs d'images » votives, actifs depuis le XIVe siècle, peut-être depuis la fin du XIIIe – auront fini par communiquer leur maîtrise technique du *réalisme par contact* (moulage, coulage de la cire, coloration du matériau) aux grands artistes du Quattrocento.

Bref, la cire, cette « chair pour croyants », sera peu à peu devenue quelque chose comme une « chair pour artistes ». Il est fascinant de voir comment ceux-ci ont pu élargir les stéréotypes techniques de l'artisanat religieux au statut d'une véritable *heuristique,* c'est-à-dire d'une expérimentation ouverte à toutes les conséquences stylistiques. Donatello, par exemple, a offert un contrepoint saisissant au visage classique de sa *Judith* en réalisant le voile qui lui couvre la tête selon une procédure que seule permettait la plasticité du matériau : il trempa un tissu réel dans de la cire chaude et le jeta sur un mannequin de carton ou de bois, afin qu'il prît son plissé le plus spontané, le plus naturel, le moins « stylisé » possible ; puis il mit l'objet durci, directement, à fondre en bronze.

Nous savons que la plupart des innombrables objets en bronze de la Renaissance furent d'abord des *modelli* en cire – cette « cire perdue » par quoi l'on nomme la technique de fonte la plus courante. Ce n'est qu'à partir du XVIe siècle, lorsque le goût esthétique pour l'esquisse se développe, que les *modelli* et *bozzetti* des sculpteurs seront préservés de la destruction par des procédés techniques plus complexes. Aussi pouvons-nous encore admirer les extraordinaires modèles en cire de Michel-Ange et de son atelier, conservés, notamment, au Victoria and Albert Museum de Londres (ill. p. 73) : nous sommes frappés d'y voir en trois dimensions ce que l'étude anatomique, chez Léonard de Vinci, offrait en deux dimensions. A savoir une « composition des surfaces » du corps humain – le terme est d'Alberti – pensée désormais à partir de la question de l'*écorché.* Comme Goethe devait plus tard le dire dans ses *Écrits sur l'art* : « L'extérieur d'une nature organique, qu'est-il d'autre que l'apparition éternellement changeante de l'intérieur? » (J. W. Goethe, 1996, p. 205).

Nous voici donc ramenés au terrain de l'anatomie humaine, comme si les usages figuratifs de la cire décrivaient un *cercle anthropologique* où tout, d'une façon ou d'une autre, devait concerner le théâtre du corps humain. La « chair pour croyants » des cires votives ne manifeste-t-elle pas avant tout l'inquiétude organique des donateurs? La « chair pour artistes » des *modelli* ne manifeste-t-elle pas avant tout la curiosité visuelle pour les rapports entre surfaces et profondeurs du corps humain ? Or, c'est bien des deux précédentes que s'infère, historiquement et techniquement, la « chair pour savants » des cires anatomiques du XVIIIᵉ siècle : outre le fait que les artistes florentins appartenaient par tradition à la Corporation des médecins et apothicaires *(Arte dei medici e speziali)*, outre le fait que c'est à l' artiste Cigoli qu'est dû le tout premier écorché anatomique en cire (l'écorché, qui date de 1600, est aujourd'hui conservé au Museo nazionale del Bargello, à Florence), le point capital réside dans la *transmission des savoirs-faire* liés à un matériau de prédilection (la cire) et à un enjeu figuratif de prédilection (la chair).

Ex-voto lungs, 18ᵗʰ century

Lunge, Votivgabe, 18. Jahrhundert

Poumons ex-voto, XVIIIᵉ siècle

Niederscheyrn, Bavaria

Ce n'est donc pas un hasard si la première grande école de céroplastie médicale est née à Florence, ce cœur de l'humanisme et du « décloisonnement » des savoirs à la Renaissance. Les grands modeleurs de la Specola – Susini, Calamai, Calenzuoli ou Tortori – ont hérité, peut-être sans clairement l'éprouver, de savoirs et de savoirs-faire qui venaient de temps fort reculés et de régions culturelles fort éloignées de toute attitude « scientifique ». Car, dans l'exacte description anatomique d'une jambe par Clemente Susini (ill. p. 74) survit encore le cadrage religieux de la jambe votive (ill. p. 86), autant que le souci artistique de celle modelée dans l'atelier de Michel-Ange (ill. p. 73).

Cercles vicieux

Il est étonnant de constater que ce « cercle anthropologique » a été parcouru dans son intégralité par un seul homme – celui-là même qui aura donné à la sculpture en cire ses chefs-d'œuvre les plus extrêmes et les plus inquiétants. Il s'agit de Gaetano Giulio Zumbo (ill. p. 55). Sa vie entière semble n'avoir été qu'un long voyage de sa Sicile natale vers le nord, et de la « chair pour croyants » (le monde des figurines dévotes) vers la « chair pour savants » (les morgues d'hôpitaux où, de Bologne à Gênes et à Paris, il réalisa d'extraordinaires modèles anatomiques). Entre les deux, Zumbo aura découvert le baroque romain puis modelé à

Florence, pour la cour des Médicis, quatre célèbres groupes allégoriques où l'étude des différents stades de la décomposition des chairs est poussée si loin qu'elle écœure et fascine tour à tour.

Exacte pourriture et mort baroque : Zumbo produit à la fois les artefacts d'une anatomie brutale, non transposée, indéfiniment observée sur de réels cadavres, – et les œuvres d'art d'une mise en scène subtile, décalée, indéfiniment réinventée à partir des formes du Bernin, voire de Poussin. La conjonction de ces deux effets produit un supplément de malaise, cela même, probablement, qui aura tenu les quatre groupes allégoriques loin du musée des Offices. Au-delà du réalisme et, même, au-delà du style : l'œuvre de Zumbo n'a cessé d'être regardée sous l'angle de la perversité, voire de la perversion. Le « cercle anthropologique » est, chez lui, si radicalement bouclé qu'il devient quelque chose comme un « cercle vicieux ». Devant cette œuvre, en effet, nous sommes dans l'élément de la ressemblance comme dans une infernale région d'inquiétude. C'est l'inquiétude des ressemblances organiques où rien – et surtout pas l'« idéalisation » d'un style académique – ne viendra nous sauver de l'informe.

Le premier auteur d'envergure à avoir reconnu l'emprise de ce « cercle vicieux » ne fut autre que le marquis de Sade. Son récit des abominations sexuelles et meurtrières de Juliette et de ses complices dans la ville de Florence dans *L'Histoire de Juliette* s'émaille, en effet, de textes issus d'un *Voyage d'Italie* écrit par Sade quelque vingt ans plus tôt : la description des œuvres de Zumbo – leur « vérité effrayante », écrit-il – est donc donnée dans un contexte où se mêlent le désir, la cruauté et la mort. Voici désormais le maître sicilien de la cire anatomique à l'origine de deux cultures généralement reconnues comme contradictoires : d'un côté, le *romantisme* noir et son destin populaire, qu'incarnent les musées de cire de Curtius, Madame Tussaud ou Grévin ; d'un autre côté, le *positivisme* et son destin populaire, incarné par ces musées anatomiques, mi-scientifiques mi-forains, qui exhibaient au XIXe siècle toutes les conséquences du vice sous la forme d'effrayants modèles pathologiques (ill. p. 89).

Il ne faut certainement pas voir dans ce « destin populaire » de la sculpture en cire – jusque dans son aspect grand-guignolesque, jusque dans sa prédilection pour les thèmes conjugués du vice sexuel et du crime sanglant – une simple vulgarisation d'inquiétudes déjà présentes dans certaines effigies votives ou funéraires. Quand Julius von Schlosser évoque le *déclassement* de la sculpture en cire au XIXe siècle, il n'oublie pas de convoquer la notion warburgienne de survivance, il n'oublie pas, en conséquence, de révoquer « toutes les prétentions téléologiques et tous les jugements de valeur » (J. von Schlosser, 1997, p. 172). Georges Bataille, de son côté, aura fait du déclassement une opération caractéristique de l'*informe*. Comment ne pas voir, dans ce mouvement même, une mise en question radicale de l'esthétique classique? Comment ne pas voir – Schlosser, lui, en aura fait toute la conclusion de son livre – que l'existence même des objets en cire déplace toute référence classique à la notion de beauté ?

Voilà bien un *déplacement* que l'esthétique contemporaine a pris en compte et radicalisé : il n'y a plus lieu de concevoir, comme le voulait Vasari, un progrès « biologique » des arts ; à cela, Nietzsche oppose l'éternel retour – un cercle vicieux – et la mêlée du dionysiaque dans l'apollinien. Il n'y a plus lieu de viser des idéaux de marbre ; à cela, Freud oppose le jeu tragique du désir et du deuil, le cercle vicieux de l'*Unheimlichkeit*. Une fois encore, la cire serait un matériau pour toutes ces chairs inquiètes, pour tous ces cercles vicieux. Un *matériau-piège* où viennent se prendre nos fantasmes. Un *matériau-fuite* où s'échangent plastiquement la ressemblance avec la dissemblance, l'apparition avec la disparition – Medardo Rosso, probablement, utilisa la cire pour cela même (ill. p. 99) –, la masse compacte des chairs avec le « souffle indistinct de l'image ».

Human Anatomy
Die Anatomie des Menschen
L´anatomie humaine

The Anatomy of the Human Body
– A unique collection of the late 18th century
Monika v. Düring

This unique collection of anatomical wax models from the museum 'La Specola', which is embedded in the tradition of European thought, gives us great insight into the knowledge and understanding of the anatomy of the human body as it existed at the end of the 18th century. If one compares the wax models with the representation of anatomical sections in woodcuts and copperplate engravings, it is clear that progress had been made since the traditional anatomical sections and illustrations of the 16th and 17th centuries, and that the production of these specimens was based upon the earlier examples.

These wax models in their three-dimensional form represent for the first time the original specimen much more accurately than a flat drawing could possibly do. The fascination of these specimens lies in the precision with which the details of the anatomical structure are reproduced. What is more, the artistic presentation is so perfected that in the model the whole body is felt to be alive — an impression which results from the representation of the human body in typical poses and gestures and complete refusal to depict a dead body. The form and shape of the human body thus appears as a living unit, with the greatest possible economy of power. Those who observe pictures of the models as much as those who visit the museum are equally impressed by the esthetic quality of human anatomy.

These models do not only represent one of the earliest macroscopic collections, but also one of the most manyfold. It is an impressive record of the skeleton and locomotor apparatus, the internal organs, the cavities of thorax, abdomen and pelvis, the circulatory and lymphatic systems, the central and peripheral nervous systems – including the sense organs – together with a large number of models depicting the relationship of these various entities in the different regions and cavities of the body.

These many exemplary specimens take the visitor on a voyage of discovery through the inner mysteries of our bodies, right down into the deeper regions where organs, vessels and nerves lie hidden. While learning anatomy, the examination of such specimens as these provides the student with a wealth of pictorial detail, bringing before his or her inner eye the image of a "transparent man".

This encyclopaedic collection, however, contains not only models for the scientific teaching of anatomy, but also models which the viewer initially regarded with displeasure and consternation. In this context one should realise that the burghers of that time were both enlightened and interested. A dissection was regarded and expirienced as a special public occasion which one not only attended but paid to attend. The promoters for their part likewise strove to satisfy the curiosity and sensationalism of the visitor, for which spectacular displays were particularly suitable.

In this presentation, the Florentine collection is for the first time made available to a wider readership in the form of a complete edition of colored illustrations. Even today it is of practical use. It offers both to the interested layman and to the medical student a variety of interesting experiences. The latter can test his anatomical knowledge by naming the various structures depicted, and will further recognize misinterpretations based upon the scientific knowledge of the time. But it will also become apparent how much detail was already known even in those days, and at the same time we become aware of the advances medicine has made with the development of new techniques of visual display.

Die anatomische Gestalt des Menschen
– Ein einmaliges Zeitdokument des ausgehenden 18. Jahrhunderts
Monika v. Düring

Diese einmalige Modellsammlung der anatomischen Wachse des
Museums La Specola vermittelt, eingebettet in die Tradition der europäischen Geistesgeschichte, den Erkenntnis- und Wissensstand der Anatomie des menschlichen Körpers im ausgehenden 18. Jahrhundert. Ver-
gleicht man die Wachspräparate mit den Darstellungen anatomischer
Sektionen auf Holzschnitten und Kupferstichen, wird deutlich, daß die
anatomische Sektions- und Abbildungstradition des 16. und 17. Jahrhunderts fortgeschrieben wurde und man sich bei der Herstellung der
Präparate an diesen Vorbildern orientierte.

In Form des gestalteten Wachsmodells gewinnt das Präparat hier
zum ersten Mal eine dreidimensionale Dimension und kommt somit
dem Originalpräparat sehr viel näher als die zweidimensionale Buchab-
bildung. Das Faszinierende dieser Präparate liegt in der Genauigkeit, mit
der die Details der anatomischen Strukturen wiedergegeben werden.
Darüber hinaus ist die künstlerische Darstellung so perfektioniert, daß
der tote Körper im Modell als lebendig empfunden wird – ein Eindruck,
der durch die Darstellung des menschlichen Körpers in typischen Posen
und Gesten und durch den vollständigen Verzicht auf die Darstellung
eines vom Tode gezeichneten Körpers entsteht. Die Form und Gestalt
des menschlichen Körpers wird auf diese Weise zu einer vitalen Einheit
von höchster Ökonomie der Kräfte. Die Modelle vermitteln dem Betrachter der Abbildungen genau wie dem Besucher des Museums eine Hu-
mananatomie von besonderer Ästhetik.

Diese Modellsammlung ist nicht nur eine der ersten makroskopischen Sammlungen, sondern auch eine der vielfältigsten. Auf beein-
druckende Weise dokumentieren dies die zahlreichen anatomischen
Präparate des Skelett- und Bewegungsapparates, der inneren Organsysteme, des Brust-, Bauch- und Beckenraums, des Blut- und Lymphgefäßsystems, des zentralen und peripheren Nervensystems – einschließlich
der Sinnesorgane – sowie eine große Anzahl von Modellen, die die Kom-
plexität der räumlichen Beziehungen verschiedener Systeme in einer
Körperregion oder Körperhöhle wiedergeben. Die Vielzahl der Detailpräparate führt den Betrachter auf eine Entdeckungsreise durch das
Innere unseres Körpers, systematisch von der Oberflächenanatomie bis

in die tieferen Regionen der Körperhöhlen mit Organen, Gefäßen und Nerven. Im anatomischen Unterricht schulte das Studium derartiger Präparate das räumliche Vorstellungsvermögen und half den Studenten, sich anhand des Modells den „gläsernen Menschen" vor seinem geistigen Auge vorzustellen.

Die enzyklopädisch reiche Sammlung enthält allerdings nicht nur Demonstrationsobjekte für den wissenschaftlichen anatomischen Unterricht, sondern auch Modelle, die der Betrachter aufgrund einer drastischen Darstellung zunächst mit Befremden und Betroffenheit betrachtet. Hierzu sollte man wissen, daß der Bürger der damaligen Zeit aufgeklärt und interessiert war. Eine Sektion wurde als ein besonderes öffentliches Ereignis empfunden und erlebt, das man besuchte und für das Eintritt zu bezahlen war. Die Veranstalter waren andererseits auch bemüht, die Neugier und Sensationslust der Besucher zu befriedigen, wozu spektakuläre Darstellungen am besten geeignet waren.

In der hier vorgelegten Ausgabe wird die Florentiner Sammlung erstmalig einem breiten Leserkreis als komplette Farbtafelsammlung zugänglich gemacht. Auch heute noch ist das Werk von praktischem Nutzen. Es bietet sowohl dem interessierten Laien wie auch dem angehenden jungen Arzt vielfältige Anregungen, der Medizinstudent kann durch Benennung der einzelnen Strukturen sein anatomisches Wissen überprüfen und wird natürlich auch die historisch bedingten Fehlinterpretationen erkennen. Im Vergleich wird deutlich, über welch genauen Detailkenntnisse man bereits zur damaligen Zeit verfügte, und gleichzeitg werden wir der Fortschritte gewahr, die die Medizin mit der Entwicklung neuer bildgebender Verfahren gemacht hat.

L'Anatomie du corps humain
– Une collection unique de la fin du XVIIIe siècle
Monika v. Düring

La collection, unique en son genre, des cires anatomiques de la Specola, replacée dans le contexte de l'histoire des sciences de l'Homme en Europe, renseigne sur l'état des connaissances en anatomie humaine à la fin du XVIIIe siècle. La comparaison des préparations en cire avec les représentations des dissections anatomiques gravées sur bois ou sur cuivre permet de constater que la tradition des dissections et de l'iconographie anatomique des XVIe et XVIIe siècles a non seulement été maintenue, mais a influencé l'élaboration des modèles en cire.

Sous la forme du modèle en cire, l'illustration anatomique devient pour la première fois tridimensionnelle, et par là se rapproche beaucoup plus de la préparation originale que de la représentation plane. Le caractère fascinant des cires de la Specola tient à la précision avec laquelle sont restitués les détails des structures anatomiques. La représentation artistique, poussée à la perfection, fait percevoir le modèle cadavérique comme un sujet vivant. Cette impression résulte de la volonté de l'artiste de faire abstraction des stigmates de la mort ; à leur place sont évoqués des positions et des gestes de la vie courante laissant transparaitre l'unicité des formes et des fonctions vitales. Ces modèles procurent à l'observateur le sentiment de cette esthétique particulière qu'éprouve le visiteur d'un musée d'anatomie.

Cette collection de modèles en cire est non seulement l'une des plus anciennes collections anatomiques macroscopiques, mais aussi l'une des plus grandes et des plus variées. Les nombreuses préparations anatomiques apportent des données remarquables sur le squelette et l'appareil locomoteur, les viscères du thorax, de l'abdomen et du petit bassin, les systèmes circulatoires sanguin et lymphatique, les systèmes nerveux central et périphérique, les organes des sens ... Un grand nombre de modèles restituent la complexité des rapports topographiques entre les différents éléments anatomiques d'une région donnée du corps ou de l'une des cavités naturelles. La multiplicité des préparations concernant des régions isolées permet à l'observateur une exploration systématique du corps depuis l'anatomie de surface jusqu'aux régions profondes où sont logés les organes, vaisseaux et nerfs. Au cours de l'enseignement de l'anatomie, l'étude de telles préparations permet l'acquisition de la notion de volume et la représentation mentale de « l'homme transparent ».

A côté des objets de démonstration pour l'enseignement de la science anatomique constituant cette collection encyclopédique, se trouvent encore des modèles qui peuvent déconcerter. voire troubler le spectateur d'aujourd'hui en raison de leur représentation radicale. Il faut savoir que l'« honnête homme » du XVIIIe siècle était instruit, et que la dissection était une manifestation publique suivie avec intérêt dont le spectacle était payant. Les organisateurs s'efforçaient en conséquence de satisfaire la curiosité et le goût du sensationnel des visiteurs par des représentations spectaculaires.

Dans le présent ouvrage, la collection de cires anatomiques de la Specola de Florence est rendue, pour la première fois, accessible à un large public sous la forme d'une série complète de photographies en couleur. A l'heure actuelle, un tel ouvrage présente encore un intérêt pratique, et ouvre de nombreuses perspectives tant au profane intéressé qu'au médecin. L'étudiant en médecine pourra notamment tester ses connaissances anatomiques en identifiant et nommant chaque structure, mais aussi en reconnaissant les fautes d'interprétation liées au contexte historique. Par comparaison avec les connaissances précises disponibles à l'époque de cette collection, il est possible de mesurer les progrès de la médecine réalisés grâce au développement de nouvelles techniques.

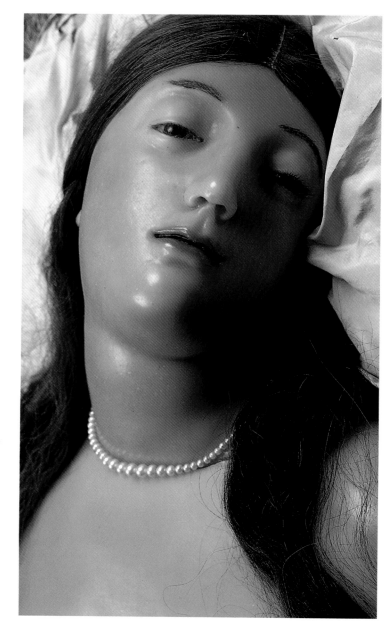

Head of whole
body specimen of a
pregnant woman.
The model can be
taken apart.

Kopfstudie des
zerlegbaren Ganz-
körperpräparates
einer Schwangeren

Tête d'une prépa-
ration démontable
du corps entier
d'une femme
enceinte

Specimen showing
the thoracic wall,
mammary gland
and abdominal wall

Darstellung der
Brustwand, der
Brustdrüse und
Bauchwand

Parois du thorax et
de l'abdomen, sein

[OSTETRICIA, 968]

Specimen showing
the thoracic and
abdominal walls

Darstellung der
Brust- und Bauch-
wand

Parois du thorax et
de l'abdomen

View into the opened thoracic and abdominal cavities. In the thorax the right and left lungs can be seen, and part of the anterior surface of the heart. The intestines are hidden behind the greater omentum.

Einblick in die eröffnete Brust- und Bauchhöhle. In der Brusthöhle sind rechter und linker Lungenflügel sowie ein Teil der Herzvorderfläche zu erkennen. Die Darmschlingen sind vom großen Netz bedeckt.

Viscères du thorax et de l'abdomen : cœur et poumons vus de l'avant, anses de l'intestin grêle recouvertes par le grand épiploon

Specimen of the
heart showing the
coronary vessels
and the great ves-
sels that enter and
leave the heart.
In the abdominal
cavity the greater
omentum has been
removed.

Präparation des
Herzens mit Dar-
stellung der Herz-
kranzgefäße und
der abgehenden
großen Gefäße
aus dem Herzen.
In der Bauchhöhle
ist das große Netz
entfernt.

Viscères du thorax
et de l'abdomen :
cœur, vaisseaux
coronaires, gros
vaisseaux de la
base du cœur, ab-
lation du grand
épiploon

Display showing
the organs in the
upper part of the
abdomen, such as
the stomach, liver
and duodenum,
and also the right
and left kidneys,
the right adrenal
gland, the abdomi-
nal aorta and the
uterus

Blick auf die Ober-
bauchorgane wie
Magen, Leber und
Zwölffingerdarm
sowie die rechte
und linke Niere, die
rechte Nebenniere,
die Bauchschlag-
ader und die
Gebärmutter

Viscères de l'abdo-
men : estomac,
foie, duodénum,
reins, glande surré-
nale droite, utérus

The right atrium,
ventricles, sto-
mach, duodenum
and uterus have
been opened

Eröffnung des rech-
ten Herzvorhofes
der Herzkammern,
des Magens, des
Zwölffingerdarmes
und der Gebärmut-
ter

Viscères du thorax
et de l'abdomen :
ouvertures de
l'oreillette droite,
des ventricules,
de l'estomac, du
duodénum et de
l'utérus

Whole body specimen of a pregnant woman. The model can be taken apart.

Zerlegbares Ganz-körperpräparat einer Schwangeren

Préparation démontable du corps entier d'une femme enceinte

[OSTETRICIA, 968]

Osteologia et Arthrologia

Bones and Joints
Knochen und Gelenke
Squelette et articulations

Bones and Joints

The form of the human body, which is genetically determined, is a particular example of the general plan underlying that of all vertebrate animals. As the supporting element in this plan, the skeleton forms the bony framework of our bodies. The high proportion of crystalline minerals in bone is responsible for the skeleton being the organic system that remains intact long after the death of the individual.

Under certain circumstances, such as the exclusion of air, or even the various forms of embalming to which the body was subjected in some cultures before burial, the bones may even survive for thousands of years. This means that long after death, the age, sex, dietary habits and health or disease of a person can be determined. The preservation of the skeleton after death also explains why it has become a symbol of death and the transitoriness of human life in the religions and cultural history of Europe.

In the first table, examples are given of the structural characteristics of various bones. These consist of a compact outer shell (the cortex) and an inner layer of fine bony trabeculae (the spongiosa), the particular structure and architecture of which is the morphological correlate revealing the organization of the pressure and tension lines of the bone under normal loading. These patterns remain dynamic throughout life, and alter in response to the functional demands made upon the bone. The red bone marrow lies between the cancellous trabeculae of the spongiosa. It contains the stem cells which during life give rise to the newly developing cells of the blood.

In the following table the many different shapes and rich variation in form of the individual bones of our bodies make up an impressive picture. Differences in size, projections, ridges and crests of whole bones or sections through bones, symmetry or asymmetry, are further clues to the interpretation of the function of the individual components of the entire skeletal system.

Considerable space is taken up by the different aspects of the bones which make up the skull, and which in their entirety form the cranium and facial skeleton. In addition to these, single vertebrae, sections of the vertebral column, the bones of the thoracic cage, the pelvis, and also the bones of the upper and lower limbs, including those of the hands and feet, are depicted.

A few specimens of joints displaying the ligaments which strengthen them and which stabilize and define their movements are

Pages · Seiten ·
Pages 116–117:

Detail from pages
134–135

Detail der Seiten
134–135

Détail des pages
134–135

also represented. Some of the joints have been opened to reveal the
articular surfaces, or particular structures such as, for instance, the
menisci of the clavicular and knee joints.

Die Gestalt des menschlichen Körpers ist genetisch festgelegt und re-
präsentiert den allgemeinen Bauplan der Wirbeltiere. Als tragender
Bestandteil dieses Bauplans bildet das Skelettsystem das knöcherne
Gerüst unserer Körperformen. Der hohe Anteil an kristallisierten Mineralien im Knochen macht das Skelett zu jenem Organsystem, das über den
Tod des Menschen hinaus erhalten bleibt. Unter bestimmten Vorausset-
zungen – wie etwa Luftabschluß, aber auch durch Konservierungsmaß-
nahmen, die in einigen Kulturen vor der Bestattung des Leichnams
durchgeführt wurden – kann der Knochen sogar über Jahrtausende
erhalten bleiben. So lassen sich am Skelett noch lange nach dem individuellen Tod, Alter, Geschlecht, Ernährungsgewohnheiten, körperliche
Leistung und Erkrankungen nachweisen und ablesen. Die postmortale
Erhaltung des Skeletts erklärt auch, warum es in der europäischen Religi-
ons- und Kulturgeschichte zum Symbol für den Tod an sich wie auch für
die individuelle Vergänglichkeit geworden ist.

Die erste Tafel zeigt Beispiele des prinzipiellen Aufbaus verschiedener Knochen, bestehend aus einer kompakten äußeren Rindenschicht
(Corticalis) und einer aus feinen Knochenbälkchen aufgebauten Innen-
schicht (Spongiosa). Die besondere Strukturierung und Architektur der
Spongiosa aus unterschiedlich feinen Knochenbälkchen ist das morphologische Korrelat für die Ausrichtung der mechanischen Druck- und
Zugspannungslinien des unter natürlicher Belastung stehenden Knochen. Diese Strukturen sind zeitlebens dynamisch und verändern sich
entsprechend der jeweiligen funktionellen Belastungen des Knochens.
Zwischen den Spongiosabälkchen befindet sich das rote Kochenmark
mit den Blutstammzellen, die zeitlebens Ursprung der Neubildung
unserer Blutzellen sind.

Auf den nachfolgenden Tafeln wird die vielfältige Gestalt sowie
der Formenreichtum der einzelnen Knochen unseres Körpers eindrucksvoll dokumentiert. Größenunterschiede, Knochenvorsprünge und Kno-
chenleisten an einzelnen Knochen oder Knochenabschnitten, Symmetrie
oder auch Asymmetrie sind weitere Kriterien der funktionellen Interpretation einzelner Knochen im Verband des Gesamtsystems.

**Knochen und
Gelenke**

Einen breiten Raum nehmen die unterschiedlichen Ansichten der Schädelknochen ein, die in ihrer Gesamtheit den Hirn- und Gesichtsschädel bilden. Darüber hinaus werden die einzelnen Wirbel, ganze Wirbelsäulenabschnitte, die Knochen des Brustkorbes, des Beckens sowie der oberen und unteren Extremitäten, einschließlich der Hand- und Fußknochen, dargestellt. Einige Knochen- und Gelenkpräparate sind um die Darstellung ihrer Bänder, die ein Gelenk stärken, stabilisieren und durch ihren Verlauf die Gelenkbewegungen definieren, ergänzt und erweitert. Zum Teil sind die Gelenke eröffnet, um die Form der miteinander artikulierenden Gelenkflächen oder auch Sondereinrichtungen, wie beispielsweise die Menisken am Schlüsselbeingelenk und Kniegelenk zu demonstrieren.

Squelette et articulations

Le squelette constitue l'armature osseuse du corps, élément de charpente de l'architecture du corps humain, comme pour tous les vertébrés. La richesse en sels minéraux des os rend leur conservation possible après la mort. Des os peuvent ainsi être conservés pendant des milliers d'années, notamment grâce à l'utilisation de techniques de conservation pratiquées dans certaines cultures avant l'inhumation. Le squelette permet de révéler, longtemps après la mort de l'individu, son âge, son sexe, ses habitudes alimentaires, ses capacités physiques, ses maladies … La conservation des os après la mort explique pourquoi le squelette est devenu, dans l'histoire des religions et des cultures européennes, le symbole de la mort et de l'existence éphémère de l'individu.

L'architecture générale des os est démontrée par la première planche qui en présente des exemples. Les os sont constitués d'une couche compacte périphérique, l'os cortical, entourant une zone profonde formée par de fines travées osseuses, l'os spongieux. La disposition et l'architecture spécifique des différentes travées de l'os spongieux sont la traduction morphologique des forces de pression et de traction exercées de façon physiologique. Ces structures évoluent de façon dynamique au cours de la vie et se transforment sous l'action des contraintes fonctionnelles. Dans l'interstice entre les travées d'os spongieux se trouve la moelle osseuse rouge contenant les cellules souches des éléments figurés du sang permettant le renouvellement des globules sanguins durant toute la vie.

La grande variété et la richesse des formes des os du corps apparaissent de façon remarquable sur la deuxième planche. La variation de taille, la présence de tubercules et d'apophyses, la symétrie ou l'asymétrie constituent des critères pour l'interprétation fonctionnelle dans l'ensemble squelettique de pièces osseuses isolées.

Différentes vues des os du crâne, articulés pour former la voûte et la base du crâne ainsi que le squelette de la face occupent une place importante de la collection. Les os de la colonne vertébrale, les os de la cage thoracique, les os du bassin, et les os des membres supérieurs et inférieurs sont ensuite représentés.

Les préparations concernant le squelette et les articulations sont complétées par la représentation de ligaments ; ceux-ci renforcent et stabilisent chaque articulation et guident les mouvements. La capsule articulaire est ouverte dans certains cas pour démontrer la cavité articulaire, la forme des surfaces articulaires, ou la présence de dispositifs intra-articulaires particuliers tels que le disque sterno-claviculaire ou les ménisques du genou.

Skeleton humanum

Human Skeleton

Menschliches
Skelett

Squelette humain

Internal structure
of long bones, skull
bones and verte-
bral bodies

Innere Struktur von
Röhrenknochen,
Schädelknochen
und Wirbelkörpern

Structure interne
d'os longs, d'os
du crâne, et de
vertèbres

View of the calvaria,
facial skeleton and
skull base

Ansicht des Hirn-
und Gesichts-
schädels sowie der
Schädelbasis

Crâne vu du dessus
(en haut), et crâne
vu du dessous (en
bas)

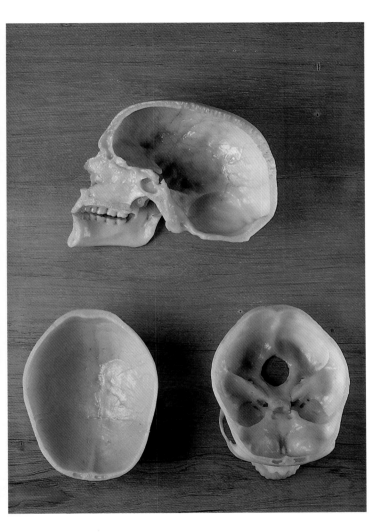

Above: median section through calvaria and facial skeleton; inner view of right half of the skull. Below: horizontal section with inner view of the skull roof and skull base

Oben: Medianschnitt durch Hirn- und Gesichtsschädel, Innenansicht der rechten Schädelhälfte. Unten: Horizontalschnitt mit Innenansicht von Schädeldach und Schädelbasis

En haut : coupe médiane du crâne : vue interne de la moitié droite.
En bas : coupe horizontale : vues endocrâniennes de la voûte et de la base du crâne

Os frontale, Maxilla, Os ethmoidale, Os sphenoidale

Frontal bone
(upper and lower
specimens)
together with two
views of the upper
jaw bone (speci-
men at side). In the
center is the eth-
moid bone.

Stirnbein (oberes
und unteres Präpa-
rat) sowie Oberkie-
ferknochen (seit-
lich gelegene
Präparate) in zwei
Ansichten. In der
Mitte ist das Sieb-
bein zu sehen.

Os frontal (en
haut et en bas) ;
os maxillaire
(à droite et à
gauche) ; os eth-
moïde (au centre)

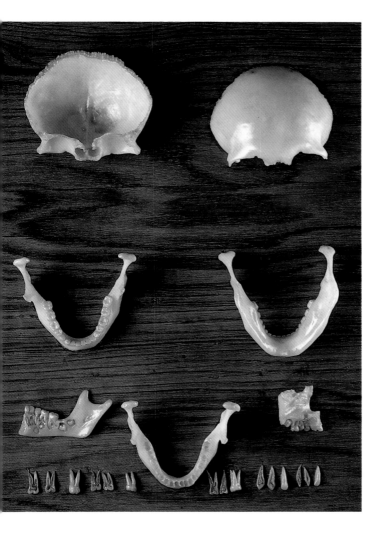

Upper specimen: two views of the frontal bone. Lower specimen: lower jaw bone with teeth. Left: milk teeth with tooth germs

Obere Präparate: Stirnbein in zwei Ansichten. Untere Präparate: Unterkieferknochen mit Zähnen; links: Milchgebiß mit Zahnanlagen

En haut : os frontal vu de l'avant et de l'arrière. En bas : mandibules d'adultes et d'enfant avec la dentition

Upper jaw bone,
temporal bone,
zygomatic bone,
nasal bone

Oberkiefer-
knochen, Schläfen-
bein, Jochbein und
Nasenbein

Os maxillaires ;
os temporaux ;
os zygomatiques
(malaire) ; os
nasaux

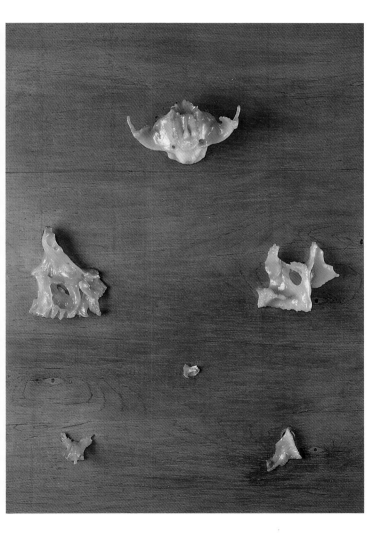

Various displays of
the paranasal sinu-
ses. Middle on left:
view into opened
maxillary sinus

Verschiedene Dar-
stellungen der
Nasenneben-
höhlen. Im Prä-
parat Mitte links:
Einblick in die
eröffnete Kiefer-
höhle

Sinus aériens de la
face. Au milieu à
gauche : sinus
maxillaire ouvert

Os petrosum

Temporal bone,
partly chiseled
away to reveal the
inner ear

Schläfenbein, zum
Teil aufgemeißelt
zur Darstellung des
Innenohres

Série d'os tempo-
raux partiellement
trépanés pour dé-
montrer l'oreille
interne

Parietal bone, occipital bone with foramen magnum, two views of the sphenoid. Middle specimen: hyoid bone

Scheitelbein, Hinterhauptsbein mit Hinterhauptsloch sowie Keilbein in zwei Ansichten, in der Mitte das Zungenbein

Os pariétal (en haut) ; os occipital avec trou occipital (au milieu) ; os sphénoïde (en bas) ; os hyoïde (au centre)

| Median section through the skull showing nasal septum, side wall of nasal cavity and nasal conchae | Medianschnitt durch den Schädel mit Darstellungen der Nasenscheidewand sowie der seitlichen Nasenwand mit ihren Nasenmuscheln | Coupes médianes du crâne : représentations de la cloison nasale et de la paroi nasale latérale avec les cornets |

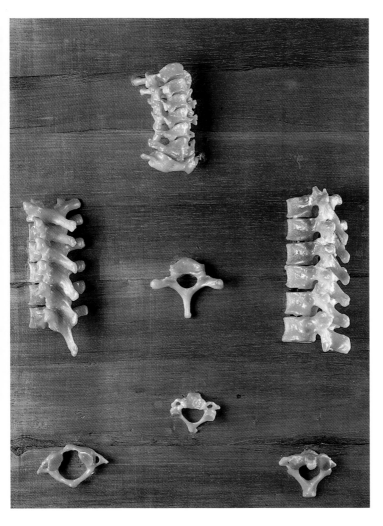

Cervical and thor-
acic vertebral
column. Below left:
the first vertebra
(atlas), which sup-
ports the skull

Hals- und Brust-
wirbelsäule. Unten
links : der den
Schädel tragende
erste Halswirbel,
der Atlas

Segments de la
colonne vertébrale
cervicale et thora-
cique; vertèbres
cervicales isolées :
atlas portant le
crâne (en bas à
gauche)

Articulationes, Ligamenta

Whole body specimen showing the ligaments,
joints and some single muscles and tendons

Ganzkörperpräparat mit Darstellung von
Bändern, Gelenken sowie einzelner Muskeln
und Sehnen

Préparation du corps entier représentant les
articulations, les ligaments et quelques muscles
et tendons

[XXVI. 428]

Lumbar vertebral
column, sacrum
and coccyx

Lendenwirbelsäule,
Kreuzbein und
Steißbein

Colonne vertébrale
lombaire ; sacrum ;
coccyx

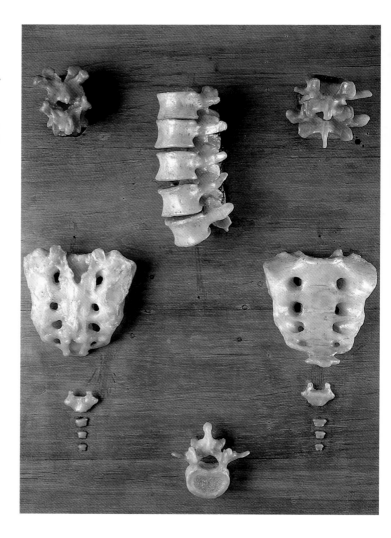

Pars cervicalis columnae vertebralis, Ligamentum longitudinale posterius, Articulatio atlantooccipitalis

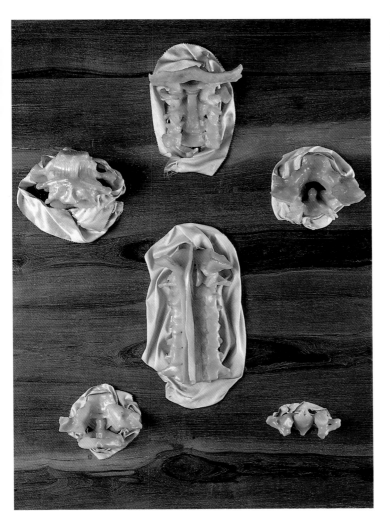

View from behind into the vertebral canal showing ligaments of the upper cervical vertebral column

Blick von hinten in den Wirbelkanal, dargestellt sind Anteile des Bandapparates der oberen Halswirbelsäule

Canal vertébral cervical vu de l'arrière ; ligaments de la jonction crâniovertébrale

Ligaments of the
upper cervical ver-
tebral column seen
from behind

Anteile des Band-
apparates der obe-
ren Halswirbelsäu-
le in der Ansicht
von hinten

Ligaments de diffé-
rents segments de
la colonne verté-
brale vus de l'ar-
rière

Ligaments of the
thoracic vertebral
column and of the
costavertebral
joints thoracic ver-
tebrae and ribs

Bandverbindungen
der Brustwirbel-
säule sowie der
Brustwirbel mit
den Rippen

Ligaments des arti-
culations de la
colonne vertébrale
thoracique et des
articulations costo-
vertébrales

Columna vertebralis, Ligamenta

External and internal ligaments of various parts of the vertebral column

Äußere und innere Bandverbindungen in verschiedenen Wirbelsäulenabschnitten

Ligaments de différents segments de la colonne vertébrale

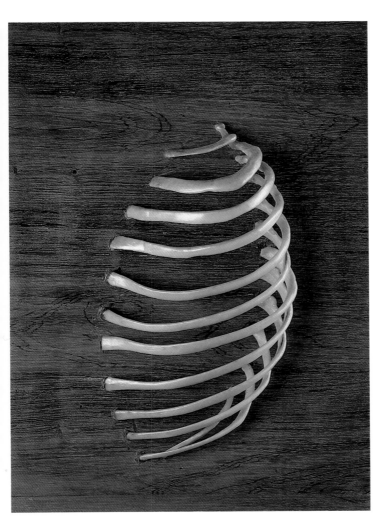

Display showing
the 12 ribs on left
side of thoracic
cage in their nat-
ural position, seen
from the side.
Above: first rib

Darstellung der 12
Rippen der linken
Brustkorbseite in
natürlichen Abstän-
den in der Vorder-
seitenansicht, erste
Rippe oben liegend

Côtes gauches
vues de côté ;
l'écartement nor-
mal entre les douze
côtes a été respecté
(la première côte
est en haut)

Costae

Display showing
the 12 ribs on left
side of the thoracic
cage in their natu-
ral position, seen
from the midline.
Above: first rib

Darstellung der 12
Rippen der linken
Brustkorbseite in
der Medianansicht,
erste Rippe oben
liegend

Côtes gauches
vues du dedans
(la première côte
est en haut)

Collarbone, breast-
bone, shoulder
blade

Schlüsselbein,
Brustbein und
Schulterblatt

Clavicule ; ster-
num ; scapula
(omoplate)

Sternum, Costae

Breastbone with rib
attachments, liga-
ments and
muscles, seen from
in front

Brustbein mit
Rippenanteilen,
Bandverbindungen
und Muskeln in der
Ansicht von vorne

Plastron sternocos-
tal vu de l'avant :
os, ligaments,
muscles intercos-
taux

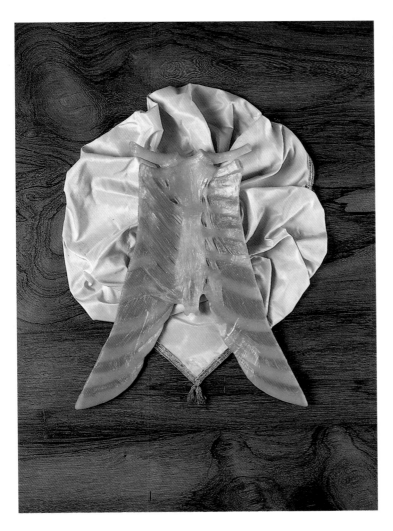

Breastbone with
collarbones and
ribs, also ligaments
and intercostal
muscles; seen from
the inside

Innenansicht von
Brustbein mit
Schlüsselbein und
Rippen sowie
Bandverbindungen
und Zwischenrip-
penmuskeln

Plastron sternocos-
tal vu de l'arrière :
os, ligaments,
muscles intercos-
taux

Upper arm and
radius

Oberarmbein und
Speiche

Humérus et radius

Two views of the
skeleton of the
right hand

Skelett der rechten
Hand in zwei
Ansichten

Squelette de la
main droite, vues
palmaire et
dorsale ; os du poi-
gnet

Ossa manus

Individual bones of
wrist and hand
bones, also bones
of fingers. Above
left: thumb with its
two phalanges

Einzelne Hand-
wurzel- und Mittel-
handknochen so-
wie Fingerglieder.
Links oben: der
Daumen mit sei-
nen zwei Finger-
gliedern

Os isolés de la
main (carpe, méta-
carpe, phalanges).
En haut à gauche :
le pouce avec deux
phalanges

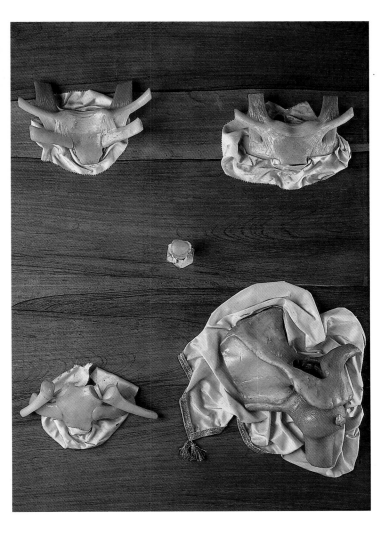

Joints connecting
the breastbone and
collarbones. Below
right: the shoulder
joint

Gelenkverbindun-
gen zwischen
Brust- und Schlüs-
selbein. Unten
rechts: das Schul-
tergelenk

Articulation sterno-
claviculaire . En bas
à droite : articula-
tions de l'épaule

Articulatio humeri

The shoulder joint,
different views

Schultergelenk
in mehreren
Ansichten

Articulations de
l'épaule (diffé-
rentes vues)

Display showing various aspects of the elbow joint

Verschiedene Dar-stellungen des Ellenbogenge-lenkes

Articulations du coude et des os de l'avant-bras

Tendines, Vaginae synoviales, Aponeurosis palmaris, Ligamenta et musculi manus

Tendons and tendon sheaths of the back of the hand. Tendinous sheet of palm, and the insertions of tendons of the flexor and extensor muscles of the fingers

Darstellungen der Sehnen und Sehnenscheiden des Handrückens sowie der Sehnenplatte der Handinnenfläche und der Ansätze der Sehnen der Fingerbeuge- und Fingerstreckmuskeln

Articulations de la main ; tendons et gaines tendineuses des muscles fléchisseurs et extenseurs des doigts

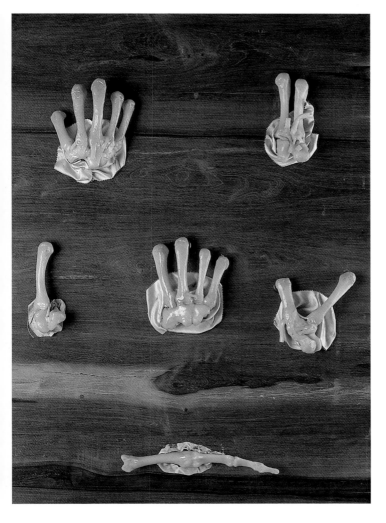

Joints of the hand
and middle finger

Gelenke der Hand-
wurzel und Mittel-
finger

Articulations de la
main et d'un doigt
(majeur)

Detail from pages | Detail der Seiten | détail des pages **134-135**

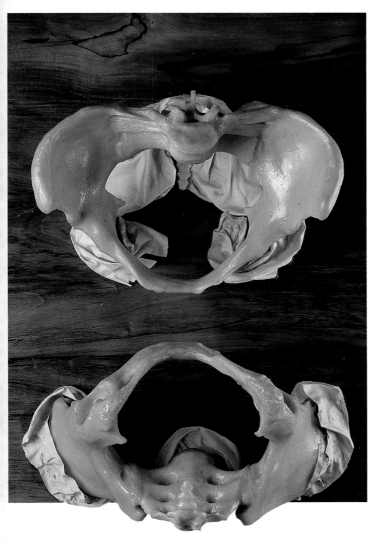

Pelvic girdle, consisting of the sacrum and two hip bones, seen from above in the upper specimen and from below in the lower specimen

Beckengürtel bestehend aus Kreuzbein und zwei Hüftbeinen, im oberen Präparat in der Ansicht von vorn oben, im unteren Präparat von unten

Articulations du bassin : vue supérieure (en haut), vue inférieure (en bas)

Cingulum membri inferioris, Os sacrum, Os coxae

Display showing
the important dia-
meters of the pelvis
at the level of the
pelvic inlet

Darstellung der
wichtigen Becken-
durchmesser der
Beckeneingangs-
ebene

Représentation des
diamètres obstétri-
caux au niveau de
l'ouverture supé-
rieure du petit
bassin

Hip bone, showing
two views of the
iliac wing

Hüftbein mit
Darmbeinschaufel
in zwei Ansichten

Os coxal vu sous
deux incidences

Pathologically
deformed pelvis
(rickets)

Krankhaft ver-
formtes Becken
(Rachitis)

Bassins patholo-
giques déformés
(rachitisme)

Specimen of the pelvis with ligaments between the sacrum and hip bones partially divided, and the cartilage between the pubic bones cut through

Darstellung des Beckens mit teilweise durchtrennten Bandverbindungen zwischen Kreuz- und Darmbein und durchtrenntem Knorpelhaft zwischen den Schambeinen

Bassins : section partielle des ligaments de l'articulation sacro-iliaque et section de la symphyse pubienne

Pathologically deformed pelvis. Ligaments between sacrum, iliac and pubic bones have been divided.

Krankhaft verformtes Becken. Die Bandverbindungen zwischen Kreuzbein, Darmbein und Schambein sind durchtrennt.

Bassins pathologiques déformés : section des ligaments et de la symphyse pubienne

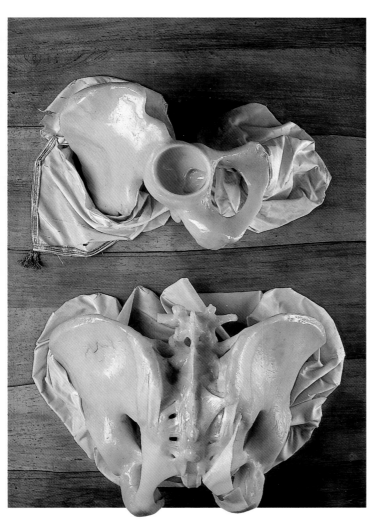

Upper specimen: hip bone with socket for the head of the femur. Lower specimen: pelvis with ligaments seen from behind

Oberes Präparat: Hüftbein mit Gelenkpfanne für den Oberschenkelkopf. Unteres Präparat: Becken von hinten mit Bändern

En haut : os coxal avec la cavité articulaire pour la tête du fémur. En bas : bassin vu de l'arrière avec les ligaments

Ligamentum sacrospinale

Hip bone with
its ligaments

Darstellung des
Hüftbeines mit
seinen Bandver-
bindungen

Os coxal avec cer-
tains ligaments

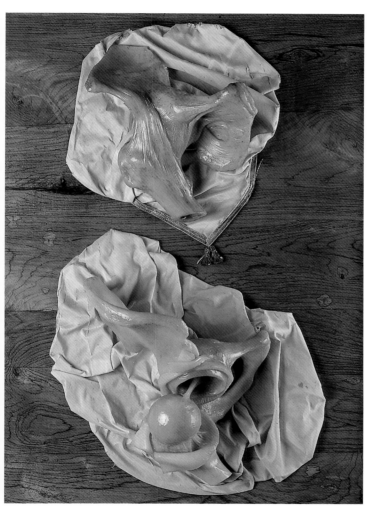

Upper specimen: right hip joint with ligaments. Lower specimen: the head of the femur has been disarticulated from the socket after dissection of the joint capsule

Oberes Präparat: rechtes Hüftgelenk mit Bandverbindungen. Unteres Präparat: der Gelenkkopf des Oberschenkelknochens ist nach Durchschneidung der Gelenkkapsel aus der Gelenkpfanne herausgedreht

En haut : articulation de la hanche droite et ligaments. En bas : tête du fémur luxée de la cavité articulaire après section de la capsule

Articulatio coxae, Articulatio genus

Left hip and knee
joints with muscle
insertions, ten-
dons, ligaments
and opened bursae
seen from behind

Linkes Hüft- und
linkes Kniegelenk
mit Muskelan-
sätzen, Sehnen
und Bändern sowie
eröffneten Schleim-
beuteln in der
Ansicht von hinten

Articulations de
la hanche et du
genou vues de
l'arrière : rapports
musculaires, ten-
dons, ligaments,
ouverture des
bourses synoviales

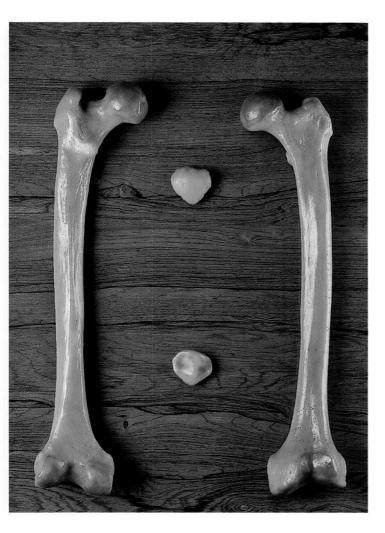

Left femur and
kneecap seen from
in front (left speci-
men) and from
behind

Linker Oberschen-
kelknochen und
Kniescheibe in der
Ansicht von vorne
(linkes Präparat)
und hinten

Fémur et patella
(rotule) gauches

Tibia, Fibula

Various aspects of
the left fibula and
shin

Linkes Waden- und
Schienbein in ver-
schiedenen Ansich-
ten

Os de la jambe
gauche : tibia et
fibula (péroné)

Skeleton of the foot

Fußskelett

Squelette du pied
et os isolés des
orteils

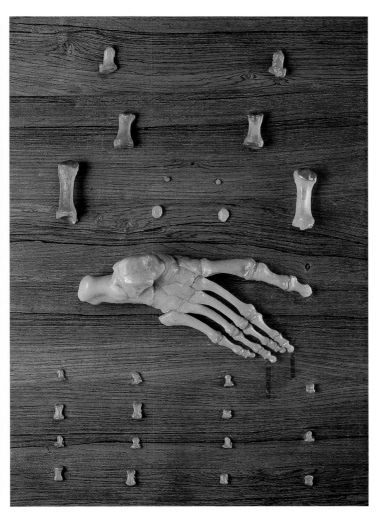

Ossa pedis

Heel-bone and
bones of the foot

Fersenbein und
Fußwurzelknochen

Os isolés du tarse

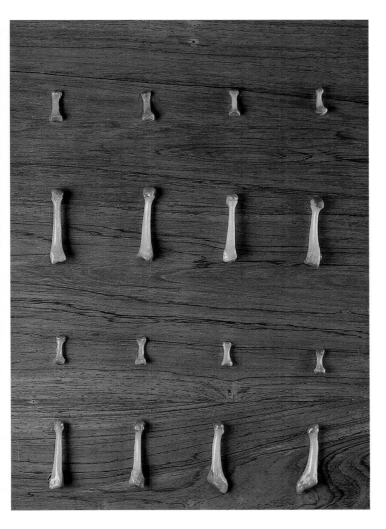

Bones of the mid-
dle part of the foot
and of the toes

Mittelfußknochen
und Zehenglieder

Os isolés du méta-
tarse et des orteils

Articulatio genus, Ligamentum patellae, Ligamenta cruciata

Upper specimen: knee joint from in front. Lower specimen: the capsule of the knee joint has been removed to show the cruciate ligaments and semilunar cartilages

Oberes Präparat: Kniegelenk in der Ansicht von vorne. Untere Präparate: das Gelenk ist zur Darstellung der Kreuzbänder und Menisken eröffnet

En haut : articulations du genou vues de l'avant. En bas : articulations ouvertes avec les ménisques et les ligaments croisés

Upper specimen: left knee joint with ligaments, tendons and muscle insertions seen from behind. Lower specimen: view of the semilunar cartilages and cruciate ligaments

Oberes Präparat: linkes Kniegelenk von hinten mit Bändern, Sehnen und Muskelansätzen. Unteres Präparat: Aufsicht auf die Menisken und Kreuzbänder

En haut : articulations du genou vues de l'arrière : ligaments, tendons et rapports musculaires. En bas : vue supérieure des ménisques et des ligaments croisés

Articulatio humeri, Articulatio genus

Shoulder and knee
joints with muscle
insertions

Schulter- und Knie-
gelenk mit Darstel-
lung der Muskel-
ansätze

Articulation de
l'épaule et articula-
tion du genou avec
tendons et rapports
musculaires

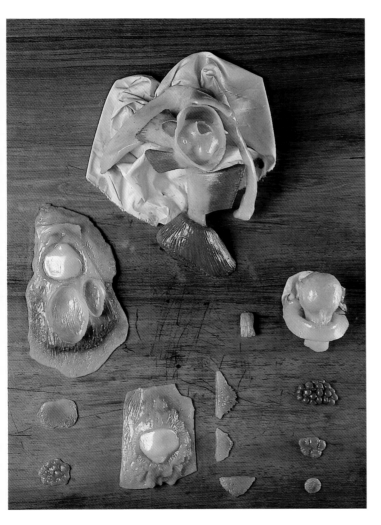

Shoulder and knee joints: the joint components, joint capsule and adipose tissue

Schultergelenk und Kniegelenk mit Darstellung von Gelenkkörpern, Gelenkkapsel und Fettgewebe

Articulation de l'épaule et articulation du genou : capsule, synoviale, corps adipeux

Ligamenta pedis

The ligaments of
the ankle joint and
foot

Darstellungen der
Bandverbindungen
des Sprunggelen-
kes und des Fußes

Articulation de la
cheville et articula-
tions du pied avec
les ligaments

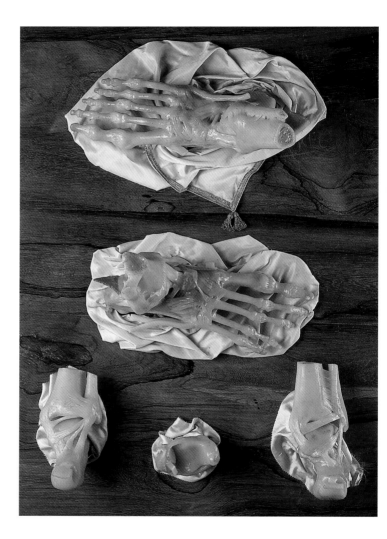

Ligamenta pedis

The ligaments of
the ankle joint and
foot

Darstellungen der
Bandverbindungen
der Sprunggelenke
und des Fußes

Articulations du
pied avec les liga-
ments (vue plan-
taire)

Myologia

Muscles
Muskeln
Muscles

Muscles and Locomotor System

The ability of human beings to walk on two feet and the postures they take up when active or at rest necessitate highly sophisticated coordination between the different groups of muscles. Our central nervous system is responsible for the neuronal control of this complex conscious and unconscious activity, all of which is carried out by motor units standing in a particular functional relationship to one another and acting on the relevant joints as the individual muscles come into play together or in sequence. In order to produce controlled movement, those muscles which act together as agonists and antagonists must be finely tuned to work in accordance with each other, since only in this way does the overall achievement of harmonious movement become possible.

Posture, walking, grasping and eye movement are probably the kinds of movement most familiar to all people, and these can be extended to include the chewing of food, breathing and speech. The morphological basis of facial expression, which reaches the maximum variety only in our species, is provided by the numerous small muscles of the face. It is not, however, only these facial muscles but the entire musculature of the whole body, which contribute to the individual "body language" by which our conscious or unconscious non-verbal self-awareness and emotions are expressed.

This extensive and remarkable collection of exhibits certainly emphasizes the extent and variety of our locomotor system, but it also illustrates the particular relationship between muscles and bones, and thus provides a key to the understanding of both simple and complex activity. The models depicting the musculature of the hand, face, eyes and larynx are extraordinarily impressive, and their representation in this medium offers a clear insight into the finely graded and highly differentiated movement of which these organs are capable.

Pages · Seiten · Pages 176–177:

Detail from page 182

Detail der Seite 182

Détail de la page 182

Der aufrechte Gang des Menschen, seine Körperhaltung in Ruhe sowie seine Körperbewegungen erfordern ein überaus differenziertes Zusammenspiel verschiedener Muskelgruppen. Unser zentrales Nervensystem übernimmt dabei die neuronale Steuerung der komplexen bewußten und unbewußten Bewegungsabläufe. Alle Bewegungsabläufe werden von funktionell in Beziehung stehenden Muskelgruppen ausgeführt, die über mehrere Gelenke hinweg ziehen können und deren individuelle Muskeln im direkten Zusammenspiel bzw. nacheinander arbeiten. Für den harmonischen Bewegungsablauf sind die agonistisch und antagonistisch arbeitenden Muskeln in ihrer Aktivität immer aufeinander abgestimmt. Nur so entsteht der Eindruck eines harmonischen Bewegungsablaufs.

Haltungs-, Stütz-, Bewegungs-, Greif- und Augenmotorik sind für den Laien die wohl bekanntesten Bewegungsformen. Einzubeziehen sind ferner die Kaumotorik bei der Nahrungsaufnahme, die Atmungsmotorik sowie die Sprachmotorik. Morphologische Grundlage der Mimik sind die zahlreichen kleinen Gesichtsmuskeln, die in dieser Vielfalt ausschließlich im menschlichen Gesicht vorkommen. Aber nicht nur diese mimischen Muskeln, sondern alle Muskeln unseres Körpers haben ihren funktionellen Anteil an der individuellen Körpersprache, mit der wir bewußt oder unbewußt non-verbal unser Selbstwertgefühl und unsere Emotionen ausdrücken.

Die vielen außergewöhnlichen Exponate vermitteln nicht nur ein umfassendes Bild von der Formenvielfalt der Muskeln unseres Körpers, sondern geben auch Aufschluß über ihre spezielle Anordnung am Skelett und tragen so zu einem funktionellen Verständnis für einfache und komplexe Bewegungsabläufe bei. Besonders beeindruckend sind die Modelle der Muskeln von Hand, Gesicht, Augen und Kehlkopf, deren plastische Darstellung ein umfassendes Verständnis der feinabgestuften und differenzierten Bewegungen ermöglicht.

Les muscles et l'appareil locomoteur

Tous les mouvements du corps humain, et en particulier la marche bipède et l'attitude érigée au repos, nécessitent la mise en jeu coordonnée de plusieurs groupes musculaires. Le système nerveux central prend en charge la régulation des mouvements complexes volontaires et involontaires. Des groupes musculaires fonctionnellement interdépendants, pouvant croiser plusieurs articulations, sont mis en jeu lors de l'exécution des mouvements. Chaque muscle participe à l'ensemble du mouvement ou prend le relai d'un autre. Le déroulement de mouvements harmonieux nécessite une coordination permanente des muscles agonistes et antagonistes.

Les aspects les plus connus de la motricité sont pour le non spécialiste le maintien d'une position, le déplacement dans l'espace, la préhension, et les mouvements de l'œil ; la mastication, les mouvements respiratoires, ou la parole articulée sont plus rarement pris en considération. Les nombreux petits muscles de la face, particulièrement développés dans l'espèce humaine, sont les supports morphologiques de la mimique. Ces muscles de la mimique ne sont pas les seuls qui interviennent dans le langage corporel, mais tous les muscles de l'organisme participent à la manifestation consciente ou inconsciente de notre personnalité et de nos émotions.

Le nombre particulièrement important des pièces de cette série ne donne pas seulement un aperçu de la variété des formes musculaires, mais renseigne aussi sur l'agencement particulier des muscles par rapport au squelette ; ces rapports permettent de comprendre la fonction de chaque muscle dans les mouvements élémentaires ou complexes. Particulièrement remarquables sont les modèles concernant la main, la face, les yeux ou le larynx, dont la représentation plastique permet la compréhension globale de mouvements différenciés fins.

Page · Seite · Page
181:

Detail from pages
406–407

Detail der Seiten
406–407

Détail des pages
406–407

Musculi faciales, Musculi colli, Musculi thoracis, Musculi abdominis, Musculi membri superioris, Musculi membri inferioris

Whole body speci-
men displaying the
superficial muscles

Ganzkörperpräpa-
rat zur Darstellung
der oberflächlichen
Muskeln

Préparation du
corps entier re-
présentant les
muscles super-
ficiels

Musculi faciales, Musculi colli, Musculi thoracis, Musculi abdominis, Musculi membri superioris, Musculi membri inferioris

Whole body specimen displaying the superficial muscles

Ganzkörperpräparat zur Darstellung der oberflächlichen Muskeln

Préparation du corps entier représentant les muscles superficiels

Musculi faciales, Musculi colli, Musculi thoracis, Musculi abdominis, Musculi membri superioris, Musculi membri inferioris, Musculi dorsi

Whole body specimen displaying the superficial and deep muscles

Ganzkörperpräparat zur Darstellung oberflächlicher und tiefer liegender Muskulatur

Préparation du corps entier représentant des muscles superficiels et profonds

Musculi faciales, Musculi colli, Musculi thoracis, Musculi abdominis, Musculi membri superioris, Musculi membri inferioris, Musculi dorsi

Whole body specimen displaying both the superficial and deep muscles

Ganzkörperpräparat zur Darstellung oberflächlicher und tiefer liegender Muskulatur

Préparation du corps entier représentant des muscles superficiels et profonds

Musculi faciales et masticatorii

Muscles of facial
expression,
muscles of masti-
cation

Mimische Muskeln
und Kaumuskeln

Muscles peauciers
de la mimique et
muscle temporal

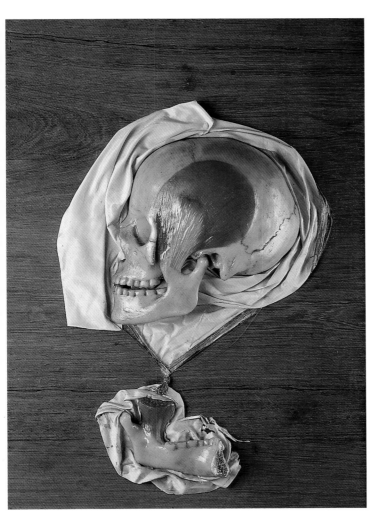

Views of the temporalis muscle. The lower specimen shows the attachment of this muscle of mastication to the lower jaw.

Darstellungen des Schläfenmuskels. Das untere Präparat zeigt den Ansatz dieses Kaumuskels am Unterkiefer.

Muscle temporal ; insertion du muscle temporal sur la mandibule (en bas)

Musculi faciales, Musculus masseter

Muscles of facial
expression (upper
specimens) and
muscle of
mastication (lower
specimens)

Darstellung von
mimischer Mus-
kulatur (obere Prä-
parate) und Kau-
muskeln (untere
Präparate)

Muscles peauciers
de la mimique
(en haut) ; muscle
masséter (en bas)

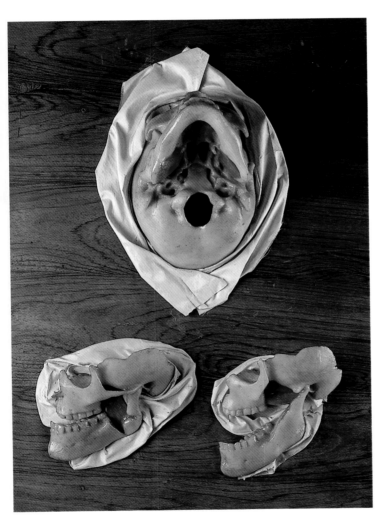

The more deeply placed muscles of mastication

Darstellung von Kaumuskeln aus einer tiefen Gesichtsregion

Muscles masticateurs des régions profondes de la face

Musculi faciales

Facial muscles surrounding the mouth, nostrils and eyes

Mimische Muskeln um Mund, Nase und Auge

Muscles peauciers de la mimique des régions des lèvres et du nez, des paupières, de l'oreille

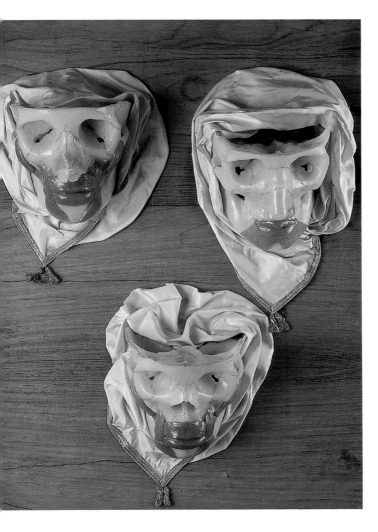

Muscles of facial
expression associ-
ated with the nose,
lips and chin

Mimische Muskeln
im Bereich der
Nase, der Lippen
und des Kinns

Muscles peauciers
de la mimique des
régions des lèvres
et du menton (en
haut)

Middle specimen: longitudinal section through the facial skeleton showing the oral cavity and throat. Above and to the side one can see the nasal conchae, orbital cavities and maxillary sinuses.

Mittleres Präparat: Längsschnitt durch den Gesichtsschädel mit Einblick in Mundhöhle und Rachen. Auf den oben und seitlich gelegenen Präparaten sind die Nasenmuscheln, die Augenhöhlen und die Kieferhöhlen zu erkennen.

Coupe médiane de la face : cavité nasale, cavité buccale, pharynx (au centre). Diverses préparations de muscles de la face

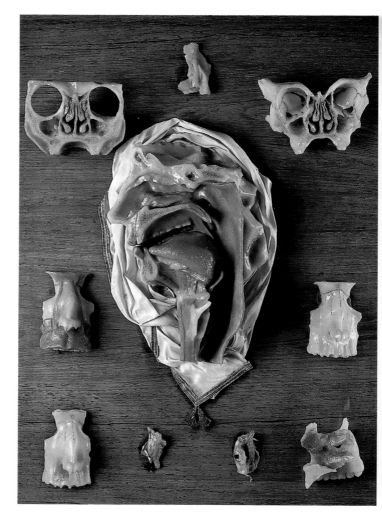

Musculus geniohyoideus, Musculus mylohyoideus, Musculus stylohyoideus

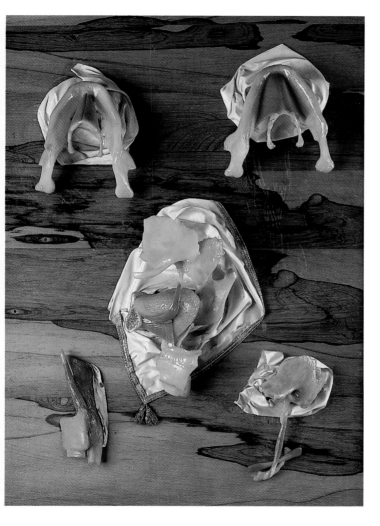

Muscles attached
to the hyoid bone

Darstellungen von
Zungenbeinmus-
keln

Muscles insérés
sur l'os hyoïde

Musculus stylohyoideus, Musculus constrictor pharyngis, Musculus palatopharyngeus

Various aspects of the muscles attached to the hyoid bone and muscles of the throat

Verschiedene Ansichten von Zungenbein- und Schlundmuskeln

Muscles du pharynx

Cavitas oris, Pharynx, Larynx, Musculus constrictor pharyngis, Musculus palatopharyngeus, Musculus stylohyoideus

Sections showing differ-
ent parts of the throat
with its muscles and also
the larynx

Verschiedene Ansichten
der Rachenabschnitte
mit ihren Muskeln und
des Kehlkopfes

Muscles du pharynx et
du larynx

Musculus omohyoideus, Musculus sternohyoideus, Musculus thyrohyoideus

Muscles attached
to the hyoid bone

Darstellungen der
unteren Zungen-
beinmuskeln

Muscles de la gor-
ge (infra-hyoïdiens)

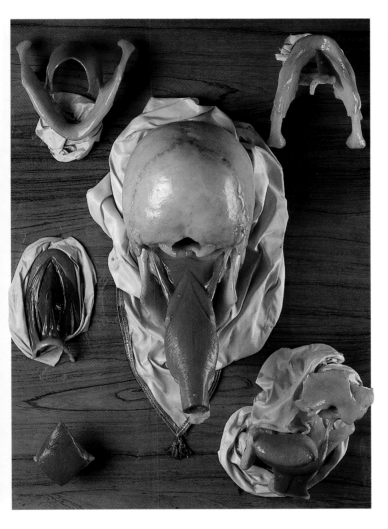

Muscles of the throat seen from behind, including individual muscles of the floor of the mouth

Schlundmuskeln, von hinten gesehen, sowie einzelne Muskeln des Mundbodens

Muscles du pharynx (vus de l'arrière) ; muscles du plancher buccal

Tunica muscularis pharyngis

Muscles of the throat seen from behind to show the arrangement of their various layers

Schlundmuskeln von hinten mit ihren unterschiedlich angeordneten Muskelschichten

Muscles du pharynx vus de l'arrière

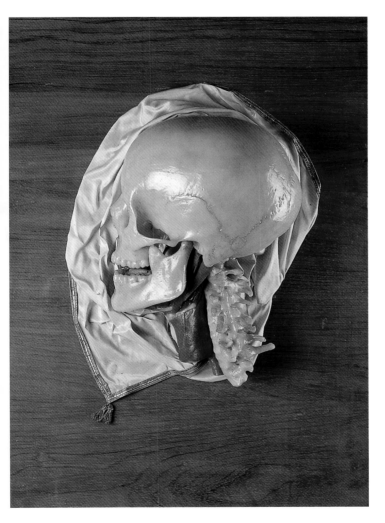

Muscles of the
throat seen from
the side

Schlundmuskula-
tur von der Seite

Muscles du pha-
rynx vus du côté
gauche

Musculus buccinator, Musculus constrictor pharyngis

Deeper plane, showing the muscles of the tongue, floor of the mouth and throat seen from the side after removal of part of the bone of the lower jaw

Zungen-, Mundboden- und Schlundmuskulatur von der Seite in einer tieferen Schicht nach Entfernung eines Teiles des Unterkieferknochens

Muscles du pharynx, de la langue, et du plancher buccal après résection d'une partie de la mandibule, vus du côté gauche

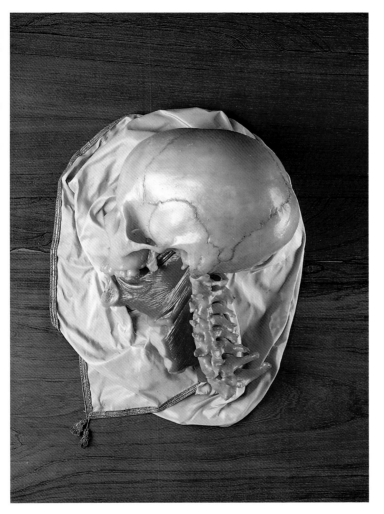

Deeper plane, showing the muscles of the tongue, floor of the mouth and throat seen from the side after removal of part of the bone of the lower jaw

Zungen-, Mundboden- und Schlundmuskulatur von der Seite in einer tieferen Schicht nach Entfernung eines Teiles des Unterkieferknochens

Muscles du pharynx et du plancher buccal après résection d'une partie de la mandibule, vus du côté gauche

Musculus constrictor pharyngis, Musculus geniohyoideus, Musculus genioglossus, Musculus hyoglossus

Deeper layer of the muscles of the floor of the mouth, tongue and throat seen from the side

Tiefere Schicht der Mundboden-, Zungen- und Schlundmuskeln in seitlicher Ansicht

Muscles de la langue, du plancher buccal, et du pharynx, vus du côté gauche

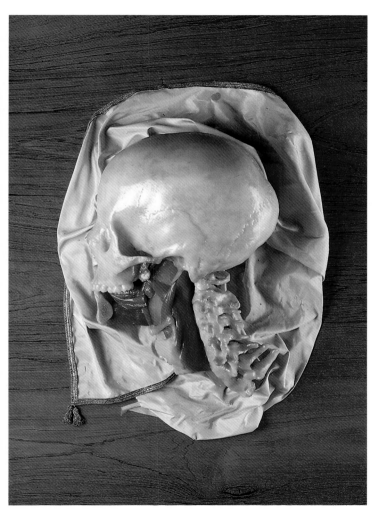

The deeper layer of muscles of the tongue, floor of the mouth and pharynx seen from the side after removal of part of the bone of the lower jaw

Zungen-, Mundboden- und Schlundmuskulatur von der Seite in einer tieferen Schicht nach Entfernung eines Teiles des Unterkieferknochens

Muscles de la langue, du plancher buccal, et du pharynx, vus du côté gauche

Pharynx, Recessus piriformis, Larynx

View from the side into the opened pharynx. Parts of the cartilaginous skeleton of the larynx can be seen.

Blick von der Seite in den eröffneten Rachenraum. Anteile des knorpeligen Kehlkopfskeletts sind sichtbar.

Muscles de la langue et du pharynx (pharynx ouvert), cartilages du larynx, vus du côté gauche

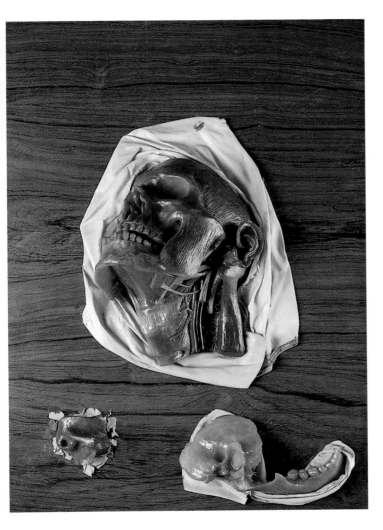

Display showing
the floor of the
mouth, muscles of
mastication and
jaw joint

Darstellung von
Mundboden, Kau-
muskulatur und
Kiefergelenk

Muscles du plan-
cher buccal et
muscles mastica-
teurs ; articulation
temporo-mandibu-
laire

Display showing
the larynx with liga-
ments and mus-
cles, the trachea
(left specimen) and
the tongue (middle
specimen)

Darstellungen des
Kehlkopfes mit
Bändern und Mus-
keln sowie der Zun-
ge (mittleres
Präparat) und der
Luftröhre (Präparat
links)

Muscles et liga-
ments du larynx:
avec la langue (au
centre), avec la
trachée (à gauche)

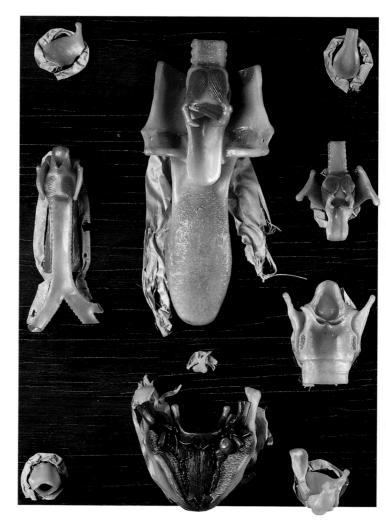

Musculus cricoarytenoideus posterior, Musculus arytenoideus obliquus, Musculus cricothyroideus, Musculus aryepiglotticus

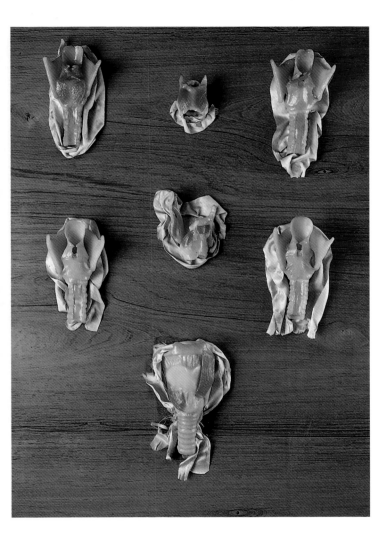

Display showing the internal and external muscles of the larynx

Darstellungen der inneren und äußeren Kehlkopfmuskeln

Muscles du larynx

Musculi laryngis

Display showing
individual muscles
of the larynx

Darstellungen ein-
zelner Kehlkopf-
muskeln

Muscles du larynx

Selected speci-
mens from the
head and neck
region

Ausgewählte
Präparate aus
dem Kopf- und
Halsbereich

Différentes prépa-
rations de détails
de la tête et du cou

Musculus longissimus

Display showing
some muscles of
the back

Darstellung eines
Teiles der Rücken-
muskulatur

Muscles érecteurs
du rachis (spinaux)

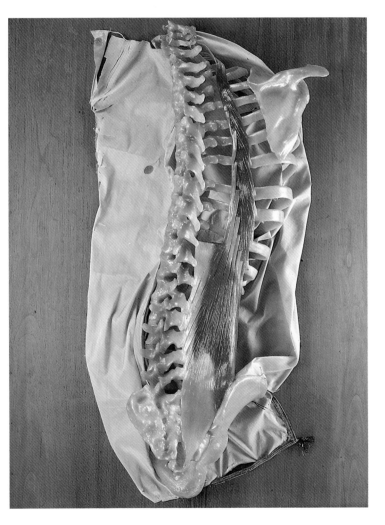

Display showing
some muscles of
the back

Darstellung eines
Teiles der Rücken-
muskulatur

Muscles érecteurs
du rachis (spinaux)

Musculus longissimus

Display showing
some muscles of
the back

Darstellung eines
Teiles der Rücken-
muskulatur

Muscles érecteurs
du rachis (spinaux)

Musculus multifidus

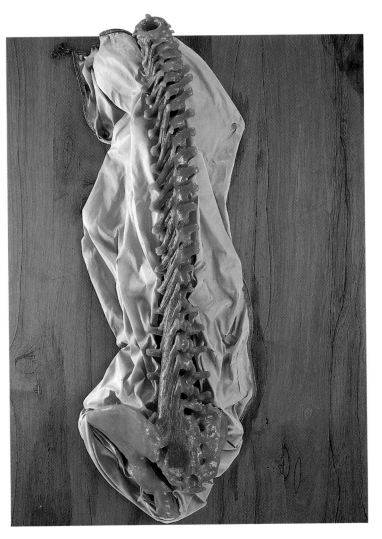

Display showing
deep muscles of
the back

Darstellung einer
tiefen Schicht der
Rückenmuskulatur

Muscles profonds
du dos insérés sur
la colonne verté-
brale

Musculus semispinalis capitis

Display showing
a deep extensor
muscle of the back

Darstellung eines
tiefen Streckmus-
kels des Rückens

Muscles du plan
profond de la
nuque insérés sur
la colonne verté-
brale

Display showing
deep extensor
muscles of the
back

Darstellung von tie-
fen Streckmuskeln
des Rückens

Muscles profonds
de la nuque insérés
sur la colonne ver-
tébrale

Musculus scalenus anterior et medius

Display showing
deep muscles at
the side of the neck

Darstellung von tie-
fen seitlichen Hals-
muskeln

Muscles profonds
de la région latérale
du cou (scalènes)

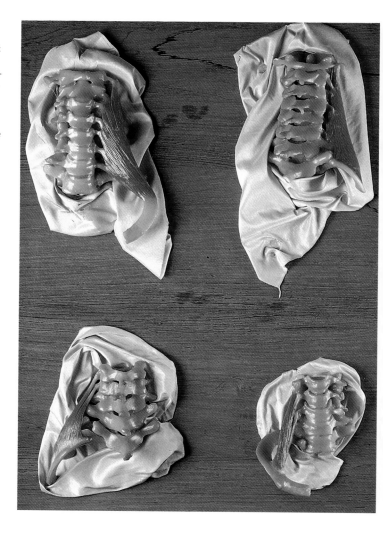

A deep neck
muscle in front of
the cervical verte-
bral column

Tiefer Halsmuskel
auf der Vorderseite
der Halswirbel-
säule

Muscles profonds
du cou dans la
région préverté-
brale

Musculi intertransversarii

Short muscles
which connect the
transverse process-
es of the vertebrae
with one another

Kurze Muskeln, die
die Querfortsätze
der Wirbel mitein-
ander verbinden

Muscles courts
tendus entre les
processus trans-
verses des ver-
tèbres cervicales

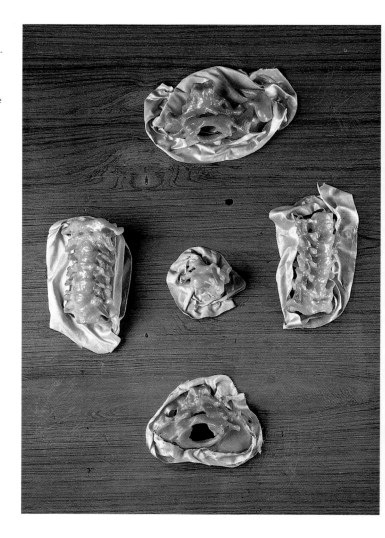

Musculus rectus capitis posterior minor, Musculus obliquus capitis inferior, Musculi interspinales, Musculi rotatores

Display showing part of the deep musculature of the neck and back

Darstellung eines Teiles der tiefen Muskulatur des Nackens und des Rückens

Muscles profonds de la nuque et du dos insérés sur la colonne vertébrale

Musculi levatores costarum, Musculi intertransversarii

Display showing
part of the deep
musculature of the
neck and back

Darstellung eines
Teiles der tiefen
Nacken- und
Rückenmuskulatur

Muscles profonds
de la nuque et du
dos insérés sur la
colonne vertébrale

Display showing
deep muscles of
the back in the tho-
racic and lumbar
regions of the ver-
tebral column

Darstellung eines
Teiles der tiefen
Rückenmuskulatur
im Bereich der
Brust- und Lenden-
wirbelsäule

Muscles profonds
du dos et des
lombes insérés sur
la colonne verté-
brale

Musculus multifidus

Deep muscles of
the back in the
lumbar region of
the vertebral
column

Tiefer Rückenmus-
kel im Bereich der
Lendenwirbelsäule

Muscles profonds
de la région lom-
baire (spinaux)

A muscle which
rotates the head
(left specimen) and
one which lies in
the skin of the neck
(right specimen)

Darstellung des
Kopfwenders (lin-
kes Präparat) und
eines in der Haut
des Halses gelege-
nen Muskels (rech-
tes Präparat)

Muscles du cou :
sterno-cléido-mas-
toïdien (à gauche),
et peaucier du cou
(à droite)

Musculus trapezius

View of the trapez-
ius muscle

Ansicht des Trapez-
muskels

Muscle superficiel
de la nuque et du
dos (trapèze)

Musculus splenius capitis, Musculus levator scapulae

View of the flat
muscles of the
back

Anteile der platten
Rückenmuskeln

Muscles du plan
intermédiaire de
la nuque

Some of the flat muscles of the back which connect the shoulder blade to the vertebral column

Anteile der platten Rückenmuskeln zwischen Schulterblatt und Wirbelsäule

Muscles fixateurs de l'omoplate à la colonne vertébrale

Musculus serratus anterior, Musculus subclavius, Musculus deltoideus

Display showing
various muscles of
the thorax and
upper arm

Darstellungen ver-
schiedener Mus-
keln von Brust und
Oberarm

Muscles attachés à
la clavicule et à
l'omoplate

View of a super-
ficial muscle of
the back

Ansicht eines ober-
flächlichen Rücken-
muskels

Muscle superficiel
des lombes et du
thorax (grand
dorsal)

Musculi faciales, Musculi colli, Musculi thoracis, Musculi abdominis, Musculi membri superioris, Musculi membri inferioris

Whole body specimen with the deep layer of muscles displayed

Ganzkörperpräparat zur Darstellung tiefer Schichten der Muskulatur

Préparation du corps entier représentant des muscles profonds

Musculi faciales, Musculi colli, Musculi thoracis, Musculi abdominis, Musculi membri superioris, Musculi membri inferioris

Whole body specimen with the deep layer of muscles displayed

Ganzkörperpräparat zur Darstellung tiefer Schichten der Muskulatur

Préparation du corps entier représentant des muscles profonds

Musculi abdominis

Superficial and
deep muscles of
the anterior
abdominal wall

Oberflächliche und
tiefe Muskeln der
vorderen Bauch-
wand

Muscles abdomi-
naux superficiels
et profonds

View of the straight
abdominal muscle
with its intermediate
tendons

Ansicht des geraden
Bauchmuskels mit
seinen Zwischen-
sehnen

Muscle droit de
l'abdomen et ses
intersections tendi-
neuses

Musculus obliquus externus abdominis

The external
oblique abdominal
muscle together
with its tendinous
sheet

Darstellung des
äußeren schrägen
Bauchmuskels
mit seiner Sehnen-
platte

Muscle oblique
externe de l'abdo-
men : corps mus-
culaire et tendon

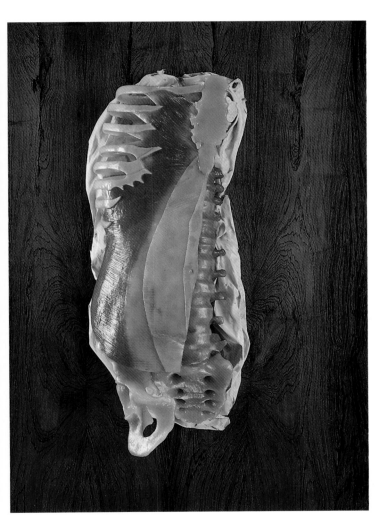

A deep oblique muscle of the anterior abdominal wall

Darstellung eines tiefen schrägen Muskels der vorderen Bauchwand

Muscle oblique interne de l'abdomen : corps musculaire et tendon ; muscle transverse du thorax

Musculus obliquus internus abdominis

The internal oblique abdominal muscle seen from the side. Below: the hip bone with its joint socket

Innerer schräger Bauchmuskel von der Seite gesehen. Unten: das Hüftbein mit der Gelenkpfanne

Muscle oblique interne de l'abdomen (vu de la gauche)

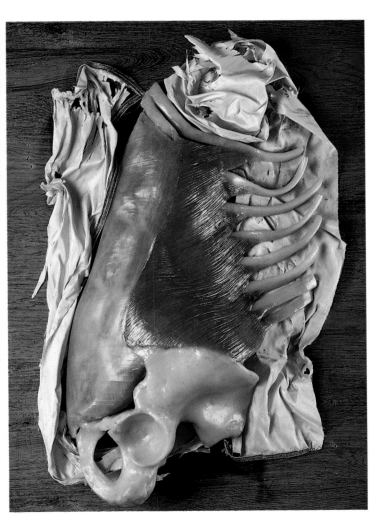

The external oblique abdominal muscle seen from the side

Äußerer schräger Bauchmuskel von der Seite gesehen

Muscle oblique externe de l'abdomen vu de la gauche

Musculus obliquus internus abdominis

Part of the internal
oblique abdominal
muscle seen from
behind

Anteil des inneren
schrägen Bauch-
muskels in der
Ansicht von hinten

Muscle oblique
interne de l'abdo-
men vu de l'arrière

View of the internal oblique muscle of the abdomen, fibers derived from which form the elevator of the testis

Ansicht des inneren schrägen Bauchmuskels und des aus Faseranteilen dieses Muskels gebildeten Hodenhebers

Muscle oblique interne de l'abdomen et fibres assurant l'élévation du testicule (crémaster)

Musculus transversus abdominis

The transverse
abdominal muscle
seen from behind

Ansicht des queren
Bauchmuskels von
hinten

Muscle transverse
de l'abdomen vu
de l'arrière

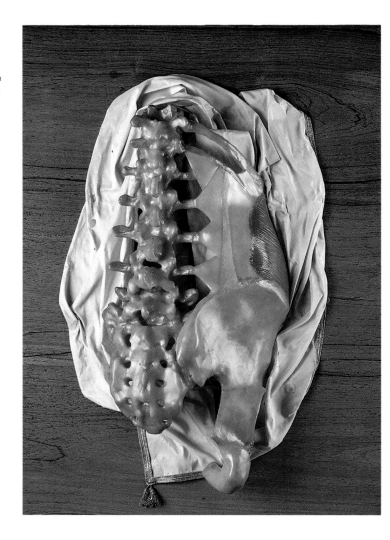

The transverse
abdominal muscle
seen from the side

Querer Bauchmus-
kel von der Seite
gesehen

Muscle transverse
de l'abdomen vu
de la gauche

Musculi intercostales externi et interni

The external and
internal intercostal
muscles

Äußere und innere
Zwischenrippen-
muskeln

Muscles intercos-
taux interne et
externe

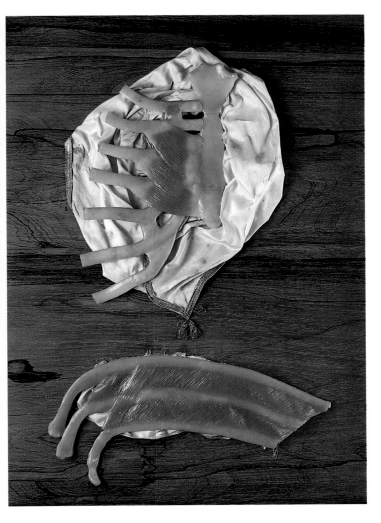

Display showing
various intercostal
muscles

Darstellung ver-
schiedener Zwi-
schenrippen-
muskeln

Muscle transverse
du thorax (en
haut) ; muscles
intercostaux

Musculi intercostales, Musculus quadratus lumborum

The posterior thoracic and abdominal walls seen from in front

Blick von vorn auf die hintere Brust- und Bauchwand

Muscles intercostaux et carré des lombes vus de l'avant

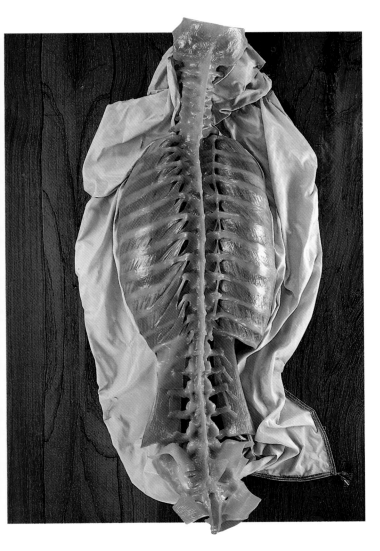

The intercostal
muscles seen from
behind

Darstellung der
Zwischenrippen-
muskeln in der
Ansicht von hinten

Muscles intercos-
taux et carré des
lombes vus de
l'arrière

Diaphragma

The diaphragm
seen from in front

Ansicht von vorn
auf das Zwerchfell

Diaphragme vu de
l'avant

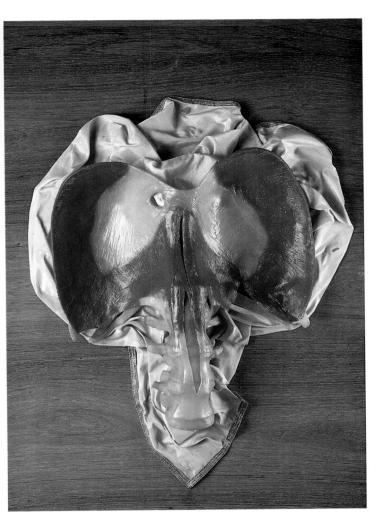

View of the abdom-
inal surface of the
diaphragm show-
ing the openings
for esophagus, aor-
ta and inferior vena
cava

Ansicht auf die
dem Bauchraum
zugewandte Seite
des Zwerchfells mit
den Durchtrittsstel-
len für Speiseröhre,
Körperschlagader
und untere Hohl-
vene

Diaphragme avec
les orifices de pas-
sage de l'œsopha-
ge, de l'aorte, et
de la veine cave
inférieure (vue in-
férieure)

Musculi faciales, Musculi colli, Musculi thoracis, Musculi abdominis, Musculi membri superioris, Musculi membri inferioris

Whole body specimen displaying the deeper layer of muscles

Ganzkörperpräparat zur Darstellung tieferer Schichten der Muskulatur

Préparation du corps entier représentant des muscles profonds

Musculi faciales, Musculi colli, Musculi thoracis, Musculi abdominis, Musculi membri superioris, Musculi membri inferioris

Whole body specimen displaying the superficial muscles

Ganzkörperpräparat zur Darstellung der oberflächlichen Muskulatur

Préparation du corps entier représentant des muscles superficiels

Musculus pectoralis major

The large muscle of
the chest seen
from in front

Großer Brustmus-
kel in der Ansicht
von vorne

Muscle grand pec-
toral vu de l'avant

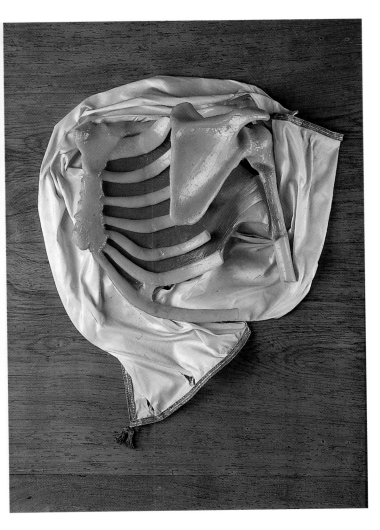

The deep surface of the large muscle of the chest, viewed from inside

Ansicht aus dem Brustraum auf die Innenfläche des großen Brustmuskels

Muscle grand pectoral vu à travers la paroi antérieure de la cage thoracique

Musculus deltoideus

The deltoid muscle

Ansicht des Delta-
muskels

Muscle deltoïde

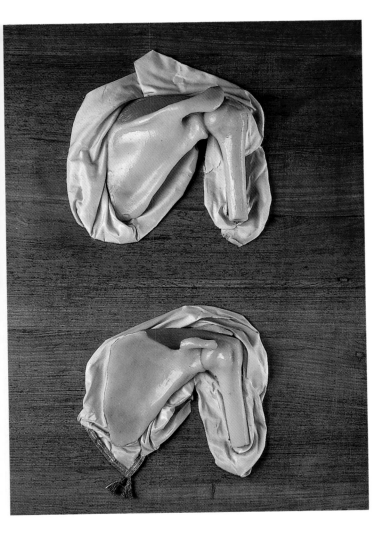

Display showing
the shoulder joint
with a muscle of its
muscular cuff

Darstellung eines
zur Muskelman-
schette des Schul-
tergelenkes gehöri-
gen Muskels

Muscle de la coiffe
des rotateurs de
l'articulation de
l'épaule (supra-
épineux)

Musculus teres major

View of a muscle
which connects the
upper arm to the
shoulder blade

Ansicht eines Mus-
kels, der Schulter-
blatt und Oberarm
verbindet

Muscle tendu
entre la scapula et
l'humérus (grand
rond)

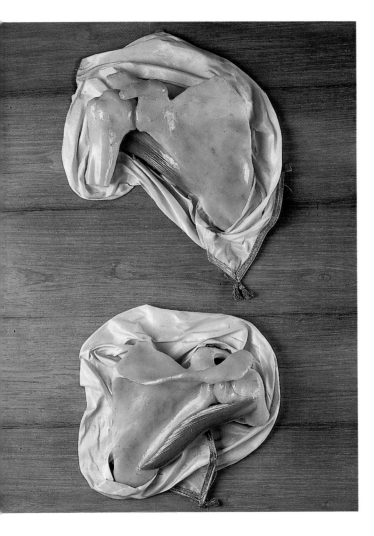

View of a muscle
which connects the
upper arm to the
shoulder blade

Ansicht eines Mus-
kels, der Schulter-
blatt und Oberarm
verbindet

Muscle tendu entre
la scapula et l'hu-
mérus (petit rond)

Display showing
shoulder muscles

Darstellung von
Schultermuskeln

Muscles de la coif-
fe des rotateurs de
l'articulation de
l'épaule

View of the biceps muscle from in front (left specimen) and from behind (right specimen)

Ansichten des Bizepsmuskels von vorn (linkes Präparat) und von hinten (rechtes Präparat)

Muscle superficiel de la région antérieure du bras (biceps brachial)

Musculus coracobrachialis

Display showing a
deep flexor muscle
of the upper arm

Darstellung eines
tiefen Oberarm-
beugemuskels

Muscle profond de
la région antérieure
du bras (coraco-
brachial)

Display showing a
deep flexor muscle
of the upper arm

Darstellung eines
tiefen Oberarm-
beugemuskels

Muscle profond de
la région antérieure
du bras (brachial)

Musculus triceps brachii

Display showing
the extensor mus-
cle of the upper
arm

Ansichten des
Oberarmstreck-
muskels

Muscle de la région
postérieure du bras
(triceps brachial)

The extensor muscles of the hand and thumb and their tendons

Streckmuskeln der Hand und des Daumens und ihre Sehnen

Muscles extenseurs du poignet et des doigts et leurs tendons

Musculus supinator

A muscle which
contributes to the
rotation of the
forearm

Ansichten eines
Muskels, der an
der Unterarmdre-
hung beteiligt ist

Muscle profond de
la loge latérale de
l'avant-bras (supi-
nateur)

Display showing
the extensor and
rotator muscles of
the forearm

Darstellungen von
Unterarmstreck-
und drehmuskeln

Muscles de la loge
latérale de l'avant-
bras (brachio-radial
et long extenseur
radial du carpe)

Musculus pronator teres, Musculus pronator quadratus

Display showing
muscles which
contribute to rota-
tion of the forearm

Darstellungen von
Muskeln, die an
Drehbewegungen
des Unterarms
beteiligt sind

Muscles de la loge
antérieure de
l'avant-bras (rond
pronateur et carré
pronateur)

Display showing the long flexor muscles of the fingers with their tendons

Darstellung der langen Fingerbeugemuskeln mit ihren Endsehnen

Muscles long fléchisseur du pouce (à gauche), et fléchisseur profond des doigts (à droite) et leurs tendons

Musculus flexor carpi radialis, Musculi palmaris longus et brevis

Muscles which
contribute to flex-
ion of the fingers

Darstellung von
Fingerbeugemus-
keln

Muscles superfi-
ciels de la loge
antérieure de
l'avant-bras (flé-
chisseur radial du
carpe et long pal-
maire)

The superficial
flexor muscle of
the fingers

Darstellung des
oberflächlich gele-
genen Fingerbeu-
gemuskels

Muscle fléchisseur
superficiel des
doigts et ses ten-
dons

Musculus extensor pollicis longus et brevis

The long extensor
muscle of the
thumb

Darstellung der
langen Daumen-
streckmuskeln

Muscles exten-
seurs du pouce

A long muscle act-
ing on the thumb

Darstellung eines
langen Daumen-
muskels

Muscle long abduc-
teur du pouce

Musculus flexor carpi ulnaris, Musculus extensor carpi radialis brevis

Display showing forearm muscles which contribute to flexion and extension at the wrist joint

Darstellung von Unterarmmuskeln, die an der Beugung und Streckung im Handgelenk beteiligt sind

Muscles de l'avant-bras (fléchisseur ulnaire du carpe et court extenseur radial du carpe)

A muscle which contributes to extension at the wrist joint

Darstellung eines Muskels, der an der Streckung des Handgelenkes beteiligt ist

Muscle de la loge latérale de l'avant-bras (long extenseur radial du carpe)

Musculus extensor digitorum, Musculus extensor carpi ulnaris

Display showing muscles bringing about extension of the fingers and sideways movement of the hand

Darstellung von Muskeln zur Streckung der Finger und Seitwärtsbewegung der Hand

Muscles de la loge postérieure de l'avant-bras (extenseur des doigts et extenseur ulnaire du carpe)

The extensor
muscle of the index
finger

Darstellung des
Streckmuskels des
Zeigefingers

Muscle extenseur
propre de l'index

Musculi interossei manus, Musculus abductor pollicis brevis, Musculus flexor pollicis brevis, Musculus adductor pollicis, Musculus abductor digiti minimi

Display showing the deep muscles in the hollow of the hand which bring about fine movements of the fingers

Darstellungen von tiefen Muskeln der Hohlhand für feinmotorische Fingerbewegungen

Muscles courts de la main (intrinsèques) pour les mouvements fins des doigts

Display showing
muscles which
contribute to fine
movements of the
fingers

Darstellung von
Muskeln, die an
den Fingerbewe-
gungen beteiligt
sind

Muscles courts de
la main (muscles
interosseux)

Musculi digitorum manus I et V, Musculus flexor digiti minimi brevis, Musculus opponens pollicis

Display showing
the muscles of the
ball of the thumb
and little finger

Darstellungen von
Muskeln des Dau-
men- und Kleinfin-
gerballens

Muscles courts
pour le pouce (émi-
nence thénar), et
pour le petit doigt
(éminence hypo-
thénar)

Display showing
the muscles
responsible for fine
movements of the
index finger and
thumb

Darstellungen von
Muskeln für die
feinmotorischen
Bewegungen von
Zeigefinger und
Daumen

Muscles courts de
la main pour le
pouce et l'index

Display showing
the joints of the
shoulder, elbow
and wrist with
muscle insertions
and tendons

Darstellung von
Muskeln, Muskel-
ansätzen und Seh-
nen von Schulter-
gelenk, Ellenbeuge
und Handbeuge-
seite

Bourses et gaines
synoviales anne-
xées aux muscles
et tendons des
articulations de
l'épaule, du coude
et de la main

Display showing
the joints of the
shoulder, elbow
and wrist with
muscle insertions
and tendons

Darstellung von
Muskeln, Muskel-
ansätzen und Seh-
nen von Schulter-
gelenk, Ellenbeuge
und Handstreck-
seite

Bourses et gaines
synoviales anne-
xées aux muscles et
tendons des articu-
lations de l'épaule,
du coude, et de la
main

Articulationes et ligamenta manus, Musculi interossei

Display showing
tendons and liga-
ments of the wrist

Darstellung von
Sehnen und Band-
verbindungen im
Bereich des Hand-
gelenkes

Tendons et liga-
ments du poignet
et des doigts ;
muscles interos-
seux

A large muscle run-
ning downwards
from the lumbar
vertebral column
viewed from in
front

Ansicht des großen
Lendenmuskels
von vorn

Muscle psoas vu
de l'avant

Musculus psoas minor

A small muscle
running down-
wards from the
lumbar vertebral
column seen from
in front

Ansicht des kleinen
Lendenmuskels
von vorn

Muscle petit psoas
(inconstant) vu de
l'avant

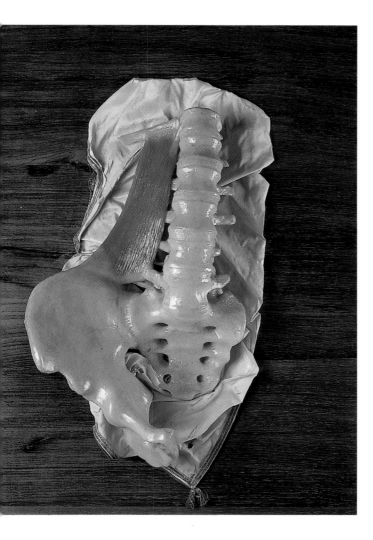

A muscle of the
posterior abdom-
inal wall seen from
in front

Blick von vorn auf
einen Muskel der
hinteren Bauch-
wand

Muscle de la paroi
abdominale posté-
rieure (carré des
lombes) vu de
l'avant

Musculus quadratus lumborum

A muscle of the
posterior abdom-
inal wall seen from
behind

Blick von hinten
auf einen Muskel
der hinteren
Bauchwand

Muscle carré des
lombes vu de l'ar-
rière

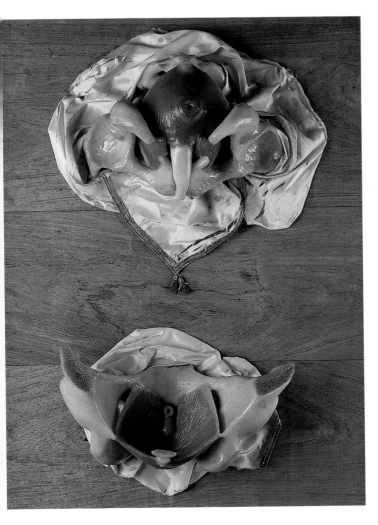

View of the muscles of the floor of the pelvis from below (upper specimen) and from above (lower specimen), also showing the circular course of the muscles of the external sphincter

Ansicht des muskulären Beckenbodens von unten (oberes Präparat) und von oben (unteres Präparat) mit Darstellung der zirkulär verlaufenden Fasern des äußeren Schließmuskels

Muscles du plancher du bassin (périnée) : vue du dessous (en haut) avec muscle sphincter de l'anus, vue du dessus (en bas)

Musculi faciales, Musculi colli, Musculi thoracis, Musculi abdominis, Musculi membri superioris, Musculi membri inferioris

Whole body specimen displaying both the superficial and deep layers of muscles

Ganzkörperpräparat zur Darstellung oberflächlicher und tiefer Schichten der Muskulatur

Préparation du corps entier représentant des muscles superficiels et profonds

Musculi colli, Musculi thoracis, Musculi abdominis, Musculi membri superioris, Musculi membri inferioris

Whole body specimen displaying the deep layer of muscles

Ganzkörperpräparat zur Darstellung tiefer Schichten der Muskulatur

Préparation du corps entier représentant des muscles profonds

Several views of the
bony pelvis and
pelvic floor

Verschiedene Dar-
stellungen des
knöchernen
Beckens mit
Beckenboden

Muscles du plan-
cher du bassin
(périnée)

A small muscle
connecting the coc-
cyx to the hip bone

Kleiner Muskel zwi-
schen Steißbein
und Hüftbein

Muscle coccygien
tendu entre le coc-
cyx et l'os coxal

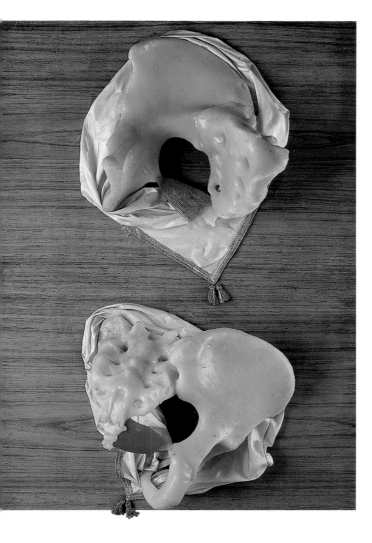

Diaphragma pelvis, Musculus levator ani

Display showing
part of the deep
muscles of the
pelvic floor

Darstellung eines
Teiles der tiefen
Beckenbodenmus-
kulatur

Muscles du plan-
cher du bassin

The large outer-
most muscle of the
buttock seen from
the side

Ansicht des großen
äußeren Gesäß-
muskels von der
Seite

Muscle superficiel
de la région fessiè-
re (grand fessier)
vu du côté droit

Musculus glutaeus medius

Display showing
part of the muscles
of the middle layer
of the buttock

Darstellung eines
Teiles der mittleren
Schicht der
Gesäßmuskulatur

Muscle moyen fes-
sier vu de l'avant et
de l'arrière

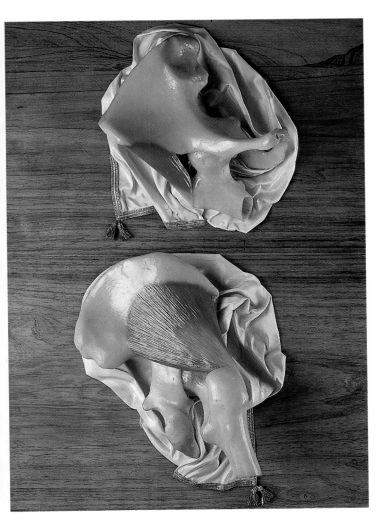

Display showing
part of the deep
muscles of the
buttock

Darstellung eines
Teiles der tiefen
Gesäßmuskulatur

Muscle le plus pro-
fond de la région
fessière (petit fes-
sier)

Musculus tensor fasciae latae

Display showing a
superficial muscle
which has a
spreading insertion
into the tendinous
sheet at the side of
the thigh

Darstellung eines
oberflächlichen
Muskels, der in die
Sehnenplatte am
seitlichen Ober-
schenkel einstrahlt

Muscle superficiel
de la région fessiè-
re (tenseur du fas-
cia lata)

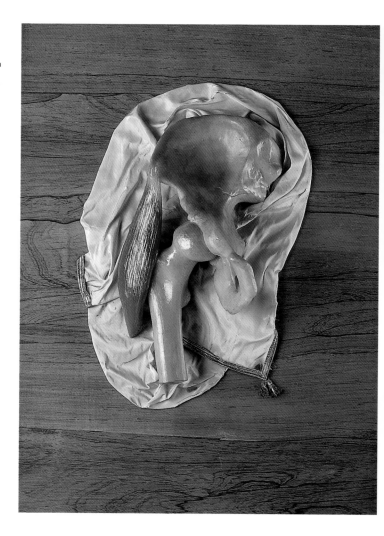

A muscle attached
to the inside of the
wing of the iliac
bone

Darstellung eines
Muskels an der
Innenseite der
Darmbeinschaufel

Muscle iliaque atta-
ché sur la face
interne du grand
bassin

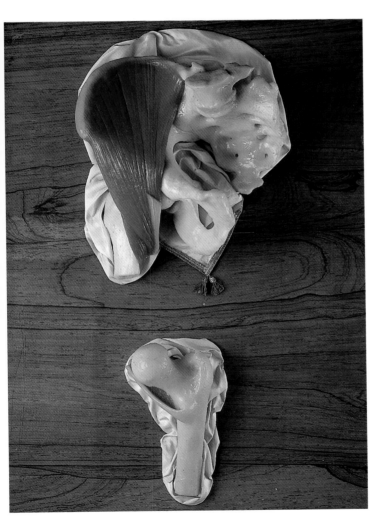

Musculi gemelli, Musculus obturatorius internus, Musculus quadratus femoris

Display showing
the deep muscles
which contribute to
rotation at the hip
joint

Darstellung von
tiefliegenden Mus-
keln, die an Dreh-
bewegungen im
Hüftgelenk betei-
ligt sind

Muscles profonds
de la région fessiè-
re rotateurs de la
cuisse (pelvi-tro-
chantériens)

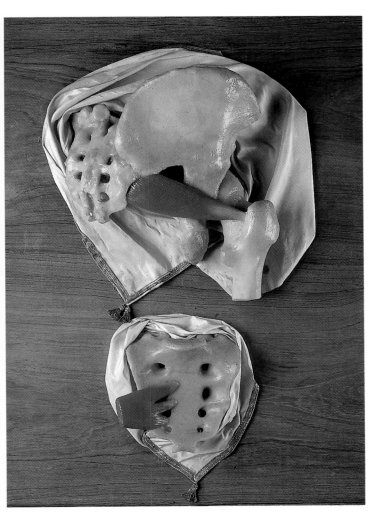

A muscle which
connects the thigh
to the sacrum

Darstellung eines
Muskels, der
Kreuzbein und
Oberschenkel ver-
bindet

Muscle piriforme
tendu entre le
sacrum et le fémur
(pelvi-trochanté-
rien)

Musculus obturatorius externus

A muscle which contributes to rotation at the hip joint

Darstellungen eines Muskels, der an Drehbewegungen im Hüftgelenk beteiligt ist

Muscle obturateur externe rotateur de la cuisse (pelvi-trochantérien)

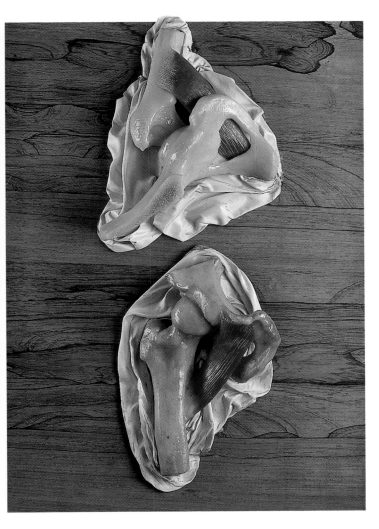

A deeply placed
muscle of the thigh

Darstellung eines
tiefliegenden Ober-
schenkelmuskels

Muscle adducteur
de la cuisse
(pectiné)

Musculus adductor brevis

A muscle which
connects the pubic
bone with the
femur

Darstellung eines
Muskels, der das
Schambein mit
dem Oberschenkel-
knochen verbindet

Muscle adducteur
tendu entre le
pubis et le fémur
(court adducteur)

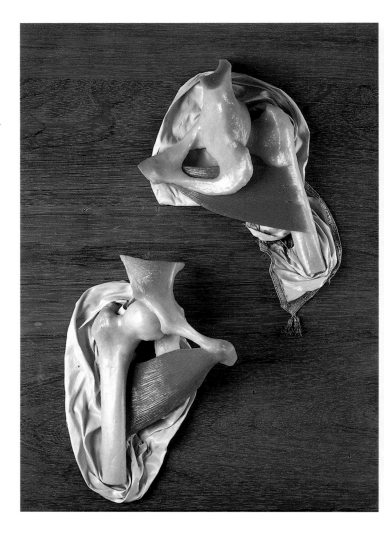

A muscle on the
inside of the thigh

Darstellung eines
Muskels der Ober-
schenkelinnenseite

Muscle adducteur
situé dans la région
interne de la cuisse
(long adducteur)

Musculus adductor magnus

A muscle on the
inside of the thigh

Darstellung eines
Muskels der Ober-
schenkelinnenseite

Muscle adducteur
situé dans la région
interne de la cuisse
(grand adducteur)

Display showing
muscles of the
thigh

Darstellung von
Oberschenkel-
muskeln

Muscles de la cuis-
se tendus entre le
bassin et le tibia
(gracile à gauche,
et couturier à
droite)

Musculus rectus femoris

Two views of a
muscle at the front
of the thigh

Muskel an der
Oberschenkelvor-
derseite in zwei
Ansichten

Portions du muscle
quadriceps de la
région antérieure
de la cuisse (droit
fémoral)

Muscles at the
inner side and back
of the thigh

Muskeln der Ober-
schenkelinnen- und
-rückseite

Muscles profonds
de la région posté-
rieure de la cuisse
(ischio-jambiers)

Musculus semitendinosus, Musculus biceps femoris

Muscles at the
back of the thigh

Muskeln der Ober-
schenkelrückseite

Muscles superfi-
ciels de la région
postérieure de la
cuisse (ischio-
jambiers)

Display showing
the deeper parts of
the four-headed
muscle of the thigh

Darstellung der tie-
feren Anteile des
vierköpfigen Ober-
schenkelmuskels

Chefs profonds du
muscle quadriceps
de la région anté-
rieure de la cuisse
(vastes)

Musculus peronaeus longus, Musculus peronaeus brevis, Musculus extensor digitorum longus, Musculus triceps surae

Superficial muscles of the lower leg and foot seen from the outer side

Oberflächliche Muskeln des Unterschenkels und Fußes in der Ansicht von der Außenseite

Muscles et tendons de la jambe et du pied

The large muscles
of the calf with the
tendon of Achilles

Darstellung des
großen Waden-
muskels mit Achil-
lessehne

Chef profond du
muscle triceps du
mollet (soléaire), et
tendon d'Achille

Display showing
some of the mus-
cles of the calf

Darstellungen
eines Teiles der
Wadenmuskeln

Chefs superficiels
du muscle triceps
du mollet ; petit
muscle accessoire
(plantaire)

A deep muscle of the calf that elevates the inner border of the foot

Darstellung eines tiefen Wadenmuskels, der an der Hebung des inneren Fußrandes beteiligt ist

Muscle profond de la jambe (tibial postérieur) élévateur du bord interne du pied

Musculus tibialis anterior, Musculus extensor digitorum longus

The long extensor
muscle of the toes

Ansicht des Zehen-
streckers

Muscles antérieurs
de la jambe (tibial
antérieur et exten-
seur des orteils)

A long muscle on the outer side of the lower leg which helps to maintain the tension of the arch of the foot

Darstellung eines langen Muskels an der Außenseite des Unterschenkels, der an der Verspannung des Fußgewölbes beteiligt ist

Muscle latéral de la jambe (long fibulaire) élévateur du bord externe du pied

Musculus peronaeus brevis

A short muscle on the outer side of the lower leg

Darstellung eines kurzen Muskels an der Außenseite des Unterschenkels

Muscle latéral profond de la jambe (court fibulaire)

Musculus extensor digitorum brevis, Musculus flexor digitorum brevis, Musculus extensor hallucis longus

Display showing muscles which contribute to movement of the toes

Darstellung von Muskeln, die an Zehenbewegungen beteiligt sind

Muscles extenseurs et muscle court fléchisseur des orteils

Musculi abductores et flexores hallucis sive digiti minimi

Display showing
muscles which
contribute to
movement of the
toes

Darstellung von
Muskeln, die an
Zehenbewegungen
beteiligt sind

Muscles courts du
pied moteurs des
orteils

Display showing muscles and tendons in the different layers of the sole of the foot

Darstellung von Muskeln und Sehnen verschiedener Schichten der Fußsohle

Plans musculaires et fibreux de la plante du pied

Musculi lumbricales, Musculi interossei plantares

Display showing
muscles and ten-
dons in the differ-
ent layers of the
sole of the foot

Darstellung von
Muskeln und Seh-
nen verschiedener
Schichten der Fuß-
sohle

Muscles et tendons
de la plante du pied

Musculus abductor hallucis, Musculus flexor digitorum brevis, Musculus flexor hallucis brevis

Display showing muscles and tendons in the different layers of the sole of the foot

Darstellung von Muskeln und Sehnen verschiedener Schichten der Fußsohle

Muscles et tendons de la plante du pied

Musculi interossei plantares

The small muscles
in the middle of the
foot

Darstellung von
kleinen Muskeln
des Mittelfußes

Muscles courts du
pied (interosseux)

The small muscles
in the middle of the
foot

Darstellung von
kleinen Muskeln
des Mittelfußes

Muscles courts du
pied (interosseux)

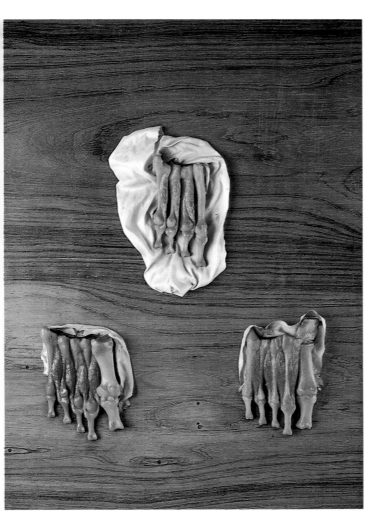

Retinacula musculi extensorum et flexorum

The superficial tendons and ligaments of the foot

Darstellung der oberflächlichen Sehnen und Bandverbindungen des Fußes

Plans fibreux et gaines tendineuses de la cheville et du pied

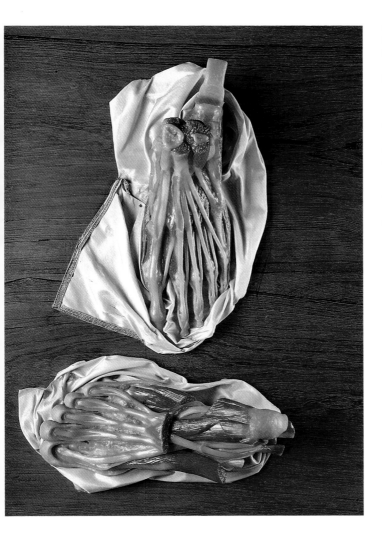

Display showing
the tendons in the
back of the foot
(upper specimen)
and sole of the foot
(lower specimen)

Darstellung der
Sehnen des
Fußrückens (obe-
res Präparat) und
der Fußsohle
(unteres Präparat)

Tendons du dos du
pied (en haut), et
de la plante du pied
(en bas)

Articulatio talocruralis, Articulatio genus

Display showing
the ankle and knee
joints

Darstellung des
oberen Sprung-
gelenkes und Knie-
gelenkes

Bourses synoviales
pour les tendons
au niveau de la che-
ville et du genou

Selected muscles of the lower leg and foot

Darstellung von ausge-wählten Muskeln des Unterschenkels und Fußes

Muscles profonds de la jambe et du pied

Musculi faciales, Musculi colli, Musculi thoracis, Musculi abdominis, Musculi membri superioris, Musculi membri inferioris

Whole body specimen displaying the superficial muscles

Ganzkörperpräparat zur Darstellung der oberflächlichen Muskulatur

Préparation du corps entier représentant des muscles superficiels

Musculi faciales, Musculi colli, Musculi thoracis, Musculi abdominis, Musculi membri superioris, Musculi membri inferioris

Whole body speci-
men with the deep
layer of muscles
displayed

Ganzkörperpräpa-
rat zur Darstellung
tiefer Schichten der
Muskulatur

Préparation du
corps entier repré-
sentant des
muscles profonds

Musculi faciales, Musculi colli, Musculi thoracis, Musculi abdominis, Musculi membri superioris, Musculi membri inferioris

Whole body speci-
men with the deep
layers of muscles

Ganzkörperpräpa-
rat zur Darstellung
tiefer Schichten der
Muskulatur

Préparation du
corps entier re-
présentant des
muscles profonds

Musculi colli, Musculi thoracis, Musculi abdominis, Musculi membri superioris, Musculi membri inferioris, Musculi dorsi

Whole body specimen with the deep layers of muscles

Ganzkörperpräparat zur Darstellung tiefer Schichten der Muskulatur

Préparation du corps entier représentant des muscles profonds

Systema cardiovasculare

Heart and Blood Circulation
Herz und Kreislauf
Cœur, artères et veines

Heart and Blood Circulation

Of all those organs which are essential to life, the heart has long occupied a unique position in our cultural history, having been accepted as the seat of the soul, and of love, feeling and the spirit. In radical contrast to this view, these wax models bear impressive witness to the state of knowledge in topographical anatomy during the 17th century. As early as 1628, the English physician William Harvey (1578–1657) discovered the relationship between the heart and circulation. Harvey's revolutionary theory of the blood circulation upset medical ideas which had been taken for granted for centuries, but it was generally accepted by the end of the 18th century.

The selection of specimens was related to the corresponding woodcuts and copperplate illustrations of the 16th and 17th centuries. These models represent many aspects of the cardiovascular system, such as the position of the heart between the lungs within the thorax, its relationship to the diaphragm, the pericardium with its nerves and vessels and the internal structure of both atria and ventricles. In some of the models one can look through openings in the anterior wall of the heart and see the position of the atrioventricular and semilunar valves on both sides of the organ.

The great vessels entering and leaving the heart and the vessels supplying the head and neck are shown in their relationship to the muscles, and the arteries and veins are clearly distinguished by their coloring. The whole distribution of the arterial system, including the large branches on the anterior abdominal wall, in the limbs and between the dissected muscles of the pelvis, can be easily followed.

Pages · Seiten · Pages 330–331:

Detail from pages 336–337

Detail der Seiten 336–337

Détail des pages 336–337

Das Herz nimmt kulturgeschichtlich unter allen lebenswichtigen Organen eine Sonderstellung ein, da es lange Zeit als Sitz der Seele, der Lie-
be, der Gefühle und des Geistes angesehen wurde. Die Wachspräparate
zeugen im Gegensatz zu dieser Betrachtungsweise eindrucksvoll vom
Kenntnisstand der makroskopischen Anatomie des 17. Jahrhunderts.
Bereits 1628 hatte der englische Anatom William Harvey (1578–1657) das
Zusammenspiel zwischen Herz und Kreislauf entdeckt. Harveys revolu-
tionäre Kreislauftheorie, die ein über Jahrhunderte gültiges Medizinkon-
zept ins Wanken gebracht hatte, war im ausgehenden 18. Jahrhundert allgemein anerkannt.

Die Auswahl der Präparate des Herzens orientiert sich an entsprechenden Holzschnitten und Kupferstichen des 16. und 17. Jahrhunderts. An diesen Modellen werden die vielfältige Aspekte des Herzens
und des Kreislaufsystems herausgearbeitet, wie etwa die topographische
Lage des Herzens im Brustkorb zwischen den Lungenflügeln, die Lage-
beziehung zum Zwerchfell, der Herzbeutel mit seinen Gefäßen und
Nerven, das Innenrelief der beiden Herzvorhöfe und -kammern. Die
Gefäßversorgung des Herzens mit Arterien, Venen und Lymphgefäßen
sowie die Nervenversorgung werden in unterschiedlichen Perspektiven
dargestellt. In einzelnen Modellen kann der Betrachter durch die aufgeschnittene Herzvorderwand in das Innere des rechten und linken Herzens blicken und die Position der Segel- und Taschenklappen einsehen.

Die großen herznahen Blutgefäße sowie die versorgenden
Gefäße der Hals- und Kopfregion sind in ihrer natürlichen Lage in den
Muskellogen wiedergegeben, wobei die arteriellen von den venösen
Gefäßen durch unterschiedliche Farbgebung klar unterschieden sind.
Der gesamte Verlauf der arteriellen Gefäße, einschließlich größerer Ver-
zweigungen an der vorderen Bauchwand, den Extremitäten sowie dem
Becken zwischen den aufpräparierten Muskelgruppen, läßt sich klar ver-
folgen.

Le cœur et l'appareil circulatoire

Le cœur occupe une place toute particulière, car il a longtemps été considéré dans l'histoire des civilisations comme le siège de l'âme et de l'esprit, de l'amour et des émotions. En opposition à ces conceptions, les modèles en cire témoignent de façon remarquable de l'état des connaissances exactes de l'anatomie macroscopique du XVIIe siècle. En 1628, l'anatomiste anglais William Harvey (1578–1657) découvre l'interdépendance du cœur et de l'appareil circulatoire ; sa théorie révolutionnaire de la circulation du sang, ébranlant un concept médical multiséculaire, est globalement admise à la fin du XVIIIe siècle.

Le choix des préparations du cœur se réfère à des gravures correspondantes, sur bois ou sur cuivre, des XVIe et XVIIe siècles. Sur les modèles en cire ressortent de nombreux aspects de la morphologie du cœur et des vaisseaux : topographie du cœur à l'intérieur de la cavité thoracique entre les deux poumons, position par rapport au diaphragme, disposition du péricarde accompagné de vaisseaux et nerfs, morphologie des cavités des oreillettes et des ventricules. La vascularisation artérielle, veineuse et lymphatique du cœur, ainsi que l'innervation, sont représentées sous différents angles. Sur des modèles du cœur isolé, une ouverture de la paroi cardiaque antérieure permet de découvrir les reliefs des cavités droites et gauches et la position des valvules cardiaques.

Les gros vaisseaux de la base du cœur, ainsi que les troncs vasculaires de la tête et du cou, sont représentés dans leur position anatomique en relation avec les loges musculaires. La distinction entre artères et veines est clairement donnée par une coloration spécifique, rouge ou bleue, de chaque type de vaisseau. Le trajet des artères entre les groupes musculaires disséqués, ainsi que le trajet des grosses branches collatérales, peut être suivi sur toute leur longueur au niveau de la paroi abdominale, du bassin, et des membres.

Page · Seite · Page 335:

Detail from pages 582–583

Detail der Seiten 582–583

Détail des pages 582–583

Arteriae

Whole body specimen showing the
arteries

Ganzkörperpräparat mit Darstellung
der Arterien

Préparation du corps entier représentant
les artères

|XXV. 446|

Larynx, Glandula thyroidea, Thorax, Mediastinum, Cor, Thymus

Thoracic cavity laid open to show the heart in its pericardium, the thymus gland and the great vessels. The lungs have been displaced sideways.

Eröffneter Brustraum mit Blick auf das Herz im Herzbeutel, die Thymusdrüse sowie die großen Gefäße und die zur Seite gedrängten Lungenflügel

Cavité thoracique ouverte : péricarde, gros vaisseaux de la base du cœur destinés au cou et aux membres supérieurs, poumons réclinés

The heart displayed in its natural position in the thoracic cavity. The pericardium has been removed and the lungs displaced sideways.

Darstellung des Herzens in seiner natürlichen Lage im Brustraum. Der Herzbeutel ist enfernt, die Lungenflügel sind zur Seite gedrängt.

Cœur en position naturelle : péricarde enlevé, poumons réclinés

Specimen showing
the heart with the
aorta, the trachea
and the main
bronchi. In the
upper specimen
a part of the
diaphragm has
been left behind.
The specimen is
displayed as if
viewed from the
inside of the
abdominal cavity.
The lower specimen
shows the anterior
surface of the heart.

Präparate des Her-
zens mit Haupt-
schlagader, Luft-
röhre und Haupt-
bronchien. Am
oberen Präparat ist
ein Teil des Zwerch-
fells belassen. Die
Ansicht entspricht
einem Blick aus der
Bauchhöhle. Das
untere Präparat
zeigt die Vorder-
fläche des Herzens.

Cœur et gros vais-
seaux de la base,
trachée et bronches
principales ; rap-
ports du cœur avec
une partie du dia-
phragme, vue du
bas et de l'arrière
(en haut) ; cœur et
artères coronaires
vus de l'avant (en
bas)

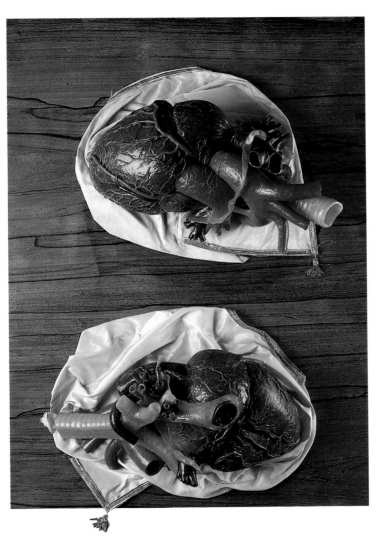

Specimens representing various aspects of the heart. The upper specimen shows the anterior surface of the heart with the coronary arteries.

Präparate des Herzens in verschiedenen Ansichten. Das obere Präparat zeigt die Vorderfläche des Herzens mit Herzkranzgefäßen.

Cœur et gros vaisseaux de la base, artères coronaires vus de l'avant (en haut) et de la droite (en bas)

Cor, Sinus coronarius, Venae pulmonales, Arteriae et venae coronariae

Upper specimen: anterior aspect of the heart seen from the left. A branch of the left coronary artery. Lower specimen: base of the heart lying on the diaphragm

Oberes Präparat: Ansicht des Herzens von links vorne. Blick auf einen Ast der linken Herzkranzarterie. Unteres Präparat: Ansicht auf die dem Zwerchfell aufliegende Herzbasis

Artères et veines du cœur (coronaires) vus de l'avant (en haut) et de l'arrière (en bas)

Cor, Arcus aortae, Arteria pulmonalis, Valvulae semilunares

The heart seen from above and from the left. Above, the trachea can be seen, in front of which lies the aortic arch, and in front of that the pulmonary artery. Lower specimens: a view into the pulmonary artery

Blick von oben links auf das Herz. Oben im Bild die Luftröhre, davor der Bogen der Hauptschlagader, vor diesem die Lungenarterie. Die unteren Präparate bieten Einblick in die Lungenarterie.

Cœur et gros vaisseaux (en haut) ; morphologie interne de l'artère pulmonaire et de ses valvules (en bas)

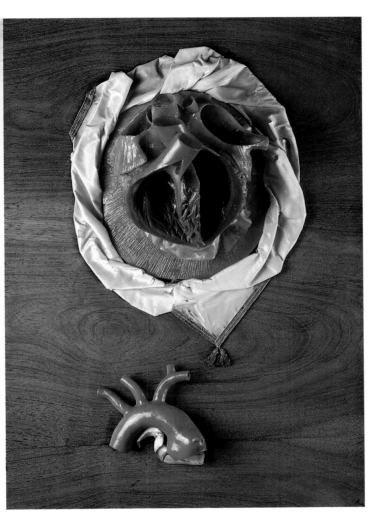

View from in front
into the opened
right and left ven-
tricles, below the
aortic arch

Blick von vorn in
die eröffnete rechte
und linke Herz-
kammer, unten der
Aortenbogen

Ventricules droit et
gauche ouverts (en
haut) ; crosse de
l'aorte isolée (en
bas)

Cor, Arteria pulmonalis, Arcus aortae, Ligamentum arteriosum Botalli

Various specimens of the heart with the ventricles laid open (above) and the atria (below). The ligamentous structure (depicted in yellow) connecting the pulmonary artery with the arch of the aorta is a remnant of the fetal circulation.

Verschiedene Präparate des Herzens mit Eröffnung der Herzkammern (oberes Präparat) und der Herzvorhöfe (unteres Präparat). Gelb dargestellt ist die bandartige Verbindung zwischen Lungenarterie und Aortenbogen, ein Relikt des fötalen Kreislaufes.

Cœur ouvert : ventricules (en haut) et oreillettes (en bas) ; en jaune (en haut) : ligament artériel, reliquat de la circulation fœtale entre l'artère pulmonaire et la crosse de l'aorte

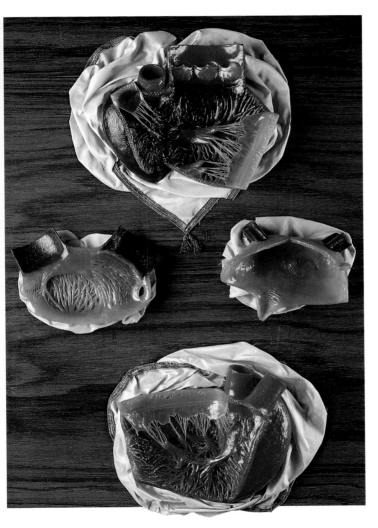

The upper and lower specimens depict the heart valves and the internal form of the ventricular muscle. The two specimens in the middle show the atrial musculature.

Oberes und unteres Präparat: Darstellung der Herzklappen und des Innenreliefs der Kammermuskulatur. Die beiden Präparate in der Mitte zeigen die Muskulatur der Vorhöfe.

Valves et valvules du cœur, reliefs des ventricules (en haut et en bas), reliefs musculaires des oreillettes (au milieu)

Various views of
the semilunar and
atrioventricular
valves

Verschiedene Dar-
stellungen von
Taschen- und
Segelklappen

Cœur ouvert :
valves et valvules
atrio-ventriculaires
et semi-lunaires

View of the heart from in front. Parts of the ventricular muscle have been removed to show the right and left atrioventricular valves.

Ansicht auf das Herz von vorn. Teile der Kammermuskulatur sind entfernt, so daß die rechte und die linke Segelklappe sichtbar werden.

Valvules atrio-ventriculaires droite et gauche vues de l'avant après ouverture des ventricules

Cor, Atrium dextrum et sinistrum

Various views of
the musculature
of the atria

Verschiedene Dar-
stellungen der
Muskulatur der
Vorhöfe

Architecture des
fibres musculaires
des oreillettes
(myocarde)

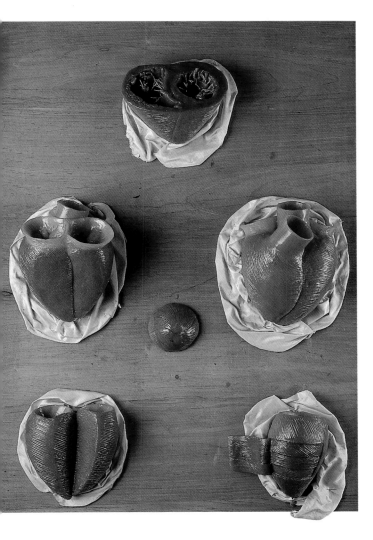

Various views
showing the
arrangement of the
fibers of the ven-
tricular muscle

Verschiedene Dar-
stellungen der
Anordnung der
Fasern der Kam-
mermuskulatur

Architecture des
fibres musculaires
des ventricules
(myocarde)

Whole body specimen showing sections of
the vascular system

Ganzkörperpräparat zur Darstellung von
Abschnitten des Gefäßsystems

Préparation du corps entier représentant
différents éléments de l'appareil circulatoire

[DEP. 15, 11]

Various views depicting the ventricular muscle. The two smaller specimens represent individual ventricles.

Verschiedene Darstellungen der Herzkammermuskulatur. Bei den kleineren Präparaten handelt es sich um Darstellungen einzelner Kammern

Architecture des fibres musculaires des ventricules

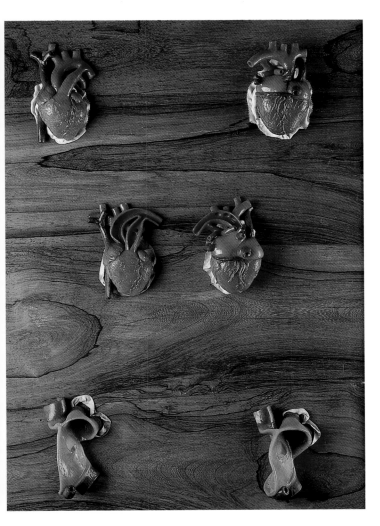

Demonstration of
the fetal heart
showing the bypass
between the pul-
monary artery and
the aortic arch, and
also between the
two atria (lower
specimen)

Darstellungen des
fötalen Herzens
mit Kurzschlußver-
bindungen von
Lungenarterie und
Aortenbogen sowie
den beiden Vorhö-
fen (untere Präpa-
rate)

Cœurs de fœtus :
communication
entre l'artère pul-
monaire et la cros-
se de l'aorte, com-
munication entre
les deux oreillettes
(en bas)

Cor fetalis, Vena umbilicalis

Demonstration of
the fetal circula-
tion. Below central:
the umbilical vein
and its tributaries
from the placenta

Darstellung des
fötalen Kreislaufes.
Unten in der Mitte:
die Nabelschnur-
vene und ihre
Zuflüsse aus dem
Mutterkuchen

Cœurs de fœtus et
circulation fœtale.
En bas au centre :
veine ombilicale et
veines du placenta

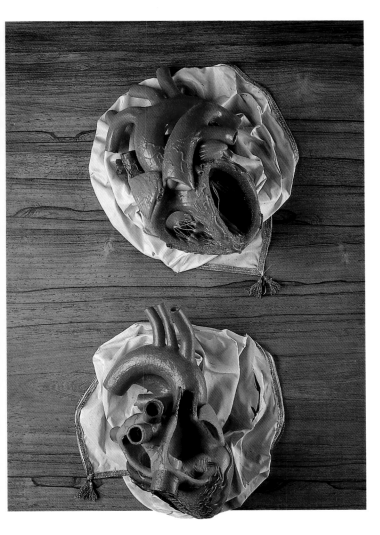

Demonstration of
the fetal heart. In
the upper speci-
men one is looking
into the opened
ventricles; in the
lower specimen,
into the atria

Darstellungen des
fötalen Herzens.
Im oberen Präparat
blickt man in die
eröffneten Kam-
mern, im unteren
Präparat in die Vor-
höfe

Cœurs de fœtus :
ventricules ouverts
(en haut) et oreil-
lettes ouvertes (en
bas)

Thoracic cavity laid
open and seen
from in front. On
the left the heart
can be seen in the
pericardium.
Behind are lying
the branches of the
pulmonary arteries
and veins and the
bronchi.

Eröffneter Brust-
korb in der Ansicht
von vorne. Links im
Bild ist das Herz
im Herzbeutel
erkennbar; dahinter
liegend die Äste
der Lungenarterien
und -venen sowie
der Bronchien.

Cage thoracique
ouverte ; en arrière
du péricarde : artè-
re et veines pulmo-
naires droites,
bronches droites,
le poumon droit
étant enlevé

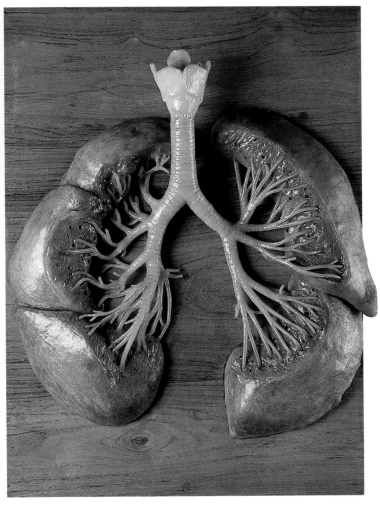

Demonstration of the respiratory tract, showing the larynx, trachea, bronchi and their subdivisions

Darstellung der Atemwege mit Kehlkopf, Luftröhre, Bronchien und ihren Verzweigungen

Appareil respiratoire : larynx, trachée, arbre bronchique disséqué dans les poumons

Pulmones, Aorta thoracica

The left and right lungs with their respective two (left) or three lobes (right) seen from behind. The aorta and its intercostal branches can also be seen.

Blick von hinten auf den linken und den rechten Lungenflügel mit den zwei (links) bzw. drei Lungenlappen (rechts) sowie auf die Hauptschlagader mit den abgehenden Zwischenrippenarterien

Viscères du thorax vus de l'arrière : lobes pulmonaires (deux à gauche et trois à droite), aorte et artères intercostales

Specimen with
both lungs and the
thoraic aorta seen
from behind

Präparat der bei-
den Lungenflügel
und der Brust-
schlagader in der
Ansicht von hinten

Viscères du thorax
vus de l'arrière :
poumons et aorte

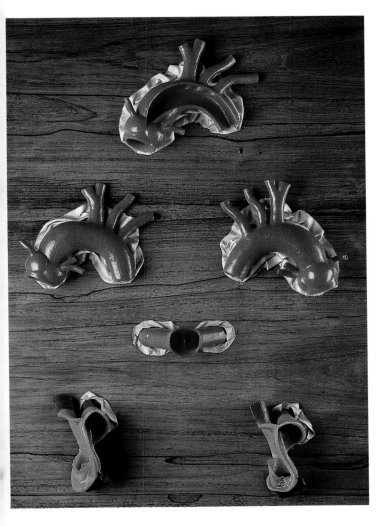

Various views of
the aortic arch. The
coronary arteries
arise from the
aortic bulb

Verschiedene Dar-
stellungen des Aor-
tenbogens. Die
Herzkranzgefäße
haben ihren Ur-
sprung im Bereich
der Auftreibung

Crosse de l'aorte et
ses branches colla-
térales ; les artères
coronaires naissent
du bulbe aortique

The aorta and the
large arteries in the
neck region

Darstellung der
Hauptschlagader
und der großen
Arterien im Bereich
des Halses

Crosse de l'aorte et
principales artères
du cou

Arcus aortae, Arteria brachiocephalica, Arteria carotis communis, Arteria subclavia,
Arteria carotis externa, Arteria vertebralis

Specimen showing
the arteries of the
head and neck. On
the left side of the
model the carotid
artery with its
branches can be
seen taking origin
from the aortic
arch.

Präparat der Arteri-
en im Bereich des
Kopfes und Halses.
Links im Bild ist die
vom Aortenbogen
abzweigende Hals-
schlagader mit
ihren Aufzweigun-
gen dargestellt.

Arbre artériel de la
tête et du cou :
ramifications de
l'artère carotide
(à gauche)

Vena cava superior, Vena brachiocephalica, Vena jugularis interna et externa, Sinus sagittalis superior, Sinus transversus, Sinus sigmoideus, Plexus venosus vertebralis internus

The veins of the
head and neck

Darstellung der
Venen im Bereich
des Kopfes und
Halses

Arbre veineux de la
tête et du cou

The veins in the region of the neck and face

Darstellung von Venen im Bereich von Gesicht und Hals

Veines de la tête et du cou

Pages · Seiten · Pages 368–369:

Detail from pages 574–575

Detail der Seiten 574–575

Détail des pages 574–575

Arteria facialis, Arteria temporalis superficialis, Arteria transversa facei, Arteria occipitalis, Vena retromandibularis, Vena facialis, Vena jugularis externa

The superficial arteries and veins of the head and neck

Darstellung von oberflächlich verlaufenden Arterien und Venen im Bereich von Kopf und Hals

Artères et veines superficielles de la tête et du cou

The veins in the
region of head and
neck

Darstellung von
Venen im Bereich
von Kopf und Hals

Veines de la tête et
du cou

Vena jugularis interna, Vena facialis, Vena occipitalis

The superficial veins of head and neck. The parotid gland and its duct can be seen lying in front of the ear.

Oberflächlich verlaufende Venen und Arterien im Bereich von Kopf und Hals. Vor dem Ohr liegt die Ohrspeicheldrüse mit ihrem Ausführungsgang.

Artères et veines de la tête et du cou ; glande parotide et conduit excréteur (de Stenon) en avant du pavillon de l'oreille

The carotid artery
and the vagus
nerve

Darstellung der
Halsschlagader
und des Vagus-
nerven

Artères carotides,
nerf vague

Arteria thoracica interna, Arteria epigastrica inferior, Arteria iliaca externa

The arteries of the
anterior thoracic
and abdominal
walls

Darstellung der
Arterien der vor-
deren Brust- und
Bauchwand

Artères des parois
antérieures du
thorax et de l'ab-
domen

Detail from

Vena cephalica, Vena basilica

The superficial
veins and cuta-
neous nerves of
the arm

Darstellung des
oberflächlichen
Venen und der
Hautnerven des
Armes

Veines et nerfs
superficiels du
membre supérieur
vus de l'avant

The muscles, vessels and nerves of the arm

Darstellung von Muskeln, Gefäßen und Nerven des Armes

Artères, veines, et nerfs du membre supérieur

Arteria profunda brachii, Arteria axillaris, Arteria brachialis

The deep arteries
of the upper arm
and forearm

Darstellung von tie-
fen Arterien des
Ober- und Unterar-
mes

Artères du membre
supérieur vues de
l'arrière

Arteria subclavia, Arteria axillaris, Arteria brachialis, Arteria radialis, Arteria ulnaris, Arcus palmaris

The arteries supplying the shoulder girdle, arm and hand

Darstellung der arteriellen Versorgung des Schultergürtels, des Armes und der Hand

Artères de l'épaule, du bras, de l'avant-bras, et de la main

Arteriae membri superioris

The arteries of the arm

Darstellung der Arterien des Armes

Arbre artériel projeté sur le squelette du membre supérieur

The veins of the
arm

Darstellung der
Venen des Armes

Réseau veineux
projeté sur le sque-
lette du membre
supérieur

Arteriae, venae et nervi membri superioris

The arteries, veins
and nerves of the
arm

Darstellung der
Arterien, Venen
und Nerven des
Armes

Artères, veines, et
nerfs du membre
supérieur projetés
sur le squelette

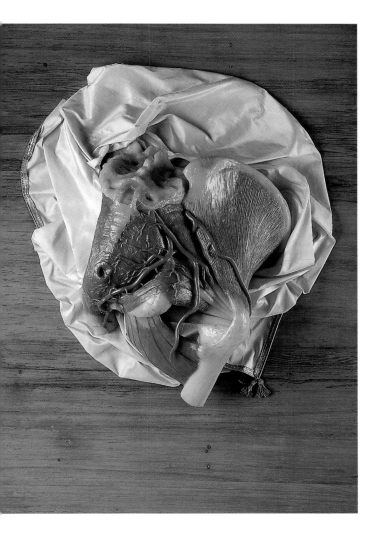

The arteries associated with the pelvic floor

Darstellung der Arterien im Bereich des Beckenbodens

Artères de la région fessière profonde et du plancher du bassin

Arteria glutaea superior et inferior

The arteries in the
region of the but-
tock after removal
of the large gluteal
muscle

Darstellung der
Arterien im Gesäß-
bereich nach Ent-
fernung des großen
Gesäßmuskels

Artères de la région
fessière profonde,
le muscle grand
fessier étant enlevé

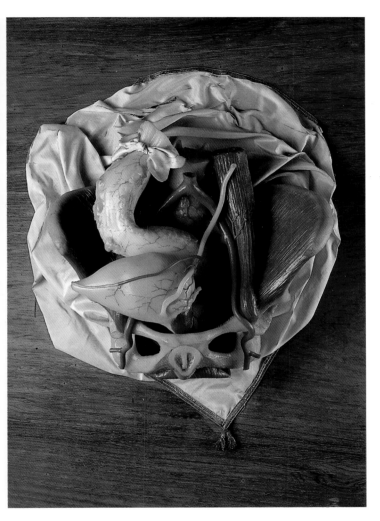

View from in front
of the organs and
arteries of a male
pelvis. The rectum
has been ligated
above, and the uri-
nary bladder dis-
placed to one side
to show the entry
of the ureter.

Blick von vorn auf
Organe und Arteri-
en eines männli-
chen Beckens. Der
Enddarm ist oben
abgebunden, die
Harnblase zur Sei-
te gedrängt, so daß
die Mündung des
Harnleiters sicht-
bar wird.

Artères et viscères
du bassin mas-
culin ; ligature du
côlon sigmoïde,
abouchement de
l'uretère dans la
vessie réclinée

View from in front
of the organs and
arteries of a female
pelvis. The uterus
can be seen lying
between the blad-
der and rectum. All
the organs have
been displaced to
one side to show
their supplying
arteries.

Blick von vorn auf
Organe und Arteri-
en eines weiblichen
Beckens. Zwischen
Harnblase und
Enddarm ist die
Gebärmutter zu
erkennen. Alle
Organe sind zur
Seite gedrängt, um
den Blick auf die
versorgenden Arte-
rien freizugeben.

Artères et viscères
du bassin féminin ;
vessie, utérus, et
côlon réclinés vers
la droite dégageant
le trajet des artères

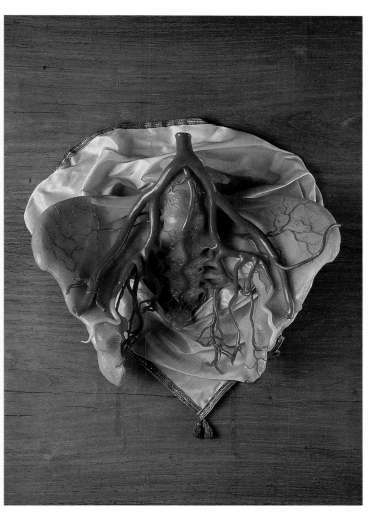

Arteries within the pelvis. The terminal part of an artery on each side is shown in yellow. This is that part of the umbilical artery which becomes obliterated after birth.

Arterien im Bereich des Beckens. Der Endabschnitt einer Arterie beidseits ist gelblich dargestellt. Hierbei handelt es sich um den beim Erwachsenen verschlossenen Teil der Nabelarterie.

Arbre artériel du bassin ; en jaune, segment terminal de l'artère ombilicale oblitéré après la naissance

Arteria iliaca externa, Arteria femoralis, Arteria femoralis profunda

The deep course of
the femoral artery

Darstellung der
Schenkelarterie in
einer tieferen
Schicht

Artère fémorale et
ses branches à la
partie supérieure
de la cuisse vues
de l'avant

Arteria femoralis

The femoral artery

Darstellung der
Schenkelarterie

Artère fémorale et
ses rapports avec
les muscles de la
cuisse vue de
l'avant

The thigh seen
from behind, show-
ing the sciatic
nerve and popliteal
artery

Ansicht des Ober-
schenkels von hin-
ten mit Darstellung
des Ischiasnerven
und der Kniekeh-
lenarterie

Artères fessières et
poplitée, nerf scia-
tique dans les
régions profondes
de la fesse, posté-
rieure de la cuisse,
et du genou

Arteria tibialis posterior, Nervus tibialis, Nervus fibularis communis

The thigh seen from behind. The superficial muscles have been removed to show the deep course of the arteries and nerves.

Unterschenkel in der Ansicht von hinten. Zur Darstellung der in der Tiefe verlaufenden Arterien und Nerven sind oberflächliche Muskeln entfernt.

Artères et nerfs profonds de la jambe visibles après ablation du muscle triceps du mollet

The arteries of the
sole of the foot

Darstellung der
Arterien der Fuß-
sohle

Artères de la plante
du pied

Lacuna vasorum

View of the super-
ficial veins of the
lower limb dis-
charging into the
femoral vein near
the inguinal liga-
ment

Blick auf die Ein-
mündung der ober-
flächlich liegenden
Beinvene in die
Schenkelvene im
Bereich des Lei-
stenbandes

Abouchement
d'une veine super-
ficielle de la cuisse
(grande saphène)
dans la veine fémo-
rale en dessous du
pli de l'aine

Specimen showing
the arterial supply
of the lower limb

Darstellung der
arteriellen Versor-
gung des Beines

Arbre artériel du
membre inférieur
projeté sur le sque-
lette

Venae membri inferioris

The venous system
of the lower limb

Darstellung des
Venensystems des
Beines

Réseau veineux du
membre inférieur
projeté sur le sque-
lette

The arteries, veins
and nerves of the
lower limb

Darstellung der
Arterien, Venen
und Nerven des
Beines

Artères, veines, et
nerfs du membre
inférieur projetées
sur le squelette

Arteriae et venae membri inferioris

The blood vessels
of the lower limb

Darstellung der
Blutgefäße des
Beines

Artères et veines
du membre in-
férieur projetées
sur le squelette

The superficial veins and cutaneous nerves of the foot

Darstellung von oberflächlichen Venen und Hautnerven des Fußes

Veines et nerfs superficiels du dos du pied et de la cheville

Venae

Whole body specimen showing the veins

Ganzkörperpräparat mit Darstellung
der Venen

Préparation du corps entier représentant
les grandes voies veineuses

[XXV. 526]

Systema lymphaticum et splen

Lymphatic System
Lymphatisches System
Système lymphatique

Lymphatic System

The lymphatic vessels, and especially the lymphatic organs such as the thymus, spleen and lymph nodes, play a central role in the immune system of our entire organism. In the 17th century Gasparo Aselli (1582–1626) had already observed the lymphatic vessels in the mesentery of a dog dissected immediately after feeding. Following the ingestion of food fats in the form of very fine droplets in the delicate lymph vessels of the intestine, the latter turned white and thus became visible. At the end of the 18th century the Italian Anatomist, Paolo Mascagni (1752–1815), used a sophisticated mercury injection technique to demonstrate that all organs possess their own widely branching lymph vessels with their associated regional lymph nodes. He described and named most of the vessels and nodes which are familiar to us today.

The models shown here summarize most impressively what was then the most up-to-date anatomical knowledge of that time. Without any doubt, these specimens must count as outstandingly graphic achievements.

Lymphatisches System

Das Lymphgefäßsystem und insbesondere die lymphatischen Organe, wie beispielsweise Thymus, Milz und Lymphknoten, nehmen eine zentrale Stellung in dem komplexen Abwehrsystem unseres Gesamtorganismus ein. Bereits Gasparo Aselli (1582–1626) entdeckte im 17. Jahrhundert die Lymphgefäße im Darmgekröse eines unmittelbar nach der Mahlzeit sezierten Hundes. Durch die Aufnahme der Nahrungsfette in Form feinster Tröpfchen in die sehr feinen Darmlymphgefäße waren diese weißlich gefärbt und dadurch sichtbar. Ende des 18. Jahrhunderts gelang es dem italienischen Anatom Paolo Mascagni (1752–1815) mittels einer raffiniert eingesetzten Quecksilber-Injektionstechnik zu zeigen, daß alle Organe über ein eigenständiges und weit verzweigtes Lymphgefäßsystem mit regionalen Lymphknoten verfügen. Er beschrieb und benannte die meisten der uns heute bekannten Lymphgefäße und Lymphknoten.

Die hier gezeigten Modelle fassen diese damals hochaktuellen anatomischen Erkenntnisse zusammen. Zweifelsohne gehören diese Präparate zu den herausragenden darstellerischen Leistungen.

Pages · Seiten · Pages 402–403:

Detail from pages 406–407

Detail der Seiten 406–407

Détail des pages 406–407

Le système lymphatique, et plus particulièrement les organes lymphatiques tels que la rate, les nœuds ou ganglions lymphatiques, et chez l'enfant le thymus, occupent une place primordiale dans la défense de l'organisme. Au XVIIᵉ siècle, Gasparo Aselli (1582–1626) avait découvert les vaisseaux lymphatiques dans le mésentère d'un chien disséqué pendant la digestion, le transport de fines gouttelettes de graisse alimentaire par les vaisseaux lymphatiques de l'intestin les rendant lactescents et donc visibles. A la fin du XVIIIᵉ siècle, l'anatomiste italien Paoli Mascagni (1782–1815) réussit à démontrer, grâce à une technique d'injection élaborée de mercure, que tous les organes sont tributaires d'une même circulation lymphatique, largement ramifiée, disposant de nœuds ou ganglions lymphatiques dans chaque région ; il a décrit et dénommé la plupart des vaisseaux et nœuds lymphatiques connus de nos jours.

Les connaissances anatomiques de cette époque, toujours valables actuellement, sont résumées de manière impressionnante par cette série de modèles en cire ; ces préparations font sans aucun doute partie des œuvres les plus représentatives de la collection.

Système lymphatique

Systema lymphaticum,
Venae epifasciales

Whole body specimen showing the superficial veins and lymphatic vessels

Ganzkörperpräparat mit Darstellung oberflächlicher Venen und Lymphgefäße

Préparation du corps entier représentant
les veines et les vaisseaux lymphatiques
superficiels

[XXVIII, 740]

Systema lymphaticum

Whole body specimen showing the
lymphatic vessels

Ganzkörperpräparat mit Darstellung des
Lymphgefäßsystems

Préparation du corps entier représentant
les grandes voies lymphatiques

[XXVII, 646]

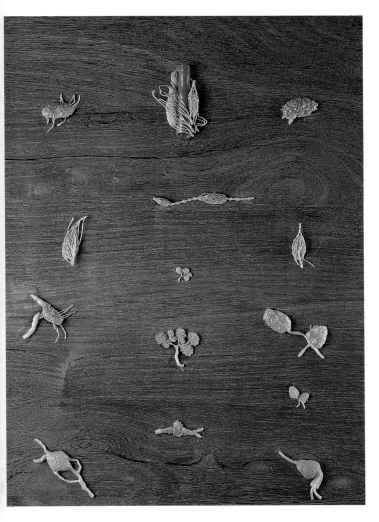

Different views of
lymph nodes with
efferent and affe-
rent lymphatic
vessels

Lymphknoten in
verschiedenen Dar-
stellungen mit zu-
und abführenden
Lymphgefäßen

Nœuds lympha-
tiques (ganglions)
avec vaisseaux lym-
phatiques afférents
et efférents

Vasa lymphatica, Nodi lymphatici submandibulares, Nodi lymphatici submentales, Nodi lymphatici retroauriculares, Nodi lymphatici cervicales superficiales

Lymphatic vessels and nodes of the head and neck. The skull has been laid open to reveal the pia-arachnoid and the brain. The lymphatic vessels of the pia-arachnoid as displayed in the specimen do not exist.

Lymphgefäße und Lymphknoten im Bereich von Gesicht, Hinterhaupt und Hals. Lymphgefäße in der weichen Hirnhaut, wie sie hier im Präparat am eröffneten Schädel dargestellt sind, existieren nicht.

Vaisseaux et nœuds lymphatiques de la face, de la nuque, et du cou. Les lymphatiques représentés au contact du cerveau n'existent pas.

View into the thoracic cage to show the thoracic duct (the main collecting lymphatic vessel), its tributaries and its opening into the great vein on the left side of the neck

Einblick in den Brustkorb mit Darstellung des Milchbrustganges (großes Lymphsammelgefäß), seinen Zuflüssen und seiner Einmündung in die linke große Halsvene

Conduit thoracique (canal collecteur lymphatique principal) : origine et trajet intra-thoracique, abouchement dans la veine jugulaire gauche

Ductus thoracicus, Vasa lymphatica pulmones superficiales

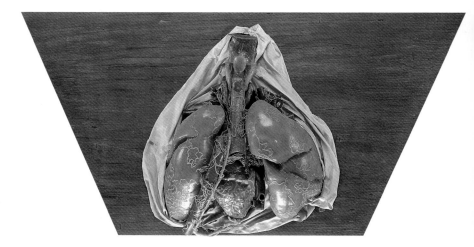

View from behind into
the thoracic cavity to
show the course of the
lymphatic vessels and
the thoracic duct

Ansicht von hinten auf
die im Brustkorb verlau-
fenden Lymphgefäße
sowie den Milchbrust-
gang

Conduit thoracique et
vaisseaux lymphatiques
des viscères du thorax
vus de l'arrière

Ductus thoracicus, Noduli lymphatici retrosternalis

Lymphatic vessels
of the liver and on
the internal surface
of the breastbone.
The thoracic duct
can be discerned as
a pale cord.

Darstellung der
Lymphgefäße der
Leber und der
Innenfläche des
Brustbeins. Als hel-
ler Strang ist der
Milchbrustgang
erkennbar.

Vaisseaux lympha-
tiques du foie et de
la face profonde de
la paroi antérieure
du thorax

Lymphatic vessels
and nodes around
the organs in the
upper part of the
abdominal cavity

Lymphgefäße und
Lymphknoten im
Bereich der Ober-
bauchorgane

Vaisseaux et
nœuds lympha-
tiques des viscères
de la partie haute
de l'abdomen (foie,
estomac)

Vasa lymphatica thoracalis et
abdominalis

Whole body specimen showing the lymphatic
vessels of the thoracic and abdominal cavities

Ganzkörperpräparat mit Darstellung des
Lymphgefäßsystems in Brust- und Bauchraum

Préparation du corps entier représentant les
veines et les vaisseaux lymphatiques des
viscères du thorax et de l'abdomen

|XXIX. 745|

Nodi lymphatici gastroomentalis

Lymphatic vessels
on the anterior sur-
face of the stomach

Darstellung der
Lymphgefäße auf
der Magenvorder-
fläche

Vaisseaux lympha-
tiques de la face
antérieure de l'es-
tomac ; pancréas
et rate

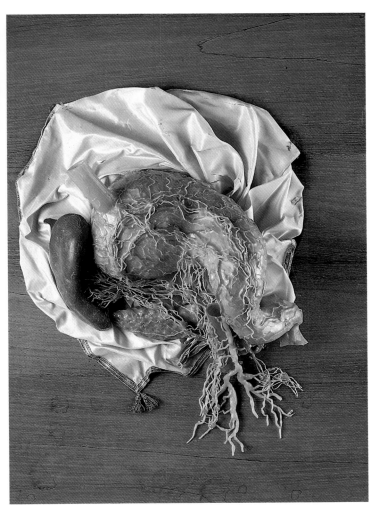

Lymph nodes and lymphatic vessels on the posterior surface of the stomach, and the thoracic duct receiving the main lymphatic tributaries

Darstellung der Lymphgefäße und Lymphknoten auf der Magenrückfläche mit Milchbrustgang und einmündenden Lymphgefäßstämmen

Vaisseaux lymphatiques de la face postérieure de l'estomac ; origine du conduit thoracique, rate

Vasa et nodi lymphatici ilei et jejuni

Lymph nodes and
lymphatic vessels
of the small intes-
tine

Darstellung der
Lymphknoten und
Lymphgefäße des
Dünndarmes

Vaisseaux et
nœuds lympha-
tiques de l'intestin
grêle et du mésen-
tère

Systema lymphaticum

Whole body specimen showing the
lymphatic vessels

Ganzkörperpräparat mit Darstellung des
Lymphgefäßsystems

Préparation du corps entier représentant
les veines et les vaisseaux lymphatiques

[XXVIII, 739]

Vasa mesenterica

Whole body specimen showing the vessels
and lymph nodes within the abdominal
cavity

Ganzkörperpräparat mit Darstellung der
Gefäße und Lymphknoten der Bauchhöhle

Préparation du corps entier représentant
les veines et les vaisseaux et nœuds
lymphatiques des viscères de l'abdomen
et du thorax

|XXIX. 747|

Systema nervosum centrale

Brain and Spinal Cord

Gehirn und Rückenmark

Encéphale

The Brain

The uniqueness of every human being is founded in his soul, i. e. his mental, religious, cultural, social and motor capabilities, which are carried out and controlled by the neuronal networks in our brains. The nerve cells are the morphological basis of the complex activities of the brain, their processes (dendrites, axons) and specialist sites of contact (synapses) serve to conduct and transmit information. Whereas two centuries ago only the vaguest concepts of their significance existed, we, by applying our modern imaging techniques, are able today to obtain detailed morphological and functional information about the individual brain without opening the skull. According to contemporary medical knowledge, the complete and irreversible cessation of the function of the cerebrum and brainstem as the site of complex and vital cerebral processes is the criterion of the individual's death. The following illustrations display the various aspects of the anatomy of the brain: an intact infant's skull after removal of the skin and muscles of the head showing the still patent anterior fontanelle, a skull laid open to reveal the connective tissue coverings of the brain (the hard and soft meninges) with their arteries and veins, the vessels on the upper and lower surfaces of the brain, including the emerging nerves and their course through the openings in the base of the skull. In contrast to these still relevant insights, the cerebral gyri bear little relationship to the original specimen, since in most models they are merely stylized. In most of the sections the visible border between the dark outer cortex and the internal white matter has been artificially emphasized.

Of great importance is the display of the points of attachment of the cranial nerves to the brain stem, as well as the various fluid-filled internal chambers (ventricles) of the brain, the position and extent of which can be very well studied in the specimens. These cerebral ventricles used to be of great interest, because they were thought during the 17th century to be the site of the spirit and the soul.

Many of the models are anatomically correct and impress one also by their great artistic merit. However, there are also certain exhibits seen from unusual points of view, the significance and meaning of which may not always be easy for the non-professional to grasp.

Pages · Seiten · Pages 428–429:

Detail from pages 424–425

Detail der Seiten 424–425

Détail des pages 424–425

Das Gehirn   Die Einzigartigkeit eines jeden Menschen ist begründet in seiner Seele, d. h. in seinen geistigen, religiösen, kulturellen, sozialen und motorischen Fähigkeiten, die von den neuronalen Netzwerken in unserem Gehirn getragen und gesteuert werden. Die morphologische Grundlage dieser komplexen Hirnleistungen bilden die Nervenzellen. Mit ihren Ausläufern und über spezielle Kontake, den Synapsen, dienen sie der Informationsleitung und -übertragung. Während vor 200 Jahren nur vage Vorstellungen über ihre Funktionsweise bestanden, können wir heute mit modernen bildgebenden Verfahren am ungeöffneten Gehirn detaillierte Aussagen über die komplexe Gestalt des individuellen Gehirns machen, und funktionelle Teilleistungen erfassen. Nach den heutigen medizinischen Erkenntnissen gilt der endgültige Ausfall der Funktion von Großhirn und Stammhirn als den Regionen komplexer und lebensnotwendiger Hirnleistungen als Todeszeichen des Menschen.

Auf den nachfolgenden Tafeln sind die verschiedensten anatomischen Ansichten zur Hirnanatomie zu sehen: ein intakter Säuglingsschädel nach Wegnahme der Kopfhaut und Kopfmuskeln mit der großen vorderen, noch offenen Fontanelle, der eröffnete Schädel mit der Aufsicht auf die Bindegewebshüllen des Gehirns (harte und weiche Hirnhaut) mit versorgenden arteriellen und venösen Blutgefäßen, die Gefäße auf der Hirnoberfläche und Hirnunterfläche, Hirnhälften mit austretenden Hirnnerven einschließlich ihrer Verläufe durch die Knochenkanäle des Schädels. Im Gegensatz zu diesen bis heute gültigen Erkenntnissen haben die in den Modellen gezeigten Hirnwindungen nur wenig oder keinen Bezug zum Originalpräparat. In den meisten Schnittpräparaten ist die sichtbare Grenze zwischen der dunkleren Hirnrinde und dem weißlichen Hirnmark herausgearbeitet.

Thematische Schwerpunkte bilden die Darstellung der Austrittsstellen der Hirnnerven am Hirnstamm sowie die verschiedenen flüssigkeitsgefüllten Innenräume (Ventrikel) des Gehirns, deren Lage und Ausdehnung an den Präparaten sehr gut studiert werden können. Diese Hirnventrikel waren von großem allgemeinen Interesse, weil man im 17. Jahrhundert in ihnen den Sitz des Geistes und der Seele vermutete.

Zahlreiche Modelle sind anatomisch korrekt und beeindrucken gleichzeitig durch ihre hohe künstlerische Qualität. Daneben finden sich aber auch Exponate in ungewöhnlicher perspektivischer Ansicht, deren Bedeutung und Aussage dem Laien nur schwer zugänglich ist.

C'est son esprit qui donne à chaque être humain son caractère unique; il capacités spirituelles, religieuses, culturelles, soziales ou motrices. Les cellules nerveuses sont la base morphologique de ces fonctions cérébrales complexes ; par leurs prolongements et à travers des zones de contact spécifiques, les synapses, elles véhiculent et transmettent les informations. Il est possible aujourd'hui, par des techniques d'imagerie, de mettre en évidence non seulement des détails de l'architecture complexe du cerveau d'un individu mais encore des localisations fonctionnelles particulières. Dans l'état actuel des connaissances médicales, l'arrêt total et définitif des fonctions du cerveau et du tronc cérébral signe la mort de l'individu.

Les vues les plus variées de l'anatomie du cerveau sont représentées dans les planches suivantes. Sur un crâne de nouveau-né, après ablation de la peau et des muscles de la tête, la grande fontanelle apparait encore ouverte, et les méninges cérébrales (dure-mère et pie-mère) sont pourvues de leur vascularisation artérielle et veineuse. Plus loin, les vaisseaux de la convexité et de la base du cerveau sont au contact des structures nerveuses. D'un hémi-cerveau partent les nerfs crâniens, dont le trajet peut être suivi jusque dans les canaux osseux de la base du crâne.

La représentation des circonvolutions cérébrales n'a que peu ou pas de relation avec la réalité anatomique, contrairement à de nombreux autres détails encore valables aujourd'hui ; les circonvolutions ont souvent été stylisées. Dans la plupart des coupes, la limite entre la substance blanche et la substance grise du cerveau a été mise en évidence.

Une attention particulière a été portée à la représentation des points d'émergence des nerfs crâniens au niveau du tronc cérébral, et à la représentation des cavités cérébrales, ou ventricules, contenant le liquide cérébro-spinal, dont la disposition et le développement peuvent être bien étudiés sur ces modèles. Les ventricules cérébraux ont suscité un grand intérêt car ils étaient considérés, au XVIIe siècle, comme le siège de l'esprit et de l'âme.

De nombreux modèles sont les témoins fidèles de la réalité anatomique et sont remarquables par leur grande qualité artistique. A côté de ces pièces de qualité, il en existe quelquesunes dont les vues perspectives inhabituelles en rendent l'interprétation difficilement accessible au non initié.

Specimen of a head. The calvaria has been removed and half of the brain can be taken out.

Präparat eines Kopfes. Das Schädeldach ist entfernt und eine Hirnhälfte herausnehmbar.

Tête ; ouverture de la voûte du crâne permettant d'enlever un hémisphère cérébral

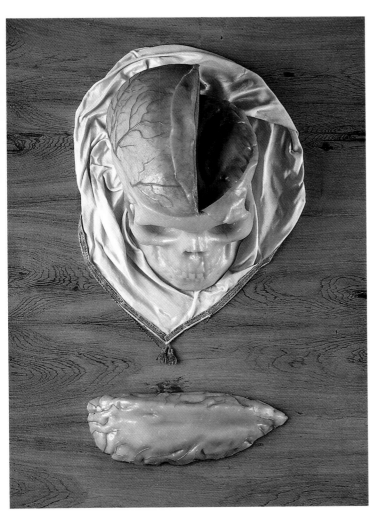

Specimen showing
the dura mater with
its arteries. The left
half of the brain
has been removed.

Präparat mit Blick
auf die harte Hirn-
haut mit ihren Arte-
rien, die linke Hirn-
hälfte ist entfernt

Méninges (dure-
mère) et artères
méningées (hémi-
sphère gauche du
cerveau enlevé)

Dura mater encephali, Sinus durae matris, Falx cerebri, Arteriae meningeae

Internal aspects of the calvaria (upper specimen) and base of skull after removal of the brain. View of the dura mater and its blood vessels. In the midline of the upper specimen one can see the sickle-shaped falx of the cerebrum.

Innenansicht von Schädeldach (oberes Präparat) und Schädelbasis nach Entnahme des Gehirns. Blick auf die harte Hirnhaut und ihre Blutgefäße. In der Mittellinie des oberen Präparates ist die Großhirnsichel erkennbar.

Voûte (en haut) et base du crâne (en bas) en vue endocrânienne recouvertes par la dure-mère avec ses vaisseaux ; la faux du cerveau est visible sur la ligne médiane de la voûte.

View of the brain after removal of the calvaria and dura mater. In the upper specimen the soft meninges with their vessels can be seen. The convolutions of the brain surface can be clearly seen in the lower specimen after removal of the meninges.

Blick auf das Gehirn nach Entfernung des Schädeldaches und der harten Hirnhaut. Im oberen Präparat ist die weiche Hirnhaut mit Gefäßen dargestellt. Das Windungsrelief des Großhirns wird nach Entfernung der weichen Hirnhaut deutlich (unteres Präparat).

Cerveau après ouverture de la voûte du crâne et de la dure-mère ; les circonvolutions cérébrales apparaissent après résection de la pie-mère et de ses vaisseaux (en bas)

The calvaria of a
fetus seen from
above, showing the
anterior fontanelle
still open (left spec-
imen) and the dura
mater after removal
of the calvaria
(right specimen).
Below: the calvaria
seen from the
inside

Blick von oben auf
das Schädeldach
eines Föten mit
offener vorderer
Fontanelle (linkes
Präparat) und auf
die harte Hirnhaut
nach Enfernung
des Schädeldaches
(rechtes Präparat).
Unteres Präparat:
Innenansicht des
Schädeldaches

Voûte du crâne du
fœtus avec la fonta-
nelle antérieure
ouverte (en haut à
gauche) ; dure-
mère après abla-
tion de la voûte (en
haut à droite). En
bas : vue endocrâ-
nienne de la voûte

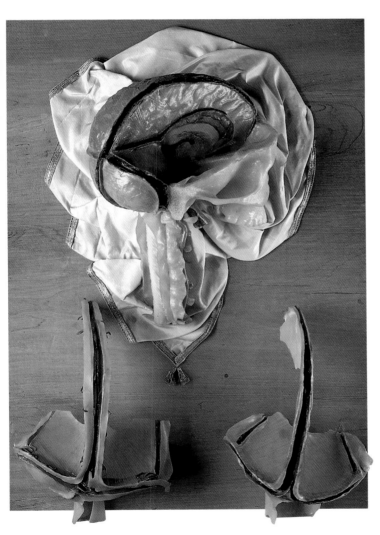

The venous si-
nuses of the dura
mater

Darstellungen der
venösen Blutleiter
in der harten Hirn-
haut

Conduits veineux
limités par la dure-
mère (sinus vei-
neux)

Sinus durae matris

The venous si-
nuses of the dura
mater

Darstellungen der
in der harten Hirn-
haut gelegenen
venösen Blutleiter

Conduits veineux
limités par la dure-
mère (sinus vei-
neux)

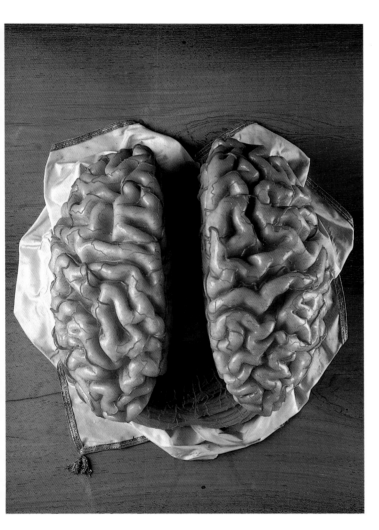

Specimen of the brain with its superficial arteries. The cerebrum has been divided in the midline and the two halves pushed aside to reveal the cerebellum (below).

Präparat des Gehirns mit oberflächlichen Arterien. Das Großhirn ist in der Mittellinie durchtrennt, die beiden Hirnhälften sind zu den Seiten verschoben, so daß der Blick auf das Kleinhirn (unten) freigegeben wird.

Artères de la convexité du cerveau ; après section médiane du cerveau, le déplacement latéral des hémisphères dégage la face supérieure du cervelet (en bas)

Arteria carotis interna, Arteria cerebri media et anterior, Arteria cerebelli posterior inferior

Specimen showing
the various arteries
at the base of the
brain

Darstellung ver-
schiedener Arterien
an der Hirnbasis

Artères de la base
de l'encéphale

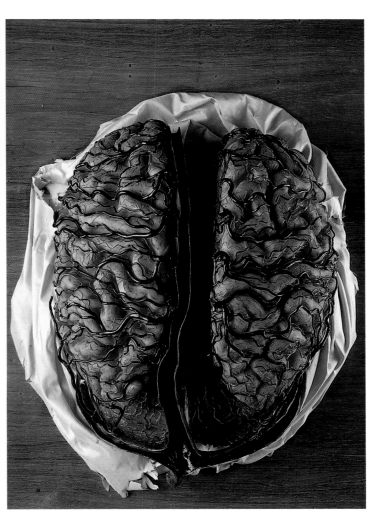

The superficial veins of the brain and their openings into the superior sagittal sinus within the falx of the cerebrum

Darstellung der oberflächlichen Hirnvenen und ihrer Mündungen in den venösen Blutleiter der Großhirnsichel

Veines superficielles de la convexité du cerveau s'abouchant dans les sinus veineux de la dure-mère

Venae cerebri superficiales, Sinus sagittalis superior

The superficial
veins of the brain
and their openings
into the superior
sagittal sinus with-
in the falx of the
cerebrum

Darstellung der
oberflächlichen
Hirnvenen und
ihrer Mündungen
in den venösen
Blutleiter der
Großhirnsichel

Veines superfi-
cielles de la
convexité du cer-
veau s'abouchant
dans les sinus vei-
neux de la dure-
mère

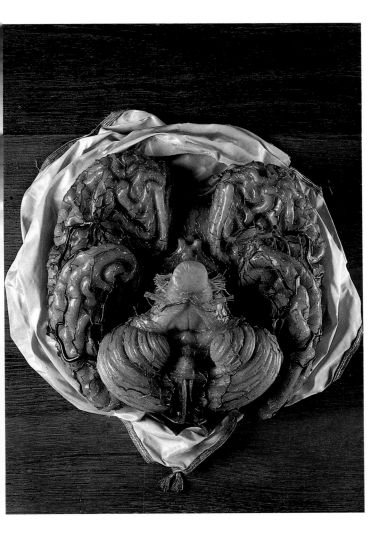

The superficial
veins at the base
of the brain

Darstellung der
oberflächlichen
Venen an der Hirn-
basis

Veines de la base
de l'encéphale

View of the arteries
and veins at the
base of the brain

Blick auf Arterien
und Venen an der
Hirnbasis

Artères et veines
de la base de l'en-
céphale

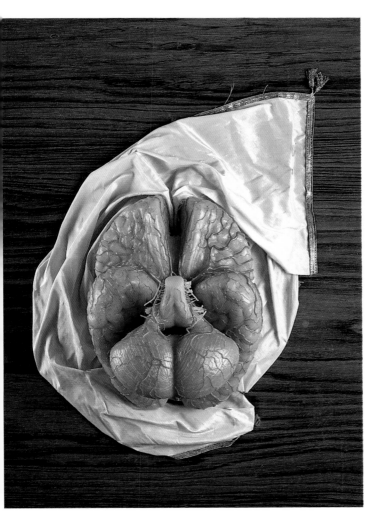

View of the arteries
at the base of the
brain

Darstellung von
Arterien der Hirn-
basis

Artères de la base
de l'encéphale

View of the arteries at the base of the brain. The lower specimen shows the confluence of the arteries which supply the brain.

Darstellung der Arterien an der Hirnbasis. Das untere Präparat zeigt den Zusammenfluß der hirnversorgenden Arterien.

Artères de la base du cerveau (en haut) ; arbre artériel montrant les anastomoses de la base (cercle de Willis) (en bas)

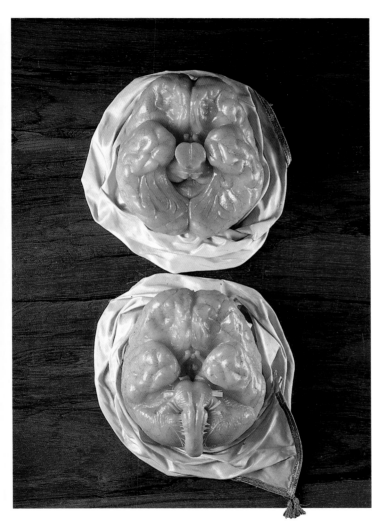

Base of the brain.
In the upper speci-
men the main pos-
terior lobes of the
brain can be seen
after the removal of
the cerebellum.

Ansichten der
Hirnbasis. Im
oberen Präparat
werden nach Ent-
fernung des Klein-
hirns die Hinter-
hauptslappen des
Großhirns erkenn-
bar.

Base de l'encé-
phale ; ablation du
cervelet découvrant
le lobe occipital
(en haut)

Thalamus

View of the base of the brain. The cerebellum and part of the brainstem have been removed. The small specimen in the middle shows the thalamus.

Ansicht der Hirnbasis. Das Kleinhirn und Teile des Hirnstammes sind entfernt. Das kleinere mittlere Präparat stellt den Thalamus dar.

Base du cerveau après ablation du cervelet (en haut) ; noyaux gris profonds du cerveau (en bas)

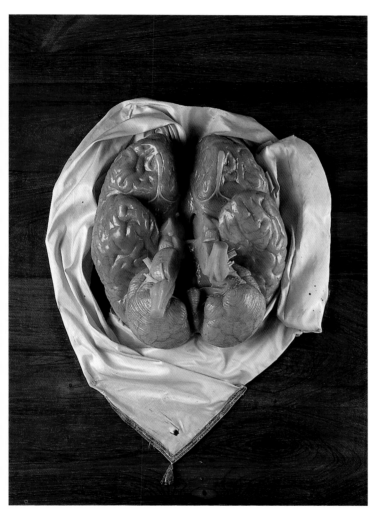

View of the base of
the brain showing
parts of the olfac-
tory bulb and tract.
The brainstem has
been divided in the
midline.

Blick auf die Hirn-
basis mit Anteilen
des Riechkolbens
und der Riechbahn.
Der Hirnstamm ist
in der Mittellinie
durchtrennt.

Base de l'encé-
phale avec tractus
olfactif; section
médiane du tronc
cérébral

Nervi cranii

View of the base of the brain. The cerebellum has been lifted up and pushed out of shape. The lower specimen shows a side view of the brainstem with the emerging cranial nerves.

Ansicht der Hirnbasis. Das Kleinhirn ist angehoben und verformt. Die unteren Präparate zeigen Seitenansichten des Hirnstammes mit austretenden Hirnnerven.

Base de l'encéphale, cervelet soulevé et déformé (en haut) ; vues latérales du tronc cérébral avec l'émergence des nerfs crâniens (en bas)

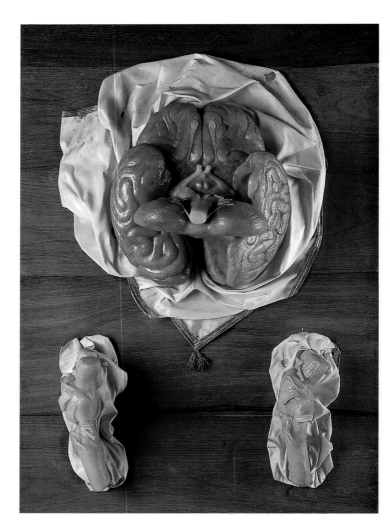

Viscerocranium, Neurocranium, Sinus sphenoidalis, Glandula pituitaria, Ventriculus tertius, Aquaeductus mesencephali, Ventriculus quartus

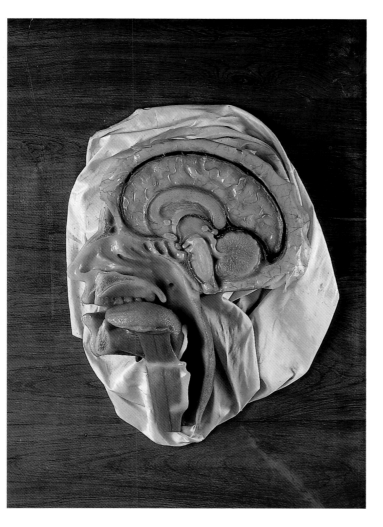

Specimen of a head which has been divided in the midline to show the relationship between cranial cavity and facial skeleton.

Präparat eines in der Mittellinie durchtrennten Kopfes, an dem die Lagebeziehungen von Hirn- und Gesichtsschädel deutlich werden.

Coupe médiane de la tête, rapports entre l'encéphale et le squelette du crâne et de la face

Specimen showing
the left half of the
brain. The C-shaped
structure below the
gyri is the corpus
callosum, which is
the main collection
of fibers connect-
ing the two halves
of the cerebrum.

Präparat einer lin-
ken Hirnhälfte.
Das C-förmig
gekrümmte Gebil-
de unterhalb der
Großhirnwindun-
gen ist der Balken,
die mächtigste
Nervenfaserverbin-
dung zwischen
beiden Großhirn-
hälften.

Hémisphère
gauche du cer-
veau ; parmi les
commissures inter-
hémisphériques, le
corps calleux en
forme de C est la
plus grosse

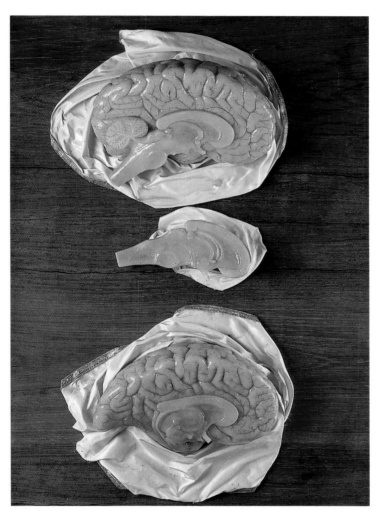

View of the left half of a brain which has been divided in the midline. In the lower specimen the brainstem and cerebellum have been removed.

Ansicht auf die linke Hirnhälfte nach Durchtrennung des Gehirns in der Mittelline. Im unteren Präparat sind Hirnstamm und Kleinhirn entfernt.

Coupes médianes de l'encéphale ; hémisphère gauche, ablation du tronc cérébral et du cervelet (en bas)

Facies superior et inferior cerebri

View of the brain
from above to
show the right and
left halves, and
from below to
show the brain-
stem and cerebel-
lum

Ansicht des
Gehirns von oben
mit rechter und lin-
ker Hirnhälfte und
von unten mit
Hirnstamm und
Kleinhirn

Cerveau vu du des-
sus (en haut), et du
dessous avec le
cervelet et le tronc
cérébral (en bas)

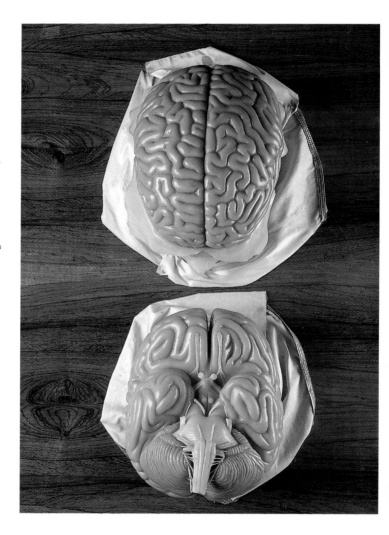

Commissura anterior, Corpus callosum, Nucleus caudatus, Ventriculus tertius cerebri, Thalamus, Glandula pinealis, Lamina quadrigemina, Ventriculus quartus

Specimens show-
ing the white sub-
stance of the brain.
In the lower speci-
men the halves of
the brain have been
separated to show
the topography of
the commissures
in relation to the
thalamus and cau-
date-putamen.

Präparate zur Dar-
stellung von Ner-
venfaserverbindun-
gen des Gehirns
(weiße Substanz).
Teile der grauen
Substanz sind ent-
fernt. Im unteren
Präparat sind die
Hirnhälften durch-
trennt.

Préparation des
faisceaux de fibres
nerveuses (sub-
stance blanche)
après ablation de
zones de substan-
ce grise ; hémi-
sphères séparés
en bas

Pars centralis et cornu inferior ventriculi lateralis, Fornix

Specimens to show
the cavities of the
brain (ventricles)

Präparate zur Dar-
stellung der Hirn-
kammern

Ventricules céré-
braux

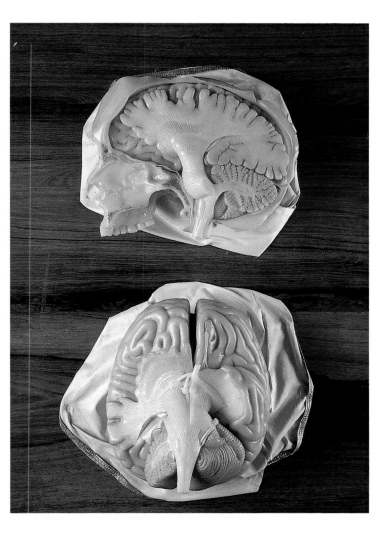

Display of the nerve fibers between the cerebrum, brainstem and spinal cord

Darstellungen von Nervenfaserverbindungen zwischen Großhirn und Hirnstamm sowie Rückenmark

Faisceaux de fibres nerveuses unissant le cerveau, le cervelet, le tronc cérébral, et la moelle épinière

Corpus callosum, Fornix, Septum pellucidum, Commissura anterior et posterior, Tentorium cerebelli

Median (above)
and paramedian
(below) sections
through the head

Medianschnitt
(oberes Präparat)
und Paramedian-
schnitt (unteres
Präparat) durch
den Kopf

Encéphale dans la
boîte crânienne :
sections médiane
(en haut) et para-
médiane (en bas)

Horizontal sections through the skull a little above the corpus callosum (upper specimen) and a little below it (lower specimen). The lower section passes through the ventricles and the caudate nucleus.

Horizontalschnitte durch den Schädel etwas oberhalb des Balkens (oberes Präparat) und unterhalb des Balkens (unteres Präparat). Das untere Präparat zeigt Abschnitte der Hirnkammern und den Schweifkern.

Coupes horizontales du crâne et de l'encéphale : au dessus du corps calleux (en haut), et en dessous avec les ventricules cérébraux (en bas)

Thalamus, Nucleus caudatus, Ventriculus tertius, Ventriculi laterales

Horizontal sections at various levels through the skull. In the upper specimen one can see the caudate nucleus, and adjacent to and directly behind it, the thalamus.

Horizontalschnitte durch den Schädel auf verschiedenen Höhen, im oberen Präparat erkennt man den Schweifkern und nach hinten direkt angrenzend den Sehhügel.

Coupes horizontales du crâne et de l'encéphale : noyaux gris profonds

Horizontal sections through the skull. In the lower specimen a part of the brain near the back of the head has been removed to reveal the more deeply placed cerebellum.

Horizontalschnitte durch den Schädel. Im unteren Präparat ist nahe am Hinterkopf ein Teil des Großhirns entfernt, so daß das tiefer gelegene Kleinhirn sichtbar wird.

Coupes horizontales du crâne et de l'encéphale : ventricules, cervelet visible après ablation de la partie postérieure du cerveau

Nucleus caudatus, Ventriculi laterales

Horizontal section
through the skull to
show the caudate
nucleus

Horizontalschnitt
durch den Schädel
mit Darstellung der
Schweifkerne

Coupe horizontale
du crâne et de l'en-
céphale : noyaux
gris profonds et
ventricules céré-
braux

Horizontal sections through the skull showing the caudate nucleus and thalamus. One can see sections passing through the ventricles.

Horizontalschnitte durch den Schädel mit Aufsicht auf den Schweifkern und den Thalamus. Man erkennt Abschnitte der Hirnkammern.

Coupes horizontales du crâne et de l'encéphale : noyaux gris profonds et ventricules cérébraux

Cornu posterius ventriculi lateralis, Ventriculus tertius

Horizontal sections through the skull showing parts of the ventricles

Horizontalschnitte durch den Schädel mit Darstellung einiger Hirnkammerabschnitte

Coupes horizontales du crâne et de l'encéphale : ventricules cérébraux

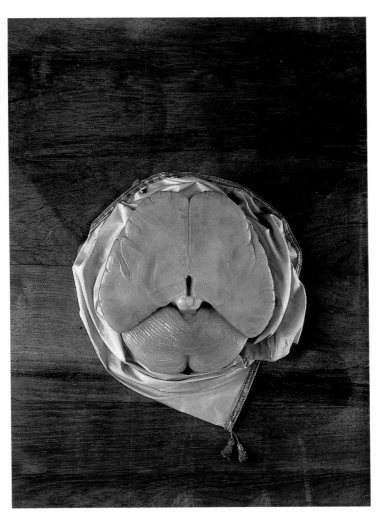

Horizontal section
through the brain
(frontal pole direct-
ed upwards). View
from above into the
third ventricle,
showing the pineal
body (or "gland")
behind it

Horizontalschnitt
durch das Gehirn
(Stirnseite oben).
Blick von oben in
die dritte Hirnkam-
mer und auf die
dahinterliegende
Zirbeldrüse

Coupe horizontale
du cerveau (lobe
frontal vers le
haut) : troisième
ventricule, épiphy-
se (glande pinéale)
au dessus du cer-
velet

Horizontal section
through the brain
(frontal pole direc-
ted downwards).
Caudate nucleus
and internal cere-
bral vein seen from
above

Horizontalschnitt
durch das Gehirn
(Stirnseite unten).
Blick von oben auf
den Schweifkern
und die innere
Hirnvene

Coupe horizontale
du cerveau (lobe
frontal vers le bas) :
vue supérieure du
noyau caudé et des
veines profondes
du cerveau

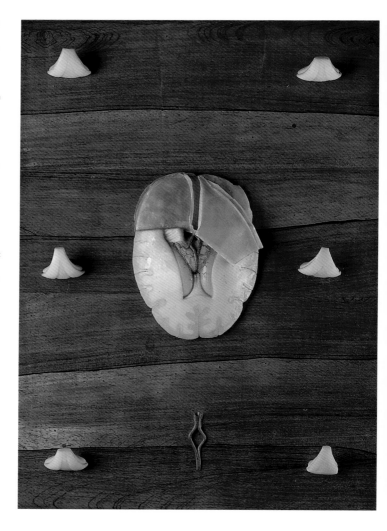

Cornu ammonis, Fornix, Nucleus caudatus, Thalamus, Ventriculus tertius, Glandula pinealis, Lamina quadrigemina

Upper specimen: hippocampus. The lower specimen shows the centrally placed cerebral nuclei such as the caudate nucleus and thalamus

Oberes Präparat: Darstellung des Hippokampus. Unteres Präparat: Darstellung zentral gelegener Kerngebiete des Gehirns wie Schweifkern und Thalamus

En haut : hippocampe disséqué. En bas : cervelet et noyaux gris profonds du cerveau : thalamus et noyau caudé

Nucleus caudatus, Thalamus, Glandula pinealis, Ventriculus tertius, Lamina quadrigemina, Corpora mamillaria, Pons

Brain specimen showing caudate nucleus and thalamus (above) and various structures at the base of the brain (below)

Ansicht auf Hirnpräparate mit Darstellung von Schweifkern und Thalamus (oberes Präparat) und verschiedener Strukturen im Bereich der Hirnbasis (unteres Präparat)

Ventricules cérébraux et noyaux gris profonds disséqués (en haut) ; base de l'encéphale (en bas)

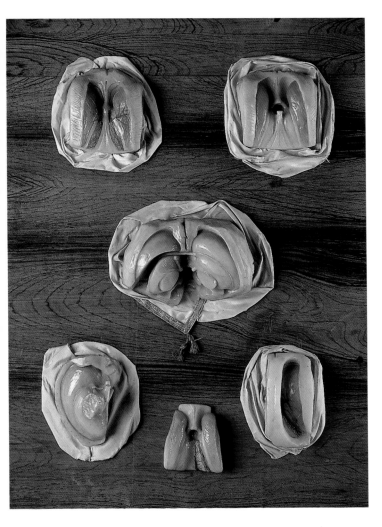

Specimens to show
nuclei in the
depths of the brain
such as the cau-
date nucleus and
thalamus

Präparate zur
Darstellung in der
Tiefe des Gehirns
gelegener Kern-
gebiete wie des
Schweifkerns und
des Thalamus

Ventricules céré-
braux et noyaux
gris profonds de
l'encéphale dissé-
qués

Cornu ammonis

Various views of
the hippocampus

Verschiedene Dar-
stellungen des Hip-
pocampus

Ventricule latéral et
hippocampe dissé-
qués

Specimens show-
ing the connec-
tions (nerve fibers)
of the hippo-
campus

Präparate zur Dar-
stellung der Ner-
venfaserverbindun-
gen des Hippo-
campus

Connexions
nerveuses de
l'hippocampe

Cornu ammonis

Specimen showing
the hippocampus
lying in the tem-
poral lobe

Präparat zur Dar-
stellung des im
Schläfenlappen
liegenden Hippo-
campus

Ventricule latéral et
lobe temporal dis-
séqués

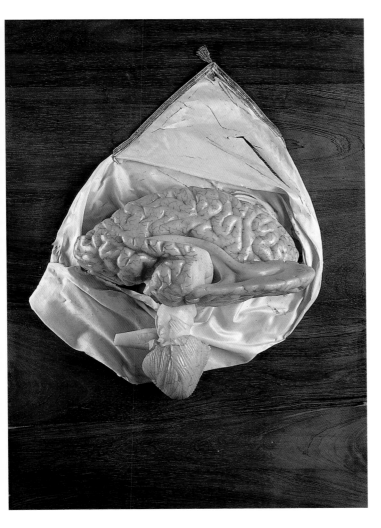

View of the corpus
callosum and a
section through a
ventricle

Darstellung des
Balkens und eines
Hirnkammerab-
schnittes

Commissure inter-
hémisphérique
(corps calleux) et
ventricule latéral

Specimens from various regions of the brain. Among other things the thalamus, caudate nucleus and hippocampus can be seen.

Präparate aus verschiedenen Hirnregionen. Dargestellt sind u. a. Thalamus, Schweifkern und Hippocampus.

Diverses régions de l'encéphale : thalamus, noyau caudé, hippocampe, tronc cérébral

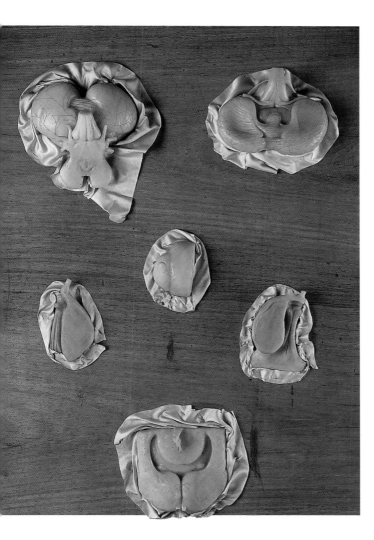

Specimens from
various regions of
the brain

Präparate aus ver-
schiedenen Hirn-
regionen

Dissections de
diverses régions de
l'encéphale

Cerebellum, Arbor vitae

Several specimens
of the cerebellum

Verschiedene
Präparate des
Kleinhirns

Cervelet : coupes
sagittales

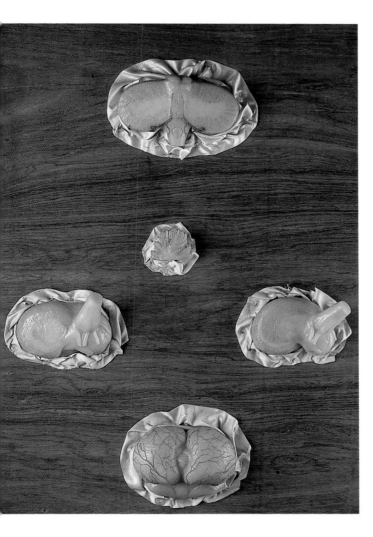

Different views of
the cerebellum

Verschiedene
Ansichten des
Kleinhirns

Cervelet

View of the inner
ear showing the
bony labyrinth
(cochlea and three
semicircular
canals, above left).
The other speci-
mens represent the
brainstem with cra-
nial nerves and the
cerebellum.

Darstellung des
Innenohres mit der
knöchernen
Schnecke und den
drei knöchernen
Bogengängen
(oben links). Die
anderen Präparate
zeigen den Hirn-
stamm mit Hirn-
nerven und Klein-
hirn.

Oreille interne :
cochlée et canaux
semi-circulaires
(en haut à
gauche) ; sur
les autres prépara-
tions : tronc céré-
bral, émergence
des nerfs crâniens,
cervelet

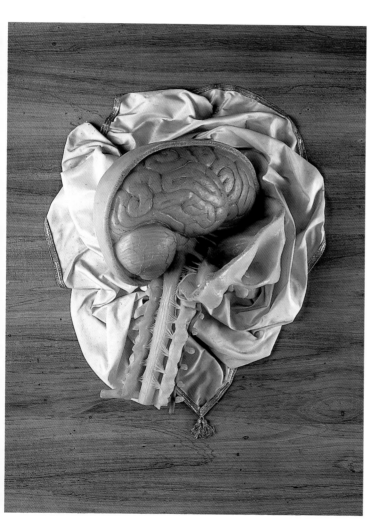

Oblique view from behind (the skull and vertebral canal have been laid open). The cerebrum and cerebellum have been lifted up to reveal the cranial nerves emerging from the brainstem.

Ansicht von schräg hinten in den eröffneten Schädel und den Wirbelkanal. Großhirn und Kleinhirn sind angehoben, um den Austritt der Hirnnerven aus dem Hirnstamm sichtbar zu machen.

Trajets intracrâniens des nerfs crâniens visibles après ouverture du crâne et du canal vertébral et après déplacement du cerveau et du cervelet (vue de l'arrière et de la droite)

Medulla oblongata, Pons, Pedunculi cerebri

Various displays
and views of the
brainstem

Verschiedene Dar-
stellungen und
Ansichten des
Hirnstammes

Tronc cérébral :
coupes diverses

View of the spinal
cord to show the
spinal nerve roots
emerging

Darstellung des
Rückenmarks mit
austretenden Ner-
venwurzeln

Mœlle épinière et
racines des nerfs
spinaux (rachi-
diens)

Medulla spinalis, Arteriae radiculares

The vertebral canal
has been laid open
from behind to
show the spinal
cord, the spinal
nerve roots and the
supplying blood
vessels

Einblick in den
eröffneten Wirbel-
kanal von hinten
mit Rückenmark,
austretenden Ner-
venwurzeln sowie
versorgenden Blut-
gefäßen

Artères de la mœlle
épinière et des
nerfs spinaux
(rachidiens) ; canal
vertébral ouvert vu
de l'arrière

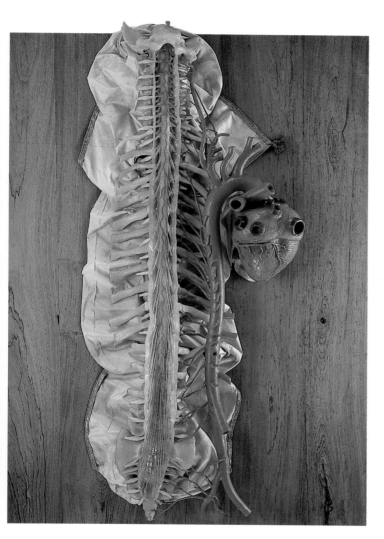

The vertebral canal
has been laid open
from in front to
show the spinal
cord, emerging
spinal nerve roots
and blood vessels

Einblick in den
eröffneten Wirbel-
kanal von vorn mit
Rückenmark, aus-
tretenden Nerven-
wurzeln sowie Blut-
gefäßen

Artères de la mœlle
épinière et des
nerfs spinaux ;
canal vertébral
ouvert vu de l'avant

Pages · Seiten ·
Pages 486–487:

Frontal view of
the specimen from
page 506

Frontalansicht des
Präparates von
Seite 506

Vue frontale de
la préparation
anatomique de la
page 506

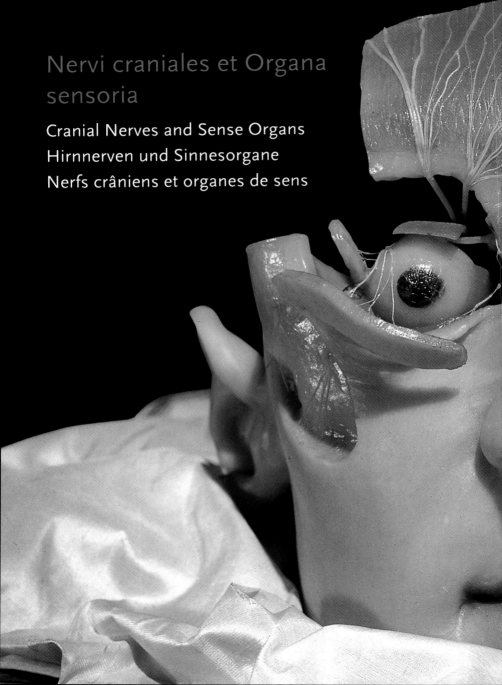

Nervi craniales et Organa sensoria

Cranial Nerves and Sense Organs
Hirnnerven und Sinnesorgane
Nerfs crâniens et organes de sens

Cranial Nerves and Sense Organs

The sense organs responsible for our perception of stimuli awakened the interest of anatomists very early on, since such special senses as hearing, sight, smell and taste have naturally always been relevant to our conscious experience.

Whereas many of the models show the detailed anatomy of the individual sense organs, other specimens display them in relationship to their central connections with the brain. This type of display is in accordance with the ideas of René Descartes (1596–1650), who interpreted the function of these organs in connection with the brain. It is indeed an essential part of cerebral function to analyze and interpret the particular stimuli which act upon our organs of special sense.

Hirnnerven und Sinnesorgane

Unsere für die Reizwahrnehmung verantwortlichen Sinnesorgane haben früh das Interesse der Anatomen geweckt, da Sinneswahrnehmungen wie Hören, Sehen, Riechen und Schmecken in unserem Bewußtsein natürlicherweise gegenwärtig sind.

Während zahlreiche Modelle im Detail die Anatomie der einzelnen Sinnesorgane dokumentieren, wird in anderen Präparaten das Sinnesorgan mit seiner nervalen Verbindung zum Gehirn gezeigt. Die Art der Darstellung lehnt sich an das Konzept von René Descartes (1596–1650) an, der die Funktionen der Sinnesorgane im Zusammenhang mit dem Gehirn interpretiert hatte. Dem Gehirn kommen dabei wesentliche Aufgaben bei der Verarbeitung der spezifischen Reize, die auf unsere Sinnesorgane einwirken, zu.

Nerfs crâniens et organes de sens

Les organes des sens, capteurs des stimulations périphériques, ont intéressé précocement les anatomistes car la perception de l'environnement par l'audition, la vue, l'odorat ou le goût est une des bases de la conscience.

L'anatomie des organes des sens isolés est démontrée en détail par de nombreux modèles en cire. Certains modèles montrent les connexions nerveuses des organes des sens avec le cerveau ; cette représentation s'appuie sur les conceptions de René Descartes (1596–1650) intégrant les fonctions des organes des sens à celles du cerveau.

Bulbus olfactorius, Nervus opticus, Nervus oculomotorius, Nervus trochlearis, Nervus trigeminus, Nervus abducens

Side view of the skull laid open to display the individual cranial nerves. The bulbous thickening right at the top is part of the olfactory system. Below: the nerves supplying the eye muscles and branches of the trigeminal nerve

Ansicht von der Seite in den eröffneten Schädel. Darstellung einzelner Hirnnerven. Oben mit der kolbigen Verdickung ein Teil des Riechsystems, darunter Augenmuskelnerven und Äste des Nervus trigeminus

Nerfs crâniens vus à travers une large ouverture du crâne : système olfactif, nerfs de la motricité de l'œil, rameaux du nerf trijumeau

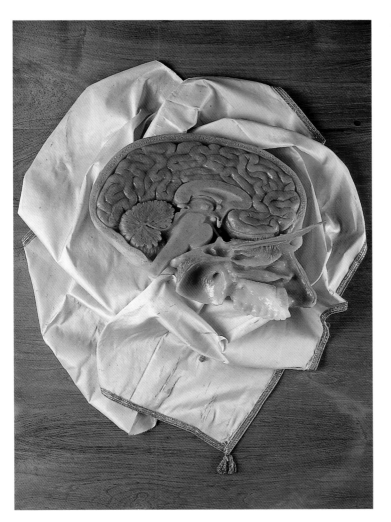

A head bisected in
the midline to
show the olfactory
fibers

In der Mittelline
durchtrennter Kopf
mit Darstellung der
Riechfasern

Coupe médiane du
crâne : trajet des
filets nerveux ol-
factifs

Fila olfactoria, Nervus trigeminus

The olfactory nerve fibers and the trigeminal nerve. The numerous olfactory fibers arise in the mucous membrane of the nose and enter the cranial cavity. Below: they are shown enlarged

Darstellung des Riechnerven und des Nervus trigeminus. Die zahlreichen Riechfasern, die aus der Nasenschleimhaut in den Schädel eintreten sind unten vergrößert dargestellt.

Filets nerveux olfactifs et nerf trijumeau (en haut) ; agrandissement des filets nerveux de l'olfaction issus de la muqueuse nasale et traversant la base du crâne (en bas)

View showing the
base of the brain
and the optic nerve

Ansicht der Hirnba-
sis mit Darstellung
des Sehnerven

Base de l'encépha-
le, nerfs optiques
et globes oculaires

Bulbus oculi

Various dissections
of the eyeball

Verschiedene
Präparationen des
Augapfels

Globes oculaires :
rétine, iris, cristal-
lin

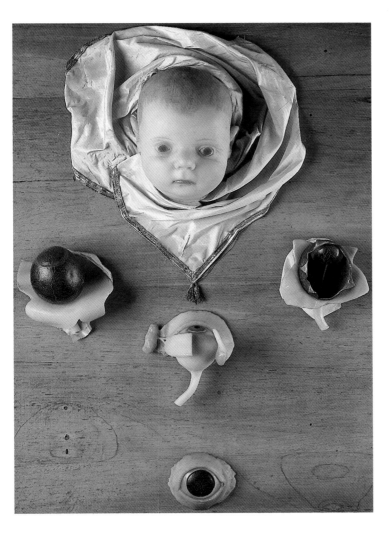

Various dissections
of the eyeball of a
fetus

Verschiedene
Präparate von
Augen eines Föten

Globe oculaire du
fœtus

Musculi bulbi oculi, Nervus opticus

Various presenta-
tions of the eyeball,
optic nerve and
external ocular
muscles

Verschiedene Dar-
stellungen von
Augapfel, Sehnerv
und äußeren
Augenmuskeln

Globes oculaires
avec nerf optique et
muscles de la
motricité de l'œil

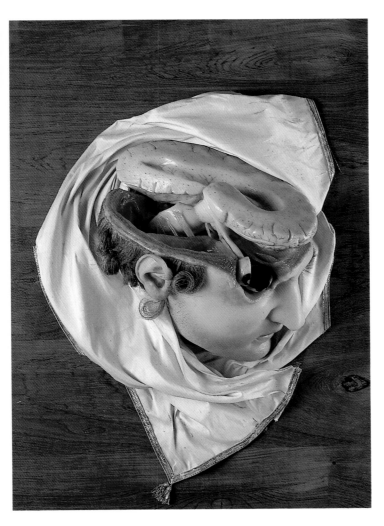

The course of the optic nerve (nerve of sight) from the eyeball to the brain

Darstellung des Sehnerven in seinem Verlauf vom Augapfel zum Gehirn

Nerf optique disséqué du globe oculaire à l'encéphale

Specimens of the orbital cavity, some with the eye muscles, nerves and vessels. The upper specimen on the left shows the eyelids with the Meibomian glands (sebaceous glands).

Darstellungen der Augenhöhle teilweise mit Augenmuskeln, Nerven und Gefäßen. Im Präparat oben links sind die Augenlider mit den Meibom'schen Drüsen (Talgdrüsen) zu erkennen.

Cavités orbitaires : globe oculaire, muscles moteurs, nerfs, vaisseaux ; paupières et glandes tarsiennes (en haut à gauche)

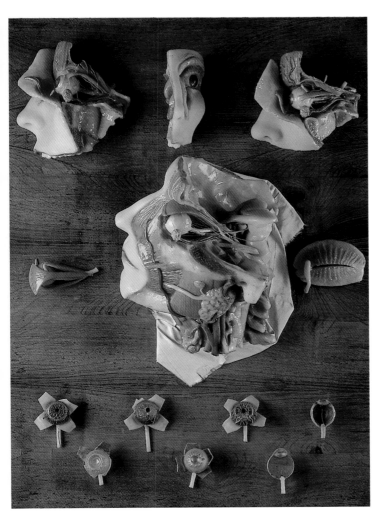

Various presentations of the eyeball and orbit. The lacrimal gland is lying against the eyeball (middle and upper specimens at the side).

Verschiedene Darstellungen von Augapfel und Augenhöhle; am Augapfel liegend die Tränendrüse (mittlere und oben seitliche Präparate)

Cavités orbitaires, globes oculaires, glandes lacrymales

Orbita, Bulbus oculi, Nervus trigeminus, Nervus oculomotorius, Nervus trochlearis, Nervus abducens

View into the
opened orbit and
maxillary sinus

Einblick in die
eröffnete Augen-
und Kieferhöhle

Cavités orbitaires :
nerfs de la motrici-
té de l'œil, sinus
maxillaire ouvert

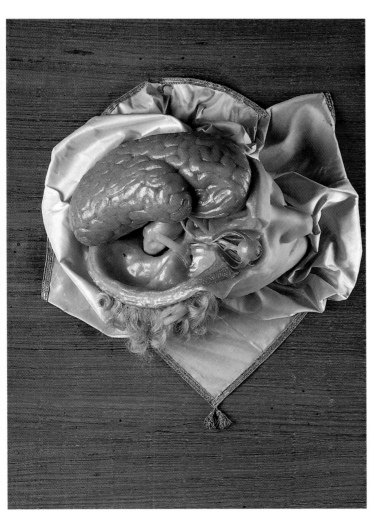

View from above
into the right orbit.
The right half of the
brain has been lift-
ed up and dis-
placed to the left.

Blick von oben auf
die rechte Augen-
höhle. Die rechte
Hirnhälfte ist ange-
hoben und nach
links verlagert.

Nerf oculomoteur,
un des nerfs
moteurs de l'œil :
trajet de l'orbite au
tronc cérébral (vue
du dessus, hémi-
sphère cérébral
droit déplacé vers
le haut et la
gauche)

Nervus abducens, Arteria carotis interna

View of the brain-stem and orbit. The brain has been lift-ed up and dis-placed to one side to show the course of one of the eye muscle nerves, the abducent nerve.

Blick auf Hirn-stamm und Augen-höhle. Das Gehirn ist angehoben und zur Seite gedrängt, um den Verlauf eines Augenmus-kelnerven, des Ner-vus abducens, zu demonstrieren.

Nerf abducens, un des nerfs moteur de l'œil : trajet de l'orbite au tronc cérébral (cerveau déplacé vers le haut et la gauche)

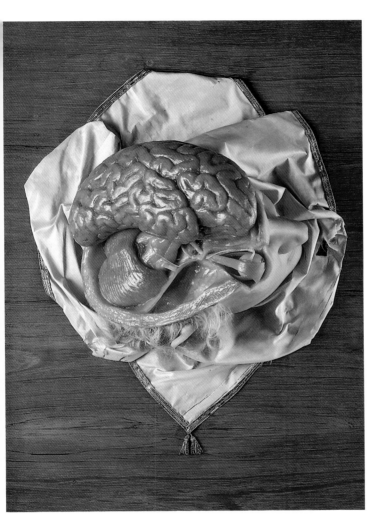

View of the brainstem and orbit. The brain has been lifted up and displaced to one side to show the course of one of the eye muscle nerves, the trochlear nerve.

Blick auf Hirnstamm und Augenhöhle. Das Großhirn ist angehoben und zur Seite gedrängt, um den Verlauf eines Augenmuskelnerven, des Nervus trochlearis, zu demonstrieren.

Nerf trochléaire, un des nerfs moteurs de l'œil : trajet de l'orbite au tronc cérébral (cerveau déplacé en haut et à gauche)

Nervus trigeminus

View of the base of the brain showing the three subdivisions of the trigeminal nerve

Ansicht der Hirnbasis mit Darstellung der drei Äste des Trigeminusnerven

Base de l'encéphale, émergence des nerfs crâniens parmi lesquels le nerf trijumeau et ses trois branches

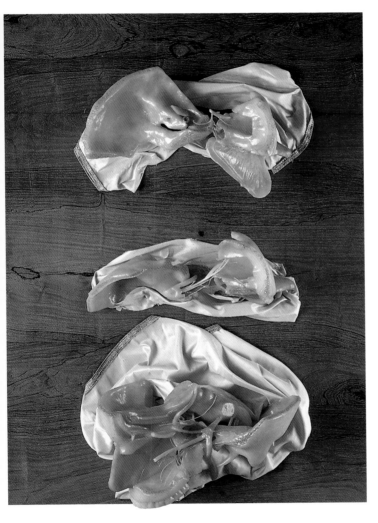

Display showing
the trigeminal
nerve and its
branches

Darstellungen des
Trigeminusnerven
mit seinen Ästen

Nerf trijumeau et
ses trois branches

Nervus trigeminus, Nervus ophthalmicus

Display showing
the first subdivi-
sion of the trigemi-
nal nerve. A part of
the frontalis mus-
cle can be seen on
the left, across
which single
branches of the
trigeminal nerve
are running.

Darstellung des
ersten Astes des
Nervus trigeminus.
Links im Bild ist ein
Teil des Stirnmus-
kels zu sehen, auf
dem einzelne Trige-
minusäste verlau-
fen.

Nerf trijumeau :
branche supérieure
ramifiée à la surfa-
ce du muscle fron-
tal

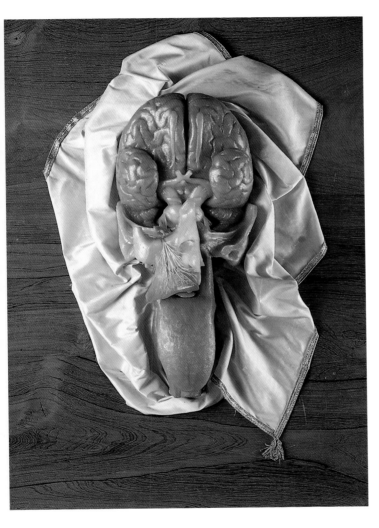

Display showing
branches of the
trigeminal nerve

Darstellung von
Ästen des Nervus
trigeminus

Nerf trijumeau :
branche supérieure
ramifiée dans la
région du front

Nervus trigeminus, portio minor

Part of the mastica-
tory muscles with
their nerve supply

Teil der Kaumusku-
latur mit nervöser
Versorgung

Nerf trijumeau :
branches pour les
muscles mastica-
teurs

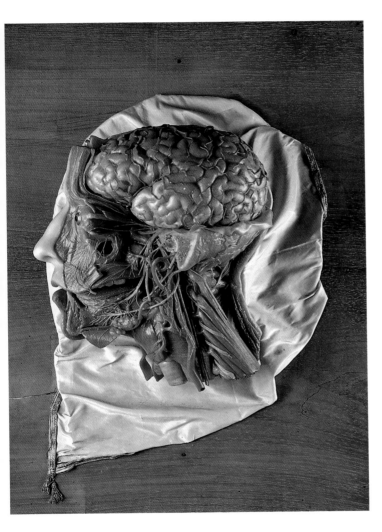

Display showing the nerves and arteries of the cavity of the mouth, tongue and throat

Darstellung der Nerven und Arterien von Mundhöhle, Zunge und Rachen

Nerfs crâniens et artères pour les régions de la bouche, de la langue, et du pharynx

Nervus lingualis

One of the sensory
nerves of the
tongue

Darstellung eines
sensiblen Nerven
für die Zunge

Nerf trijumeau :
branches pour la
sensibilité de la
langue

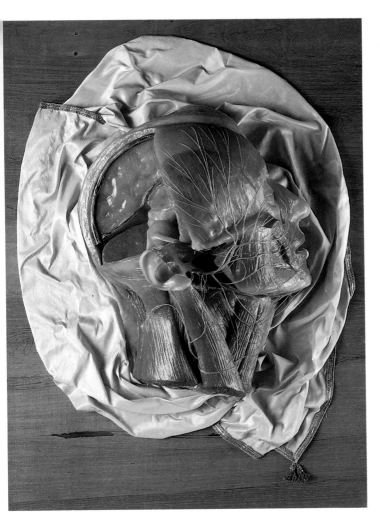

Display showing
the facial nerve,
which supplies the
muscles of facial
expression

Darstellung des
Nervus facialis, der
die mimische Mus-
kulatur innerviert

Nerf facial :
branches pour les
muscles peauciers
de la mimique

Specimen of the
ear with the exter-
nal auditory mea-
tus, eardrum,
middle ear and
Eustachian tube

Präparat einer Ohr-
muschel mit äuße-
rem Gehörgang,
Trommelfell, Mit-
telohr sowie der
Ohrtrompete

Pavillon de l'oreille,
conduit auditif
externe, tympan,
caisse du tympan,
et trompe auditive
(d'Eustache)

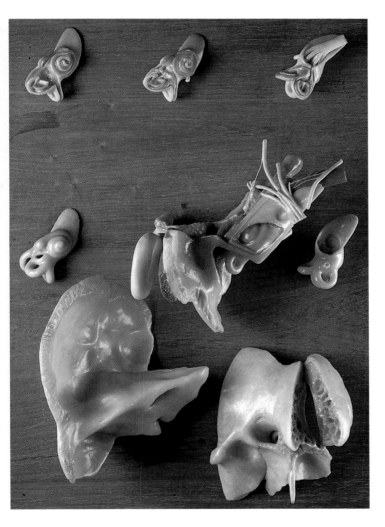

Various presentations of the inner ear with the cochlea and semicircular canals

Verschiedene Darstellungen des Innenohres mit knöcherner Schnecke und Bogengängen

Oreille interne : cochlée et canaux semi-circulaires

Specimen of the petrous temporal bone partly chiseled away to show the organs of hearing and balance (greatly enlarged). Below on the right are the individual auditory ossicles.

Darstellung des aufgemeißelten Felsenbeines mit Gehör- und Gleichgewichtsorgan (stark vergrößert). Die Präparate unten rechts zeigen die einzelnen Gehörknöchelchen.

Organes de l'audition et de l'équilibration dans l'os temporal trépané fortement agrandis ; osselets de l'ouïe isolés (en bas à droite)

Os temporale, Cavum tympani, Stapes, Incus, Malleus, Musculus tensor tympani, Musculus stapedius

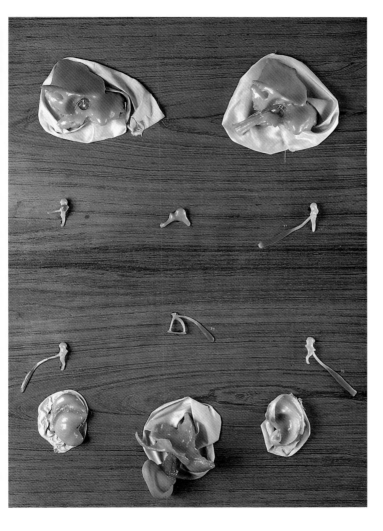

The auditory ossicles and the muscles of the middle ear

Gehörknöchelchen und Muskeln des Mittelohres

Osselets de l'ouïe et muscles de l'oreille moyenne

Nervus cochlearis, Genu externus nervi facialis

Display showing
the organs of hear-
ing and balance,
and the motor
nerve of the face
passing through
the petrous tem-
poral bone

Darstellung von
Gehör-, Gleichge-
wichts- und motori-
schem Gesichts-
nerv im Felsenbein

Nerf de l'audition
et de l'équilibra-
tion, nerf de la
mimique (facial)
dans l'os temporal

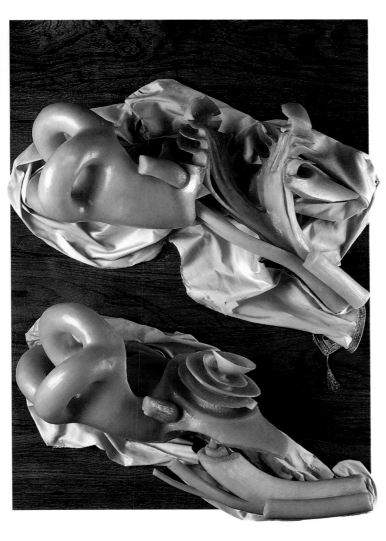

Greatly enlarged specimen of the inner ear showing the semicircular canals and the convolutions of the cochlea

Darstellung des stark vergrößerten Innenohres mit Bogengängen und Windungen der Schnecke

Oreilles internes fortement agrandies : canaux semicirculaires, tours de spire de la cochlée

Cochlea, Canales semicirculares

Greatly enlarged
specimen of the
inner ear showing
the semicircular
canals and the con-
volutions of the
cochlea

Darstellung des
stark vergrößerten
Innenohres mit
Bogengängen und
Windungen der
Schnecke

Oreilles internes
fortement agran-
dies : cochlée et
canaux semi-circu-
laires ouverts (en
haut)

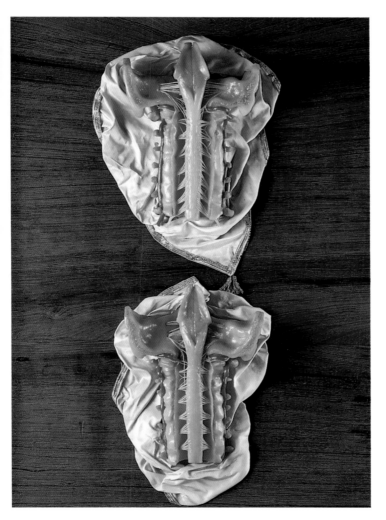

Specimen showing the brainstem and upper part of the spinal cord with the attached spinal nerves roots; seen from behind

Präparat des Hirnstammes und des oberen Rückenmarks mit austretenden Nervenwurzeln in der Ansicht von hinten

Tronc cérébral et mœlle épinière cervicale vus de l'arrière, racines de nerfs crâniens et spinaux, artère vertébrale

The brainstem and upper part of the spinal cord seen from behind. Variations in the course of the eleventh cranial nerve can be observed.

Hirnstamm und oberes Rückenmark in der Ansicht von hinten. Die Varianten im Verlauf des elften Hirnnerven sind sichtbar.

Tronc cérébral et mœlle épinière cervicale vus de l'arrière, variations du trajet du nerf accessoire, onzième nerf crânien

Display showing
the tenth cranial
nerve, the vagus
nerve

Darstellung des
zehnten Hirnner-
ven, der Vagusnerv

Nerf vague, dixiè-
me nerf crânien

Nervus vagus, Nervus hypoglossus, Plexus cardiacus

Nerves in the region of the neck and thoracic cage. The vagus nerve follows an almost directly vertical course near the midline

Nerven im Bereich des Halses und des Brustkorbes. Nahezu senkrecht in der Mitte verlaufend der Vagusnerv

Nerfs du cou et des viscères du thorax, nerf vague descendant verticalement au milieu

The viscera of neck
and thorax showing
the course of the
vagus nerve

Hals- und Brustein-
geweide, in der
Mitte der Vagus-
nerv

Nerf vague droit,
plexus nerveux
cardiaque, plexus
nerveux cervical et
brachial

Nervus vagus, Plexus brachialis

Specimen showing
the left vagus nerve

Darstellung des lin-
ken Vagusnerven

Nerf vague gauche

Specimen in which the head has been powerfully hyperextended backwards. The lower jaw has been removed. The neurovascular bundle of the neck including the vagus nerve is displayed.

Präparat mit stark nach hinten überstrecktem Kopf. Der Unterkiefer ist entfernt. Dargestellt ist die Gefäßnervenstraße des Halses mit dem Vagusnerv.

Nerf vague, nerfs et artères du cou (tête en forte extension, mandibule enlevée)

Nervus vagus, Nervus laryngeus recurrens, Plexus cardiacus, Truncus sympathicus, Pars cervicalis

The neurovascular bundle of the neck

Darstellung der Gefäßnervenstraße des Halses

Nerf vague, axes nerveux et artériels du cou

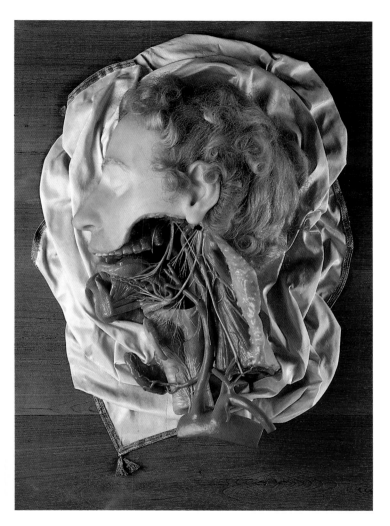

Neck dissected to show the nerves and vessels. Display showing the innervation of the tongue, floor of the mouth and larynx

Präparierter Hals mit Nerven und Gefäßen. Darstellung der Innervation von Zunge, Mundboden und Kehlkopf

Nerfs et artères du cou : innervation de la langue, du plancher de la bouche, et du larynx

Nervus hypoglossus, Nervus laryngeus recurrens, Nervus vagus, Nervus laryngeus superior

Upper specimen: display showing the innervation of the tongue. Lower specimen: the innervation of the mucous membrane and muscles of the larynx

Darstellung der Innervation der Zunge (oberes Präparat) sowie der Kehlkopfschleimhaut und -muskulatur (unteres Präparat)

Innervation de la langue (en haut), de la muqueuse et des muscles du larynx (en bas)

Display showing
the vagus nerve
and the area inner-
vated by it in the
thoracic and
abdominal cavities

Darstellung des
Vagusnerven mit
seinen Innervati-
onsgebieten in
Brust- und Bauch-
höhle

Nerf vague : inner-
vation des viscères
du thorax et de
l'abdomen

Nervus vagus

Display showing
the vagus nerve
and its area of
innervated thoracic
and abdominal cav-
ities

Darstellung des
Vagusnerven mit
seinen Innervati-
onsgebieten in
Brust- und Bauch-
höhle

Nerf vague : inner-
vation des viscères
du thorax et de
l'abdomen

Display showing the vagus nerve and the area innervated by it in the thoracic and abdominal cavities

Darstellung des Vagusnerven mit seinen Innervationsgebieten in Brust- und Bauchhöhle

Nerf vague : innervation des viscères du thorax et de l'abdomen

Nervus accessorius

Variations in the
origin and course
of the eleventh
cranial nerve

Varianten im
Ursprung und Ver-
lauf des elften
Hirnnerven

Nerf accessoire
(spinal), onzième
nerf cranien : varia-
tions de l'origine et
du trajet

Display showing
the course of the
eleventh cranial
nerve to the trapez-
ius muscle

Darstellung des
Verlaufes des elften
Hirnnerven zum
Trapezmuskel

Nerf accessoire :
innervation du
muscle trapèze

Display showing
the course of the
eleventh cranial
nerve to the trapez-
ius muscle

Darstellung des
Verlaufes des elften
Hirnnerven zum
Trapezmuskel

Nerf accessoire :
innervation du
muscle trapèze

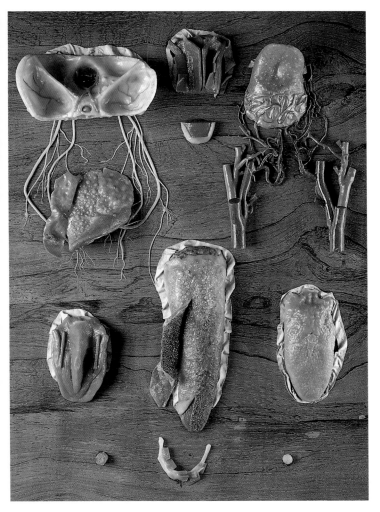

Nerves and vessels
of the tongue

Nerven und Gefäße
der Zunge

Nerfs et vaisseaux
de la langue

Nervus hypoglossus, Nervus lingualis, Nervus vagus, Nervus laryngeus superior et inferior

Display showing the innervation of the tongue; the lingual nerve running down in front of, and the hypoglossal nerve behind, the ear

Darstellung der Innervation der Zunge, des Nervus lingualis (vor dem Ohr absteigend) und Nervus hypoglossus (hinter dem Ohr absteigend)

Innervation de la langue : nerf lingual (en avant de l'oreille), nerf hypoglosse (en arrière de l'oreille)

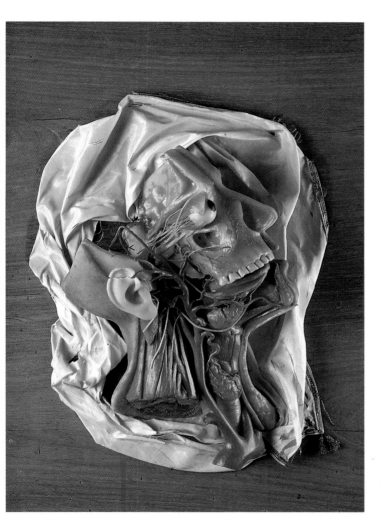

The nerves and
arteries of the orbit,
tongue and neck

Darstellung von
Nerven und Arteri-
en der Augenhöhle,
der Zunge und des
Halses

Nerfs et artères de
la cavité orbitaire,
de la langue, et du
cou

Lingua, Papillae circumvallatae

Median section of
the scull. One can
discern the bony
roof of the oral cav-
ity and the papillae
of the tongue.

In der Mitte durch-
trennter Schädel.
Man erkennt das
knöcherne Dach
der Mundhöhle
und die Papillen
der Zunge.

Organes du goût :
papilles de la
langue (cavité buc-
cale vue après sec-
tion médiane du
crâne et écarte-
ment des deux
moitiés)

Tactile organs in
the skin of the
palms

Darstellung der
Tastorgane der
unbehaarten Haut
(Leistenhaut)

Organes du tact :
peau des doigts et
de la paume de la
main

Systema nervosum peripheriale et autonomicum

Spinal Nerves and Autonomic Nervous System
Spinalnerven und autonomes Nervensystem
Nerfs spinaux et système nerveux autonome

Spinal Nerves and Autonomic Nervous System

The spinal nerves – or nerves of the spinal cord – are shown in their relationship to the central nervous system, similar to the models displaying the course of the cranial nerves. The models show very clearly that the basic principle of segmentation of the spinal cord, together with the emergence of the nerve roots and ganglia and their position within the spinal canal, was already recognized by the end of the 18th century. It is striking to observe how the alternating topographical relationship between the nerves and the adjacent vertebrae is reproduced in the models. Some of the specimens display the large nerve plexuses which lie at the side of the cervical and lumbar vertebrae. It is remarkable how well they reproduce the complexity of the nerve trunks which innervate (that is to say, carry the nerve impulses for) the limbs. In the neck, thoracic and pelvic regions, elements of the sympathetic trunk as branches of the autonomic nervous system can be recognized.

In many of the models of all regions of the body one can fully understand the course and topography of the peripheral nerves. In many cases the complete course of the connective tissue septa and the muscle segmentation are displayed. Again, in other specimens, the most striking thing is the impressive way in which the fine autonomic nerve plexuses of the heart, hilum of the liver and mesentery have been reproduced.

Spinalnerven und autonomes Nervensystem

Die Spinal- oder Rückenmarksnerven werden – ähnlich den Modellen der Hirnnervenverläufe – in ihrem Bezug zum zentralen Nervensystem dargestellt. Diese Modelle zeigen deutlich, daß bereits im ausgehenden 18. Jahrhundert das Grundprinzip der Rückenmarksgliederung, die austretenden Nervenwurzeln und Ganglien sowie die Aufhängung im Wirbelkanal, erkannt war. Die topographische Beziehung der Nervenaustritte zwischen benachbarten Wirbelkörpern ist in bemerkenswerter Weise im Modell umgesetzt. Einige Präparate zeigen die großen Nervengeflechte, die im seitlichen Bereich der Hals- und Lendenwirbelsäule liegen. Sie dokumentieren eindrucksvoll, wie komplex die Nervenstämme zusammengesetzt sind und wie sich schließlich die Nerven für die Innervation (die Reizübertragung durch die Nerven) der Extremitäten formieren. Im Hals-, Brust- und Beckenbereich sind Abschnitte des Truncus sympathicus als einem der Schenkel des autonomen Nervensystems zu erkennen.

Pages · Seiten ·
Pages 540–541:

Detail from page 587

Detail der Seite 587

Détail de la page 587

In einer großen Anzahl von Modellen aus allen Regionen unseres Körpers kann der Betrachter die Verläufe sowie die Topographie der peripheren Nerven nachvollziehen. Vielfach sind zur Darstellung des gesamten Verlaufes die Bindegewebssepten und Muskellogen aufgeschnitten. In anderen Präparate wiederum liegt das Hauptaugenmerk auf der Wiedergabe der sehr feinen autonomen Nervenfasergeflechte des Herzens, der Leberpforte und des Darmgekröses.

Les nerfs spinaux, ou nerfs rachidiens, sont représentés, comme les nerfs crâniens, en connexion avec le système nerveux central. Ces préparations montrent clairement qu'à la fin du XVIIIᵉ siècle étaient connus les principes fondamentaux de la subdivision de la mœlle épinière, la disposition des racines et des ganglions des nerfs spinaux, leurs moyens de suspension dans le canal vertébral. Les rapports topographiques des nerfs spinaux entre deux vertèbres voisines sont représentés de façon remarquable. Quelques préparations montrent les grands plexus nerveux disposés de part et d'autre des segments cervical et lombaire de la colonne vertébrale ; elles montrent la complexité de la formation des troncs nerveux et la constitution des nerfs destinés aux membres. Au niveau du cou, du thorax et du bassin, peuvent être reconnus des éléments du tronc sympathique, composante du système nerveux végétatif.

Le trajet et les rapports topographiques des nerfs périphériques peuvent être suivis et analysés sur de nombreux modèles concernant toutes les régions du corps ; souvent l'ouverture des cloisons fibreuses et des loges musculaires permet de suivre un nerf sur tout son trajet. Sur certaines préparations, au niveau du cœur, du hile du foie, ou du mésentère, l'attention est attirée sur la disposition des réseaux nerveux constitués par les fines fibres nerveuses végétatives.

Nerfs spinaux et système nerveux végétatif

Nervus ischiadicus

Whole body speci-
men with muscles
and nerves from
behind

Ganzkörperpräpa-
rat zur Darstellung
der Muskulatur
und Nervenläufe
an der Körperrück-
seite

Préparation du
corps entier représ-
sentant les nerfs
des régions posté-
rieures

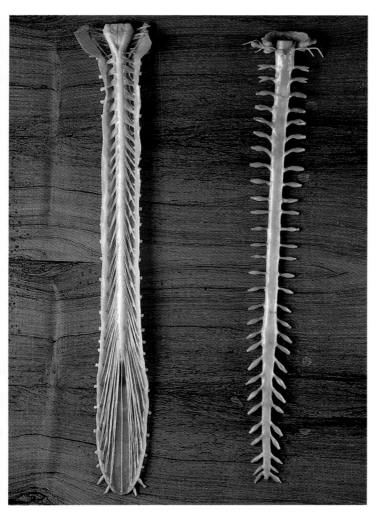

View of the spinal cord from behind. Left: with the dura mater. Right: showing the spinal ganglia

Blick auf das Rückenmark von hinten; links mit harter Rückenmarkshaut, rechts mit Darstellungen der Spinalganglien

Mœlle épinière et racines des nerfs spinaux vus de l'arrière ; méninges ouvertes (à gauche), méninges intactes et ganglions spinaux (à droite)

Plexus brachialis, Ganglia autonomia, Ganglion trigeminale

Below: display
showing the nerve
plexus of the arm.
Above: the trigem-
inal ganglion

Darstellungen von
Nervenfaserge-
flechten u. a. des
Armnervengeflech-
tes (untere Präpa-
rate) und des Trige-
minusganglions
(obere Präparate)

Plexus nerveux:
plexus brachial (en
bas), ganglion du
nerf trijumeau (en
haut)

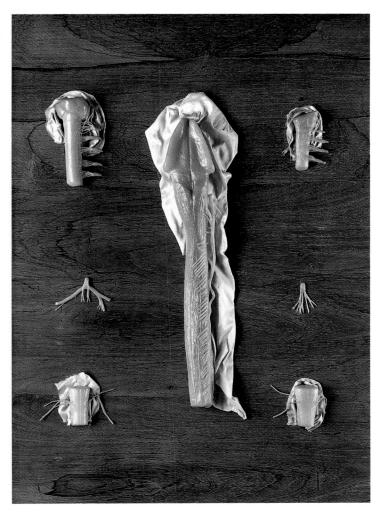

Brainstem and upper spinal cord seen from behind. The nerve roots are sometimes only shown on one side.

Hirnstamm und oberes Rückenmark in der Ansicht von hinten. Die Nervenwurzeln sind z. T. nur auf einer Seite dargestellt.

Tronc cérébral et mœlle épinière cervicale vus de l'arrière, racines des nerfs spinaux représentées d'un seul côté

Plexus cervicalis, Ganglion cervicale superius

View of the cervical
nerves and of the
back of the head
after removal of the
skin

Aufsicht auf Hals-
nerven und auf den
Hinterkopf nach
Entfernung der
Kopfhaut

Nerfs de la région
occipitale après
section du cuir che-
velu, nerfs du cou

Display showing
the nerves at the
back of the head
and the neurovas-
cular bundles in
the deep region of
the neck

Darstellung der
Hinterhauptsner-
ven und der Gefäß-
Nervenstraße in
der tiefen Hals-
region

Nerfs de la région
occipitale, artères
et nerfs des régions
profondes du cou

Nervus occipitalis major

Display showing
the course of a
nerve at the back
of the head

Darstellung des
Verlaufes eines
Hinterhaupts-
nerven

Nerf grand occi-
pital

Nervus occipitalis major, Nervus occipitalis minor

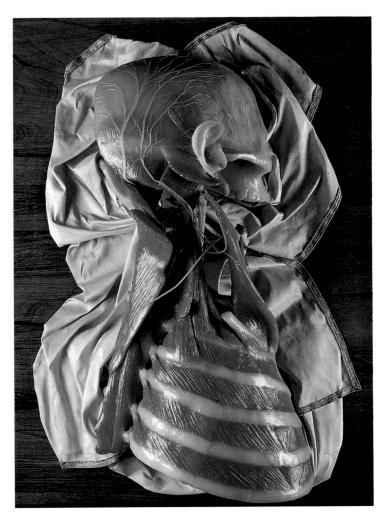

Display showing
the nerves at the
back of the head

Darstellung der
Hinterhaupts-
nerven

Nerfs occipitaux

Nervus facialis, Punctum nervosum

Display showing
the branches of the
facial nerve and the
cutaneous branch-
es of the cervical
plexus

Darstellung von
Ästen des Nervus
facialis und von
Hautästen des
Halsnerven-
geflechtes

Rameaux du nerf
facial et rameaux
cutanés du plexus
nerveux cervical

Display showing
the cutaneous
nerves at the side
of the neck

Darstellung von
Hautnerven in der
seitlichen Hals-
region

Plexus nerveux cer-
vical dans la région
superficielle du
cou, nerfs cutanés

Plexus cervicalis

Display showing a
deeper layer of the
cervical plexus

Darstellung des
Halsnervengeflech-
tes in einer tiefer
gelegenen Schicht

Plexus nerveux cer-
vical dans les ré-
gions profondes
du cou

The cervical plexus

Darstellung des Halsnervengeflechtes

Plexus nerveux cervical dans les régions profondes du cou

Plexus cervicalis, Nervus phrenicus, Nervus hypoglossus, Ansa cervicalis profunda, Plexus brachialis

View of the deep region of the neck and into the opened thoracic cage. The heart can be seen. Observe the nerves supplying the diaphragm running along the side of the pericardial wall.

Blick auf die tiefe Halsregion und in die eröffnete Brusthöhle mit Herz. Man beachte den Verlauf des Zwerchfellnerven entlang der seitlichen Herzbeutelwand.

Nerfs des régions profondes du cou et des viscères thoraciques ; trajet du nerf du diaphragme (phrénique) le long du péricarde

The nerve plexus of
the upper limb

Darstellung des
Armnervengeflech-
tes

Plexus nerveux bra-
chial au niveau du
cou

Plexus cervicalis, Plexus brachialis

The nerves in a deeper layer of the neck. Above the thoracic cage one can see parts of the nerve plexus of the upper limb.

Nerven des Halses in einer tiefen Schicht. Oberhalb des Brustkorbs erkennt man Anteile des Armnervengeflechtes.

Nerfs des régions profondes du cou, plexus nerveux brachial au dessus de la première côte, nerfs intercostaux

Deeper layer show-
ing cervical plexus
and plexus of the
upper limb

Hals- und Armner-
vengeflecht in einer
tiefen Schicht

Plexus nerveux cer-
vical et brachial,
rameaux des nerfs
intercostaux

Plexus brachialis

The nerve plexus of
the upper limb

Darstellung des
Armnervengeflech-
tes

Plexus nerveux
brachial

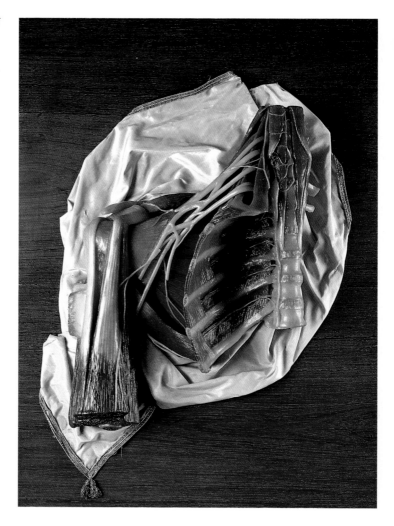

The nerve plexus of
the upper limb
seen from the side

Blick auf das Arm-
nervengeflecht von
der Seite

Plexus nerveux bra-
chial vu de la droite

Nervi membri superioris

The nerves of the upper limb and side of the chest wall

Darstellung der Nerven der seitlichen Brustwand sowie des Armes

Nerfs du membre supérieur vus du côté droit

The nerves and
muscles of the
upper limb

Darstellung von
Muskeln und Ner-
ven des Armes

Nerfs, artères, et
muscles du
membre supérieur

Plexus brachialis

The nerves and
plexus of the upper
limb

Darstellung von
Armnerven und
Armnervengeflecht

Plexus nerveux bra-
chial et nerfs du
bras gauche

The skeleton of the left arm and shoulder seen from in front. The nerves and plexus of the arm, together with the associated region of the spinal cord, can also be seen.

Präparat eines linken Arm- und Schulterskelettes in der Ansicht von vorn mit Armnerven, Armnervengeflecht und zugehörigem Rückenmarksabschnitt

Plexus brachial et nerfs projetés sur le squelette du membre supérieur

Nervi intercostales

Display showing the intercostal nerves

Darstellung der zwischen den Rippen verlaufenden Nerven

Nerfs intercostaux vus de la cavité thoracique

Rami cutanei rami dorsales nervi spinales, Nervi intercostales, Nervus iliohypogastricus, Nervus ilioinguinalis

Display showing
the cutaneous
nerves of thorax,
abdomen and back

Darstellung der
Nerven von Brust-,
Bauch- und
Rückenhaut

Nerfs intercostaux
vus de l'arrière,
rameaux cutanés

Plexus lumbosacralis

A male pelvis divided in the midline; view of the nerve plexus of the lower limb

In der Mittellinie durchtrenntes männliches Becken mit Blick auf das Beinnervengeflecht

Plexus nerveux sacré, nerf honteux (coupe médiane du bassin masculin)

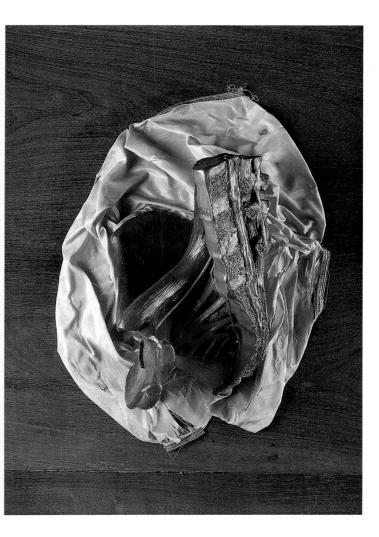

Pelvis divided in
the midline; view of
the nerve plexus of
the lower limb

In der Mittellinie
durchtrenntes
Becken mit Blick
auf das Beinner-
vengeflecht

Plexus nerveux
lombo-sacré à l'ori-
gine de nerfs du
membre inférieur
(coupe médiane du
bassin)

Nervi membri inferiores

The nerves and
muscles of the
lower limb

Darstellung der
Nerven und Mus-
keln des Beines

Nerfs et muscles
du membre infé-
rieur

Display showing
the nerves supply-
ing the muscles
and skin of the sole
of the foot

Darstellung der
Nerven für die Fuß-
sohlenmuskulatur
und Haut

Nerfs des muscles
et de la peau de la
plante du pied

Nervi membri inferioris

Inner view of a specimen of the right lower limb and hip bone. The nerves and their plexuses are also shown

Präparat eines rechten Beines mit Hüftknochen in der Ansicht von innen. Dargestellt sind die Beinnerven und ihre Beinnerven-geflechte

Plexus nerveux et nerfs du membre inférieur droit pro-jetés sur le sque-lette

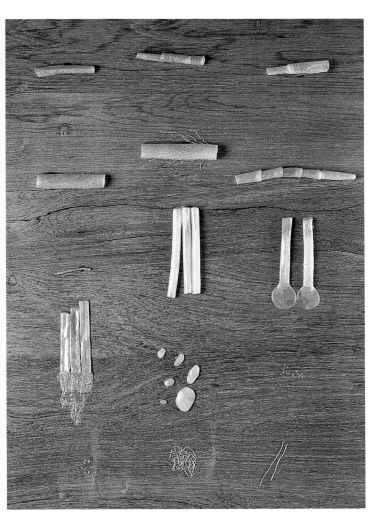

Specimens show-
ing the effect of
nerve fiber trans-
section (based on
microscopic obser-
vations)

Darstellung von
Reaktionen auf
Nervendurchtren-
nungen nach
mikroskopischen
Präparaten

Processus de cica-
trisation des nerfs
après section
(d'après des obser-
vations microsco-
piques agrandies)

Arteriae

Whole body specimen showing the
arteries

Ganzkörperpräparat mit Darstellung der
Arterien

Préparation du corps entier représentant
des nerfs et artères

[XXV, 445]

Truncus sympathicus, Plexus lumbosacralis, Plexus pelvinus

The autonomic
nerve plexuses of
the thoracic and
abdominal cavities

Darstellung vegeta-
tiver Nervenfaser-
geflechte der Brust-
und Bauchhöhle

Système nerveux
végétatif pour les
viscères du thorax,
de l'abdomen, et
du bassin

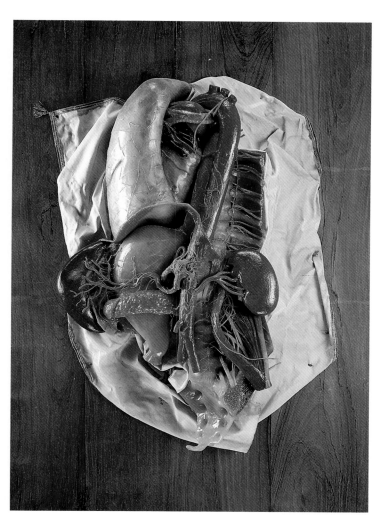

Specimen showing
the viscera with the
arteries and their
associated auto-
nomic nerve fiber
plexuses

Eingeweidepräpa-
rat mit Arterien
und begleitenden
vegetativen Ner-
venfasergeflechten

Système nerveux
végétatif autour
des artères se des-
tinant aux viscères
de l'abdomen

Ganglion coeliacum, Plexus mesentericus

Display showing
the autonomic
nerve plexuses
near the vertebral
column and asso-
ciated with the
abdominal arteries

Darstellung von
vegetativen Ner-
venfasergeflechten
im Bereich der seit-
lichen Wirbelsäule
und der Baucharte-
rien

Système nerveux
végétatif dans la
région latéro-verté-
brale et autour des
artères de l'abdo-
men

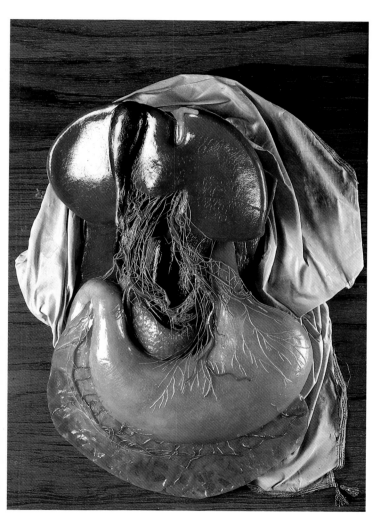

Display showing
the autonomic
nerve plexus asso-
ciated with stom-
ach and liver

Darstellung der
vegetativen Ner-
venfasergeflechte
an Magen und
Leber

Système nerveux
végétatif de l'esto-
mac et du foie

Truncus sympathicus, pars cervicalis, Ganglion cervicale superius et medius, Ganglion stellatum

Display showing the sympathetic nerves and their ganglia in the deep region of the neck	Darstellungen sympathischer Nerven und ihrer Ganglien im Bereich der tiefen Halsregion	Nerfs et ganglions sympathiques de la région profonde du cou

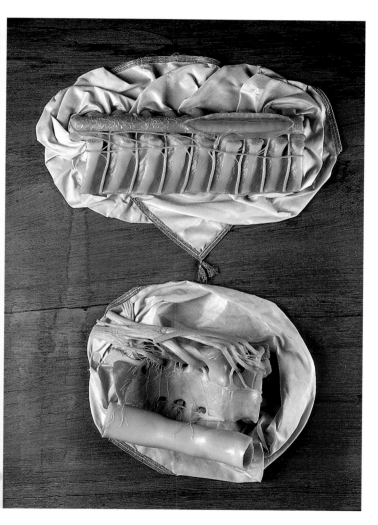

Display showing
the sympathetic
nerves and their
ganglia in the
region of the tho-
racic cage (upper
specimen) and in
the region of the
sacrum (lower
specimen)

Darstellung sympa-
thischer Nerven
und ihrer Ganglien
im Bereich des
Brustkorbs (oberes
Präparat) und im
Bereich des Kreuz-
beines (unteres
Präparat)

Nerfs et ganglions
sympathiques de la
région thoracique
(en haut) et sacrée
(en bas)

Systema digestorium et respiratorium

Viscera
Eingeweide
Appareil digestif, appareil respiratoire

Viscera

The recognition of surgery as a legitimate part of the medical faculty coincided in time with the collecting of these models and had a lasting effect on anatomical teaching and research. As a result of the new status acquired by surgery, accurate anatomical knowledge acquired a new significance. Particular attention was paid to the anatomical dissection of the organs of the thorax, abdomen and true pelvis. Continued developments dissection techniques led to increasingly detailed specimens representing the topographical (spatial) relationship between individual organs, and also their blood and nerve supply. In contrast to the drawings and woodcuts, the preparation of wax models of original specimens gave an entirely new impetus to the study of anatomy, allowing the complex structures to be represented in three dimensions.

A large number of the models in this collection show the organs within the thoracic and abdominal cavities in their natural positions. Beginning with these overall displays, many of the detailed models also show the complete extent of the individual organs together with their blood supply, and for this purpose adjacent organs were displaced from their natural relationship or completely removed from the body. In these specimens the arteries and veins are clearly distinguished, and colored either red or blue. Sections of the various organs are arranged to show their internal structure, including the relative internal measurements of hollow organs, as in the case of sections through the digestive tract in which the internal surfaces are also illustrated.

Pages · Seiten · Pages 582–583:

Whole body specimen showing the lymphatic vessels in the thoracic and abdominal cavities

Ganzkörperpräparat mit Darstellung der Lymphgefäße in Brust- und Bauchraum

Préparation du corps entier représentant les vaisseaux lymphatiques des cavités thoracique et abdominale
[XXIX, 746]

Die Anerkennung der Chirurgie als Fach der Medizin fiel zeitlich mit der **Eingeweide**
Herstellung der Modellsammlung zusammen und hatte nachhaltigen
Einfluß auf die Lehr- und Forschungsinhalte der Anatomie. In der prakti-
schen Umsetzung durch die Chirurgie erlangten die genauen Kenntnisse
der Anatomie einen neuen Stellenwert. Das besondere Interesse galt der
anatomischen Sektion der Organsysteme von Brust- und Bauchhöhle
sowie des kleinen Beckens. Immer weiter entwickelte Sektionstechniken
ermöglichten eine zunehmend detaillierte präparatorische Darstellung
der topographischen (räumlichen) Beziehungen der einzelnen Organe
sowie ihrer Gefäß- und Nervenversorgung. Im Gegensatz zu Zeichnungen und Holzschnitten eröffneten die vom Originalpräparat hergestell-
ten Wachsmodelle dem anatomischen Studium eine völlig neue Dimension, indem sie die komplexen Strukturen des menschlichen Körpers
dreidimensional wiedergaben.

Eine Vielzahl von Modellen dieser Sammlung zeigt die Organe
des Brust- und Bauchraums in ihrer natürlichen Lage. Ausgehend von
diesen Übersichtsdarstellungen sind in vielen Detailmodelle zusätzlich
die Organe in ihrer gesamten Ausdehnung sowie ihre Gefäßversorgung
zu sehen. Hierzu wurden benachbarte Organe aus ihrer natürlichen
Position verlagert oder ganz herausgenommen. Arterien und Venen sind
in diesen Präparaten zur klaren Differenzierung rot bzw. dunkelblau
koloriert. Anschnitte der verschiedenen Organe zeigen deren inneren
Aufbau, einschließlich der luminalen Größenverhältnisse von Hohlorga-
nen, wie dies beispielsweise der Anschnitt des Darms mit dem Schleim-
hautrelief verdeutlicht.

Les viscères   La chirurgie a été reconnue comme discipline médicale à part entière à l'époque où a été réalisée la collection de modèles de la Specola ; cette intégration de la chirurgie a influencé l'enseignement et la recherche en anatomie. Les connaissances précises en anatomie ont été valorisées par leur transposition dans la pratique chirurgicale.

La dissection des organes et appareils contenus dans le thorax, l'abdomen et le bassin a été l'objet d'un intérêt particulier. Le perfectionnement continu des techniques de dissection a entrainé une représentation de plus en plus détaillée des rapports topographiques entre les différents organes ainsi que la mise en évidence de leur vascularisation et de leur innervation. Contrairement aux dessins et aux gravures, le modèle en cire réalisé à partir d'une préparation originale offrait à l'étude de l'anatomie une dimension entièrement nouvelle par la représentation tridimensionnelle des structures complexes du corps humain.

Les organes du thorax ou de l'abdomen dans leur situation naturelle sont présentés par un grand nombre de modèles de cette collection. A côté de ces représentations d'ensemble, des détails des organes sont aussi représentés par de nombreux modèles comme par exemple les pédicules vasculaires. Pour permettre ces observations, les organes voisins sont alors déplacés de leur position naturelle ou entièrement enlevés. Les artères et les veines sont clairement différenciées dans ces cires par l'emploi des couleurs rouge ou bleu foncé respectivement. Les tranches de section des différents organes permettent de voir leur structure interne, ou le relief de la lumière des viscères creux comme par exemple celui de la muqueuse intestinale.

Whole body speci-
men with thoracic
and abdominal cav-
ities laid open. The
loops of the small
intestine have been
removed to display
the arteries, veins
and nerves.

Ganzkörperpräpa-
rat mit eröffneter
Brust- und Bauch-
höhle. Die Dünn-
darmschlingen
sind entfernt. Dar-
stellung von Arteri-
en, Venen und Ner-
ven

Préparation du
corps entier repré-
sentant des vis-
cères du thorax et
de l'abdomen,
l'arbre artériel et
les troncs nerveux
(les anses de l'in-
testin grêle sont
enlevées)

Ventriculus, Hepar, Vesica fellea, Omentum majus et minus

Specimen showing
the viscera, includ-
ing the stomach,
liver and lesser and
greater omentum.
The liver has been
lifted up to show
the gallbladder.

Eingeweidepräpa-
rat mit Magen,
Leber, sowie dem
kleinen und großen
Netz. Durch Anhe-
ben der Leber wird
die Gallenblase
sichtbar.

Viscères de l'abdo-
men : estomac, foie
relevé avec vésicule
biliaire, petit et
grand épiploon
(péritoine)

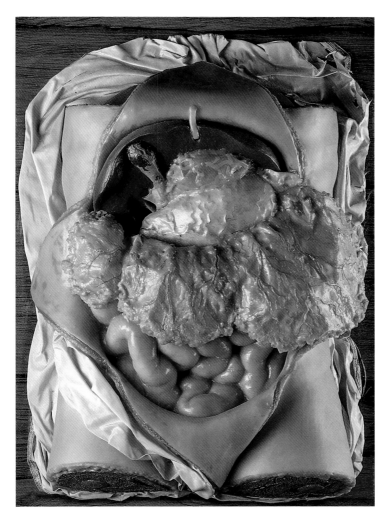

Specimen showing the viscera, including the stomach, liver and greater and lesser omentum, as well as the loops of the small intestine

Eingeweidepräparat mit Magen, Leber, großem und kleinen Netz sowie Dünndarmschlingen

Viscères de l'abdomen : estomac, foie, vésicule biliaire, anses de l'intestin grêle, petit et grand épiploon

Specimen showing
the viscera, includ-
ing the stomach,
liver, large intestine
and the lesser and
greater omentum

Eingeweidepräpa-
rat mit Magen,
Leber, Dickdarm
sowie dem kleinen
und großen Netz

Viscères de l'abdo-
men : estomac,
foie, gros intestin,
petit et grand épi-
ploon

View showing the
stomach bed

Blick auf den hinter
dem Magen gele-
genen Abschnitt
der Bauchhöhle

Région de la cavité
de l'abdomen
située en arrière de
l'estomac

Colon, Ligamentum falciforme, Ligamentum teres hepatis

View showing the loops of the small intestine and parts of the large intestine after removal of the greater omentum

Blick auf Dünndarmschlingen und Dickdarmabschnitte nach Entfernung des großen Netzes

Viscères de l'abdomen après résection du grand épiploon : foie, estomac, intestin grêle, gros intestin

View showing the loops of the small intestine and a part of the large intestine after removal of the greater omentum

Blick auf Dünndarmschlingen und einen Dickdarmabschnitt nach Entfernung des großen Netzes

Anses de l'intestin grêle et partie du gros intestin après résection du grand épiploon

View into the
abdominal cavity.
The loops of the
small intestine
have been
removed.

Einblick in die
Bauchhöhle. Die
Dünndarmschlin-
gen sind entfernt.

Cavité abdominale
après résection des
anses de l'intestin
grêle, vue du
mésentère

View of the stomach bed. The stomach has been divided

Blick in den Bauchhöhlenabschnitt hinter dem Magen. Der Magen ist durchtrennt.

Région de la cavité abdominale située en arrière de l'estomac, section de l'estomac et du grand épiploon

View of the large
intestine after
removal of the
small intestine. The
vermiform appen-
dix can be seen on
the left.

Blick auf den Dick-
darm nach Heraus-
nahme des Dünn-
darmes. Der
Wurmfortsatz ist
links im Bild zu
erkennen

Gros intestin (cae-
cum, colon) après
résection de l'intes-
tin grêle, appendice
visible en bas à
gauche

Display showing the vermiform appendix and the entry of the small into the large intestine. The opened specimens show the valve in the region of the entry.

Darstellung des Wurmfortsatzes und der Mündungsstelle des Dünndarmes in den Dickdarm. Die aufgeschnittenen Präparate zeigen die Klappe in der Mündungsregion.

Abouchement de l'intestin grêle (iléon) et de l'appendice dans le gros intestin, valve iléo-caecale

Vena mesenterica superior

Display showing
the venous
drainage of the
various parts of the
large and small
intestines

Darstellung der
venösen Abflüsse
verschiedener
Abschnitte des
Dünn- und Dick-
darmes

Réseaux veineux de
l'intestin grêle et
du gros intestin

Display showing
the arterial blood
supply of the large
intestine

Darstellung der
arteriellen Versor-
gung des Dickdar-
mes

Artères du gros
intestin

Truncus coeliacus, Arteria mesenterica superior

Display showing
the arterial blood
supply of the stom-
ach, liver, spleen
and pancreas

Darstellung der
arteriellen Versor-
gung von Magen,
Leber, Milz und
Bauchspeichel-
drüse

Artères de l'esto-
mac, du foie, de la
rate, et du pan-
créas

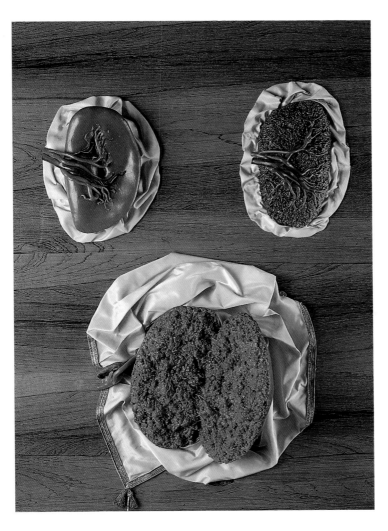

Specimens of the spleen and its vessels. The lower specimen is a bisection of the spleen.

Präparate der Milz mit ihren Gefäßen. Das untere Präparat zeigt die aufgeschnittene Milz.

Artères et veines de la rate (spléniques) ; coupe de la rate (en bas)

Truncus coeliacus

Display showing
the arterial blood
supply of the stom-
ach, liver and gall-
bladder

Darstellung der
arteriellen Versor-
gung von Magen,
Leber und Gallen-
blase

Artères de l'esto-
mac, du foie, et de
la vésicule biliaire

Specimen showing the upper abdominal organs including the hilum of the liver

Präparat der Oberbauchorgane. Magenausgang und Zwölffingerdarm sind eröffnet. Hinter dem Zwölffingerdarm liegt die Bauchspeicheldrüse.

Viscères de la partie supérieure de l'abdomen ; ouverture de la partie terminale de l'estomac et du duodénum, pancréas en arrière, foie et vésicule biliaire

Display showing the stomach, duodenum, gallbladder and pancreas

Darstellung von Magen, Zwölffingerdarm, Gallenblase und Bauchspeicheldrüse

Estomac, duodénum, vésicule biliaire, et pancréas

Display showing
the stomach
(upper specimen)
and the pancreatic
duct as far as its
entry into the duo-
denum (lower
specimen)

Darstellung des
Magens (oberes
Präparat) und des
Ausführungsgan-
ges der Bauchspei-
cheldrüse bis zu
seiner Mündung
im Zwölffinger-
darm (unteres
Präparat)

Estomac (en haut) ;
conduit excréteur
du pancréas jus-
qu'à son abouche-
ment dans le duo-
dénum (en bas)

Vena splenica

Stomach, pancreas
and splenic vein

Darstellung von
Magen, Bauchspei-
cheldrüse und
Milzvene

Estomac, duodé-
num, pancréas,
rate, et vaisseaux

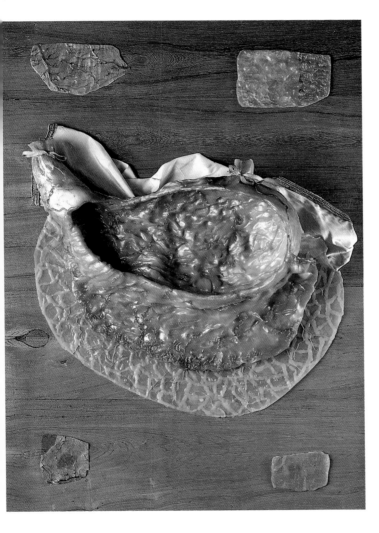

View into the
opened stomach

Blick in den eröff-
neten Magen

Estomac ouvert :
muqueuse gas-
trique

Upper specimen: stomach, duodenum, liver and gallbladder. Lower specimen: the C-shaped form of the duodenum and the pancreatic duct

Das obere Präparat zeigt Magen, Zwölffingerdarm, Bauchspeicheldrüse sowie Leber und Gallenblase. Das untere Präparat stellt die Ringfalten des Zwölffingerdarms sowie den Ausführungsgang der Bauchspeicheldrüse dar.

Duodénum, pancréas, foie et voies biliaires (en haut) ; abouchement des voies biliaires et du conduit excréteur du pancréas dans le duodénum ouvert (en bas)

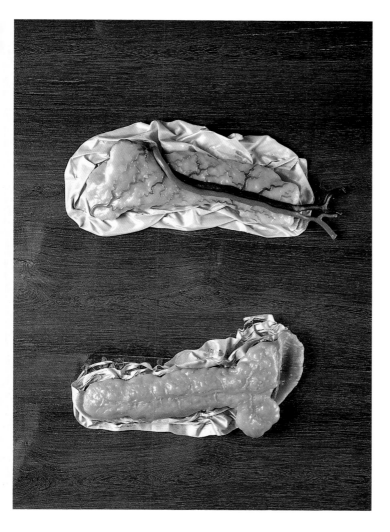

The pancreas; in
the upper speci-
men with the
splenic vessels

Darstellungen der
Bauchspeichel-
drüse, im oberen
Präparat mit Milz-
gefäßen

Pancréas et vais-
seaux spléniques

Diaphragma, Hepar, Ligamentum falciforme

Display showing
the relationship of
the liver to the
diaphragm

Darstellung der
Lagebeziehungen
von Leber und
Zwerchfell

Foie et ligament du
péritoine le reliant
au diaphragme

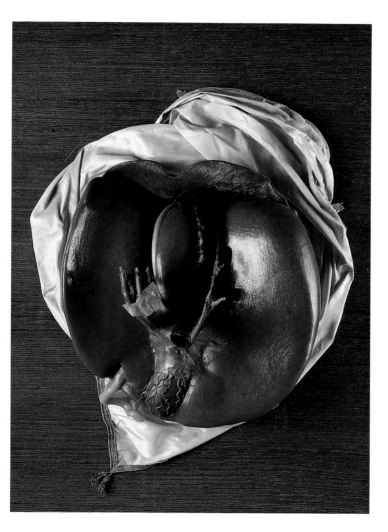

Posterior surface of
the liver showing
its various lobes
and the related
course of the infer-
ior vena cava

Leberrückfläche
mit verschiedenen
Lappen und vorbei-
ziehender unterer
Hohlvene

Face inférieure du
foie : lobes hépa-
tiques, vésicule
biliaire, hile du foie,
veine cave infér-
ieure

Vena portae

Posterior surface of
the liver showing
the vessels of the
liver

Leberrückfläche
mit Darstellung der
Lebergefäße

Face inférieure du
foie : branches de
l'artère hépatique
et de la veine porte
disséquées

Specimen showing the
diaphragm, peritoneum,
kidneys and ureters,
seen from behind

Blick von hinten auf ein
Präparat mit Zwerchfell,
Bauchfell und Nieren mit
Harnleiter

Viscères de l'abdomen
vus de l'arrière : péritoine
pariétal, reins et ure-
tères, portion de dia-
phragme conservée

Systema urogenitale et genitale

Urinary and Reproductive System
Harn- und Geschlechtsorgane
Appareil urinaire, appareil génital

Fama di un giovane eseguita da Luigi Calamai per commiss.e al posto di modellatore in cera

Urinary and Reproductive System

The wide range of exhibits in this section reflect very clearly the enlightened interest so characteristic of that time, and which was so far removed from the later prudery of the Victorian era.

The models are anatomically correct representations of the female and male reproductive organs shown in their natural position in the true pelvis. In addition, detailed specimens of functionally related organs are displayed from various points of view. Additional information is given by sections through organs which allow the observer a view into the wide or narrow inside space. Particular emphasis has been laid upon presentations of the uterus taken from the various stages of pregnancy.

The models of embryos are especially informative, as well as those which record the different stages of fetal development up to the time of delivery. Observing the specimens of infants in which the thoracic and abdominal organs are represented in detail, it is the difference in relative size of these organs as compared with those of the adult which is particularly impressive.

Harn- und Geschlechtsorgane

Das breite Spektrum der Exponate in diesem Kapitel spiegelt den aufgeklärten und interessierten Geist der damaligen Zeit eindrucksvoll wider, der sich deutlich von der späteren Prüderie des viktorianischen Zeitalters abhebt.

Die Modelle zeigen anatomisch korrekt die weiblichen und männlichen Geschlechtsorgane in ihrer natürlichen Lage im kleinen Becken. Zudem werden funktionell zueinander in Beziehung stehende Organe als Detailpräparate in verschiedenen Ansichten dargestellt. Zusätzliche Informationen liefern die Schnittpräparate der Organe, die dem Betrachter Einblicke in die verschiedenen weit oder eng gestalteten Innenräume erlauben. Einen thematischen Schwerpunkt bildet die Darstellung der Gebärmutter in den verschiedenen Stadien der Schwangerschaft.

Besonders informativ sind die Modelle der Embryonen sowie die Präparate, die die fötalen Entwicklungsstadien bis zum geburtsreifen Neugeborenen dokumentieren. Bei der Betrachtung der Säuglingspräparate mit Detaildarstellungen der Brust- und Bauchorgane sind besonders die – im Vergleich zur Organanatomie des Erwachsenen – anderen Größenverhältnisse der sich noch in der Entwicklung befindlichen Organe auffällig.

Pages · Seiten · Pages 614–615:

Male torso with the thoracic and abdominal cavities laid open

Männlicher Torso mit Einblick in die eröffnete Brust- und Bauchhöhle

Viscères du thorax, de l'abdomen, et du bassin masculin
[XXX, 447]

Le large choix des pièces concernant les organes génitaux et la grossesse reflète l'état d'esprit éclairé et intéressé qui régnait à l'époque de leur réalisation.

Des représentations anatomiques exactes des organes génitaux féminins et masculins en place dans le petit bassin sont données par plusieurs modèles en cire. A ces vues d'ensemble sont adjointes des préparations plus détaillées d'organes ayant des rapports fonctionnels mutuels, vus sous différentes incidences. Des sections et coupes apportent des précisions supplémentaires en donnant à l'observateur une vue dans les diverses cavités, plus difficilement explorables autrement.

La représentation de l'utérus aux différents stades de la grossesse est aussi un thème particulièrement étudié. Les modèles d'embryons ou les préparations démontrant les stades du développement du fœtus jusqu'à la naissance sont particulièrement instructifs. Des préparations montrent avec précision les organes thoraciques et abdominaux de nouveaux-nés ; il ressort remarquablement de leur observation les différences de proportions entre les organes du nouveau-né et ceux de l'adulte.

View of the posterior abdominal wall after removal of the abdominal viscera. Kidneys, upper urinary tract, urinary bladder, aorta and inferior vena carva

Blick auf die hintere Bauchwand nach Entfernung der Bauchorgane. Darstellung der Nieren, der Harnleiter, der Blase sowie der Bauchschlagader und der unteren Hohlvene

Reins, uretères, vessie, aorte abdominale et veine cave inférieure contre la paroi postérieure de l'abdomen après résection des autres viscères

Male urogenital tract with its blood supply. The left kidney has been cut open to reveal the calyces and renal pelvis.

Darstellung des männlichen Urogenitaltraktes mit Gefäßversorgung. Die linke Niere ist aufgeschnitten zur Darstellung der Nierenkelche und des Nierenbeckens.

Appareils urinaire et génital masculins avec leur vascularisation artérielle, coupe d'un rein : calices, bassinet

Various aspects
of the kidney

Verschiedene Dar-
stellungen der
Niere

Reins : morpholo-
gie, structure, vas-
cularisation

Specimen of the male urogenital tract showing bladder wall with seminal vesicles and prostate

Präparat des männlichen Urogenitaltraktes mit Blick auf die hintere Blasenwand mit Bläschen- und Vorsteherdrüse

Appareils urinaire et génital masculins : vessie vue de l'arrière, glandes séminales, prostate, testicules

Organs on the posterior abdominal wall of a male fetus. In the true pelvis the right and left testes can be seen. At this stage of development they have not yet reached the scrotum.

Blick auf die Organe der hinteren Bauchwand eines männlichen Föten. Im Bereich des kleinen Beckens sind rechts und links die Hoden zu erkennen, die zu diesem Zeitpunkt noch nicht im Hodensack liegen.

Appareils urinaire et génital du fœtus masculin : testicules dans la cavité abdominale et non encore descendus dans les bourses

Coverings of the
testis in a newborn
infant

Darstellung der
Hodenhüllen von
einem Neugebore-
nen

Appareil uro-géni-
tal d'un nouveau-
né : enveloppes du
testicule

Penis, Prostata, Vesica urinaria, Rectum

Specimen of a male
pelvis which has
been divided in the
midline

Präparat eines
median durch-
trennten männ-
lichen Beckens

Bassin masculin,
coupe médiane

External view of the
floor of the pelvis
showing the root of
the penis with its
nerves and vessels

Präparat des äuße-
ren Beckenbodens
sowie der Peniswur-
zel mit Nerven und
Gefäßen

Plancher du bassin
masculin (périnée) :
racine du pénis,
artères, nerfs

Vesica urinaria, Ureter, Radix penis

View into a hemi-
sected male pelvis

Einblick in ein hal-
biertes männliches
Becken

Viscères du bassin
masculin : vessie,
rectum

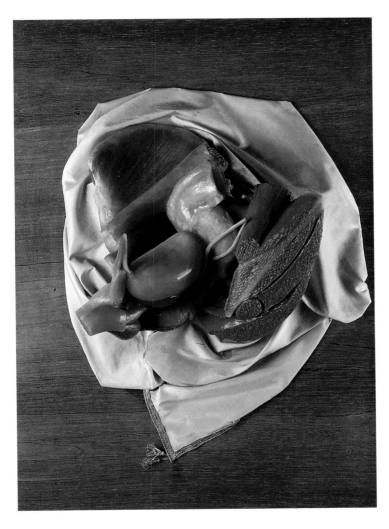

View into the male
pelvis showing
urinary bladder and
rectum

Einblick in ein
männliches Becken
mit Harnblase und
Mastdarm

Viscères du bassin
masculin : vessie,
rectum

Various aspects of male urinary bladder with prostate gland. The upper specimen on the left has been opened to show the urinary bladder and urethra.

Männliche Harnblase mit Vorsteherdrüse in verschiedenen Ansichten. Das obere linke Präparat zeigt die eröffnete Harnblase und Harnröhre.

Vessie chez l'homme, prostate, artères ; vessie et urèthre ouverts (en bas à droite)

Specimen of the male genital organs. Above center: the urethra has been laid open. Below right: the urinary bladder seen from behind and the chestnut-shaped prostate gland

Präparte von männlichen Geschlechtsorganen. Im oberen zentral gelegenen Präparat ist die eröffnete Harnröhre dargestellt. Das Präparat rechts unten zeigt die Harnblase von hinten und die kastanienförmige Vorsteherdrüse

Organes uro-génitaux masculins : urèthre ouvert (au milieu) ; vessie, prostate en forme de châtaigne, glandes séminales, vus de l'arrière (en bas à droite)

Various aspects of
the blood supply of
the penis

Verschiedene Dar-
stellungen der Blut-
versorgung des
Penis

Pénis : artères,
veines, et nerfs

Vesica urinaria, Glandula vesiculosa, Prostata, Utriculus prostaticus, Glandula bulbourethralis

Male bladder, prostate, seminal vesicle and bulbourethral gland

Darstellungen der männlichen Harnblase, Vorsteherdrüse und Bläschendrüse

Vessie chez l'homme, prostate, glandes séminales, conduit déférent

Specimen of the male urinary bladder und prostate

Darstellungen der männlichen Harnblase und Vorsteherdrüse

Vessie chez l'homme, prostate

Various aspects of testis, epididymis and their coverings

Verschiedene Darstellungen des Hodens, Nebenhodens und ihrer Hüllen

Testicules, épididyme, et enveloppes, cordon spermatique

Glandula vesiculosa, Prostata, Musculus levator ani, Musculus bulbospongiosus, Musculus bulbocavernosus

View of the male
pelvic floor from
below

Blick von unten auf
ein Präparat des
männlichen
Beckenbodens

Plancher du bassin
masculin vu du
dessous

Specimens of the
female breast

Präparate der weib-
lichen Brust

Seins, glande
mammaire

Glandula mammaria, Papilla mammae

Various specimens of the female mammary gland after removal of the skin

Verschiedene Präparate der weiblichen Brustdrüse nach Entfernung der Haut

Seins sans la peau, glande mammaire

Specimens showing the
milk ducts of the mam-
mary gland

Präparate der Milchgän-
ge der Brustdrüse

Glande mammaire,
conduits lactifères

Female urogenital
tract with its blood
supply

Darstellung des
weiblichen Uroge-
nitaltraktes mit
Gefäßversorgung

Appareils urinaire
et génital féminins
et leur vasculari-
sation

Vesica urinaria, Ureter, Uterus, Tuba uterina, Pars ampullaris tubae uterinae, Arteria et vena uterina, Arteria umbilicalis

View from in front onto the internal genital organs and urinary bladder of a woman. Above: uterine tube with the infundibulum for reception of the ova

Blick von vorne auf die inneren Geschlechtsorgane und die Harnblase der Frau. Das obere Präparat zeigt den Eileiter mit dem Trichter für die Aufnahme der Eizellen.

Organes génitaux internes féminins et vessie vus de l'avant (en bas) ; trompes utérines rattachées à l'utérus (en haut)

View from behind
onto the internal
genital organs and
urinary bladder of
a woman (lower
specimen). Above:
the clitoris and its
muscles

Blick von hinten
auf die inneren
Geschlechtsorgane
und die Harnblase
der Frau (unteres
Präparat). Das obe-
re Präparat zeigt
die Klitoris mit
ihrer Muskulatur.

Organes génitaux
internes féminins :
utérus, trompes,
vagin, et vessie vus
de l'arrière (en
bas) ; clitoris et ses
muscles (en haut)

Various aspects of
the female internal
reproductive
organs

Verschiedene Dar-
stellungen der
inneren weiblichen
Geschlechtsorgane

Organes génitaux
internes féminins

Ovar, Tuba uterina, Ligamentum teres uteri, Uterus, Portio vaginalis uteri, Vesica urinaria

Above: view of the external os ("outer mouth") of the uterus, vagina laid open. View into the opened urinary bladder

Oberes Präparat: Darstellung des äußeren Muttermundes nach Eröffnung der Scheide. Unteres Präparat: Einblick in die eröffnete Harnblase

En haut : organes génitaux internes féminins : col de l'utérus visible après ouverture du vagin. En bas : vessie ouverte

The internal repro-
ductive organs of a
woman

Darstellungen
der inneren Ge-
schlechtsorgane
der Frau

Organes génitaux
internes féminins,
artères (en haut) et
veines (en bas)

Internal reproductive organs and urinary bladder of a woman

Darstellung der inneren Geschlechtsorgane der Frau und der Harnblase

Organes génitaux féminins et vessie et leur vascularisation

View into the
opened uterus
and vagina

Einblick in die von
hinten eröffnete
Gebärmutter und
Scheide

Utérus et vagin
ouverts, vus de
l'arrière

Placenta

Pathologically
affected placenta

Krankhaft verän-
derte Plazenta

Placenta dégénéré
par une maladie

Various specimens
of the female repro-
ductive organs with
ovary, tube, uterus
and vagina

Verschiedene
Präparate der weib-
lichen Geschlechts-
organe mit Eier-
stock, Eileiter,
Gebärmutter und
Scheide

Organes génitaux
féminins : ovaire,
trompe utérine,
utérus, vagin

Specimen of a
female pelvis div-
ided in the midline

Präparat eines
median durch-
trennten weib-
lichen Beckens

Bassin féminin,
coupe médiane

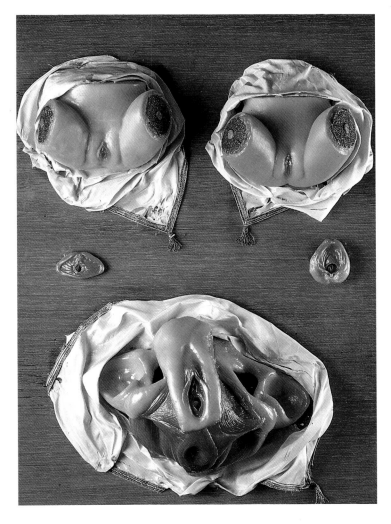

External genital
organs of a female
infant

Äußere Ge-
schlechtsorgane
eines weiblichen
Säuglings

Organes génitaux
externes féminins
du nourrisson

Organa genitalia femina externa

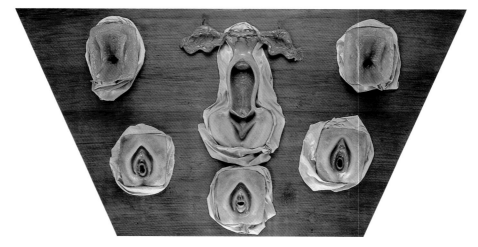

Female external genital
organs

Präparate der äußeren
weiblichen Geschlechts-
organe

Organes génitaux
externes feminins

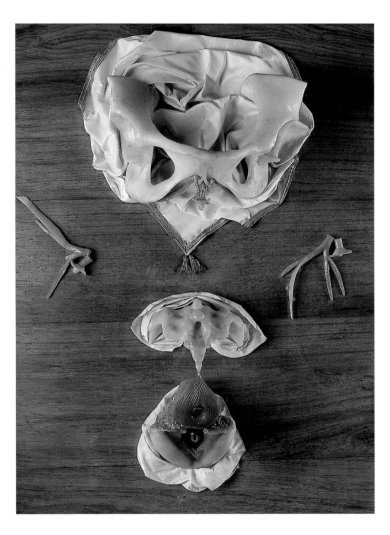

Above: female
pelvis with clitoris.
Below: view of the
coccyx and part of
the pelvic floor,
seen from below

Oberes Präparat:
Weibliches Becken
mit Darstellung der
Klitoris. Unteres
Präparat: Ansicht
auf das Steißbein
und Teile des
Beckenbodens von
unten

Bassin osseux avec
clitoris (en haut) ;
sacrum, coccyx et
partie du plancher
du bassin (en bas)

Vulva

Female external
genital organs

Darstellung der
äußeren weiblichen
Geschlechtsorgane

Organes génitaux
externes féminins
(position gynécolo-
gique)

*Pages · Seiten ·
Pages 652–653:*

Whole body
specimen seen
from below
(cf. pp. 582–583)

Ganzkörperprä-
parat in Untersicht
(vgl. S. 582–583)

Préparation du
corps entier, vu du
bas (cf. p. 582–583)

Female external
genital organs

Darstellung der
äußeren weiblichen
Geschlechtsorgane

Organes génitaux
externes féminins
(position gynécolo-
gique)

Uterus gravidus

Lower part of the belly of a pregnant woman; abdominal cavity laid open

Präparat eines Unterleibes einer Schwangeren mit eröffneter Bauchhöhle

Utérus pendant la grossesse après ouverture de la paroi abdominale

Lower part of the
belly of a pregnant
woman; abdominal
cavity laid open

Präparat eines
Unterleibes einer
Schwangeren mit
eröffneter Bauch-
höhle

Utérus à la fin de la
grossesse après
ouverture de la
paroi abdominale

Uterus gravidus

Lower part of the belly of a pregnant woman; abdominal cavity laid open. The superficial layers of the uterine wall have been removed to show the blood vessels.

Präparat eines Unterleibes einer Schwangeren mit eröffneter Bauchhöhle. Oberflächliche Schichten der Gebärmutterwand sind zur Darstellung der Blutgefäße entfernt.

Utérus à la fin de la grossesse : après ouverture de la paroi abdominale et dissection des couches superficielles de l'utérus, mise en évidence des vaisseaux utérins

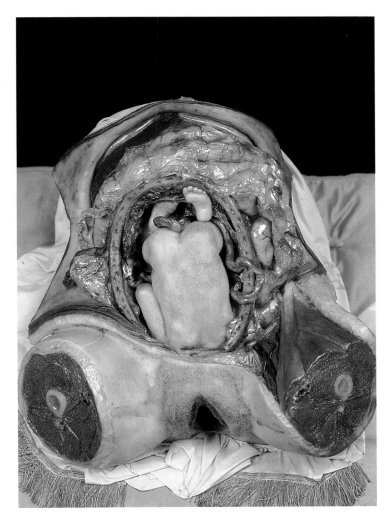

View into the
opened uterus of a
pregnant woman
during parturition

Einblick in die
eröffnete Gebär-
mutter einer
Schwangeren
während des
Geburtsvorganges

Fœtus dans l'uté-
rus ouvert

Uterus of a preg-
nant woman laid
open; dilatation of
external os

Präparat einer
eröffneten Gebär-
mutter einer
Schwangeren mit
sich öffnendem
Muttermund

Fœtus jumeaux
dans l'utérus
ouvert, béance du
col utérin

Uterus of a pregnant woman laid open

Präparat einer eröffneten Gebärmutter einer Schwangeren

Fœtus dans l'utérus ouvert

Uterus after deliv-
ery of child and
placenta

Präparat einer
Gebärmutter nach
der Geburt des Kin-
des und des Mut-
terkuchens

Utérus juste après
l'accouchement et
l'expulsion du pla-
centa (coupe
médiane)

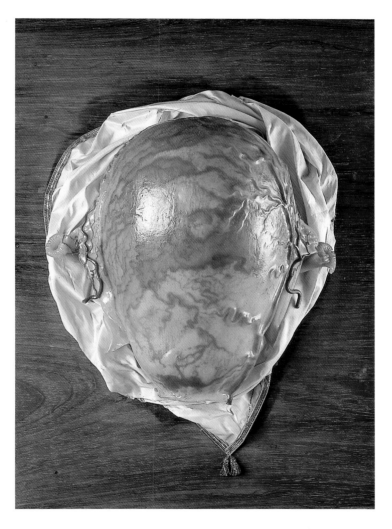

Uterus of a preg-
nant woman

Präparat der Gebär-
mutter einer
Schwangeren

Utérus pendant la
grossesse

Uterus gravidus

Uterus of a pregnant woman; deeper layer showing blood vessels

Präparat der Gebärmutter einer Schwangeren, tiefere Schicht mit Darstellung der Blutgefäße

Utérus pendant la grossesse : artères et veines

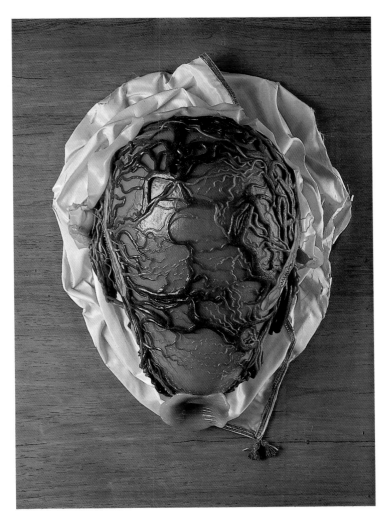

Uterus of a pregnant woman; deeper layer showing blood vessels

Präparat der Gebärmutter einer Schwangeren, tiefere Schicht mit Darstellung der Blutgefäße

Utérus pendant la grossesse : artères et veines

Uterus gravidus

Uterus of a pregnant woman; deeper layer showing blood vessels

Präparat der Gebärmutter einer Schwangeren, tiefere Schicht mit Darstellung der Blutgefäße

Utérus pendant la grossesse : couches profondes, réseaux vasculaires

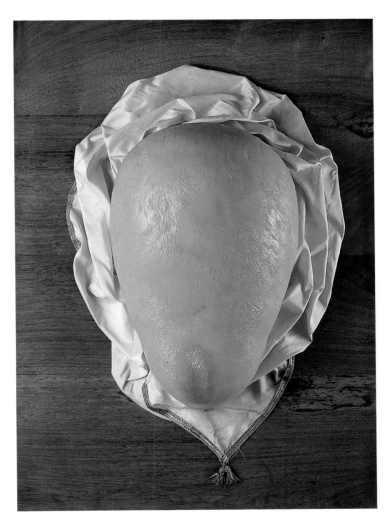

Uterus of a preg-
nant woman; uter-
ine musculature
displayed

Präparat der Gebär-
mutter einer
Schwangeren mit
Darstellung der
Gebärmuttermus-
kulatur

Utérus pendant la
grossesse : organi-
sation des fibres
musculaires

Uterus gravidus

Uterus of a pregnant woman; uterine musculature displayed

Präparat der Gebärmutter einer Schwangeren mit Darstellung der Gebärmuttermuskulatur

Utérus pendant la grossesse : organisation des fibres musculaires

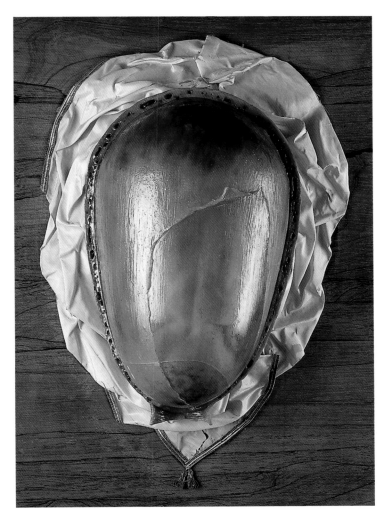

Uterus with am-
niotic sac

Präparat einer
Gebärmutter mit
Fruchtblase

Utérus ouvert et
enveloppes du
fœtus (sac amnio-
tique)

Uterus with a fetus

Präparat einer
Gebärmutter mit
Fötus

Fœtus dans l'uté-
rus ouvert

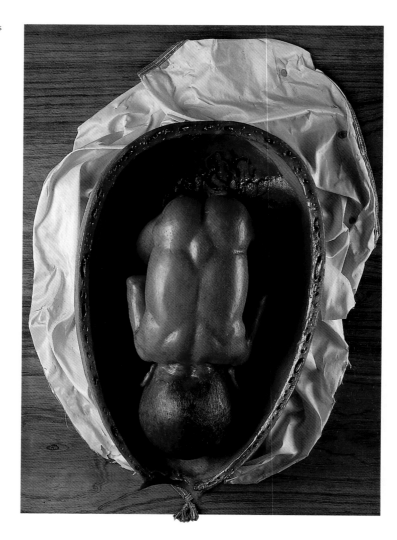

Uterus with
placenta

Präparat einer
Gebärmutter mit
Mutterkuchen

Utérus ouvert avec
le placenta

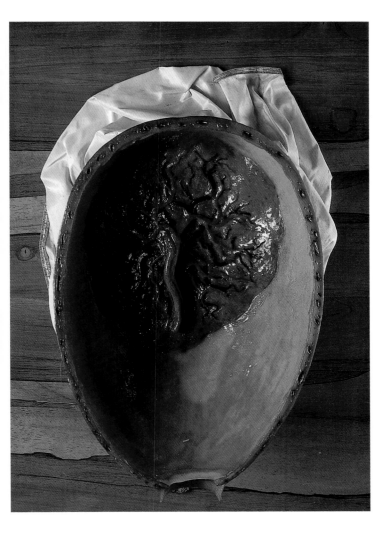

Uterus post partum

Uterus after deliv-
ery of the placenta

Präparat einer
Gebärmutter nach
der Geburt des
Mutterkuchens

Utérus ouvert
après l'expulsion
du placenta

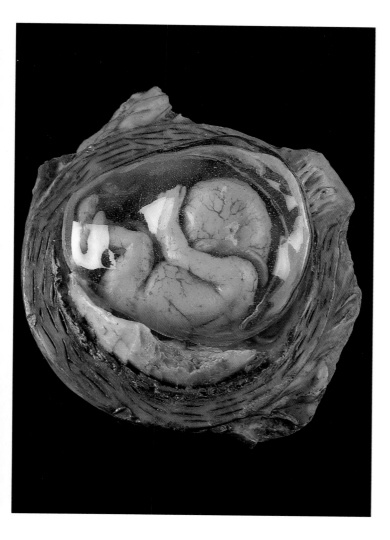

Specimen showing
a fetus within the
amniotic sac

Darstellung eines
Fötus in der Frucht-
blase

Fœtus dans le sac
et le liquide amnio-
tique dans l'utérus
ouvert

Uterus gravidus, Fetus

View of a fetus
inside the uterus

Darstellung eines
Föten in der Gebär-
mutter

Fœtus dans l'uté-
rus ouvert

View of a fetus
inside the uterus

Darstellung eines
Föten in der Gebär-
mutter

Fœtus dans l'uté-
rus ouvert

Uterus gravidus, Fetus

View of a fetus
inside the uterus

Darstellung eines
Föten in der Gebär-
mutter

Fœtus dans l'uté-
rus ouvert

The uterus of a
pregnant woman
containing the
placenta

Darstellung der
Gebärmutter einer
Schwangeren mit
Mutterkuchen

Utérus ouvert avec
le placenta

Uterus gravidus, Placenta, Fetus

The uterus of a
pregnant woman
with amniotic sac,
fetus and placenta

Darstellung der
Gebärmutter einer
Schwangeren mit
Fruchtblase, Fötus
und Mutterkuchen

Fœtus dans le sac
amniotique et pla-
centa dans l'utérus
ouvert

A newborn infant
with the thoracic
and abdominal cav-
ities laid open. The
arms and legs of
the specimen have
been damaged.

Darstellung eines
Neugeborenen
mit Einblick in den
Brust-und Bauch-
raum. Das Präparat
ist an den Armen
und Beinen
beschädigt.

Nouveau-né : vis-
cères thoraciques
et abdominaux
(membres supé-
rieurs et inférieurs
endommagés)

Graviditas extrauterina

Specimen showing
abdominal preg-
nancy

Darstellung ver-
schiedener Typen
von Bauchhöhlen-
schwangerschaften

Présentation de dif-
férents types de
grossesses extra-
utérines

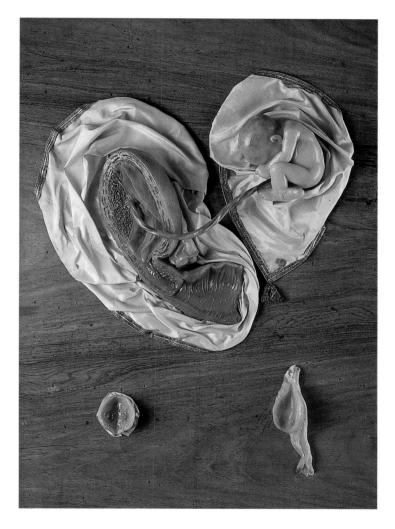

Uterus with placenta, umbilical cord and fetus

Präparat der Gebärmutter mit Mutterkuchen, Nabelschnur und Fötus

Fœtus, cordon ombilical, placenta, utérus ouvert

Placenta, Funiculus umbilicalis

Newborn infant
with umbilical cord
and placenta

Präparat des Mut-
terkuchens mit
Nabelschnur und
Neugeborenem

Nouveau-né,
cordon ombilical,
placenta

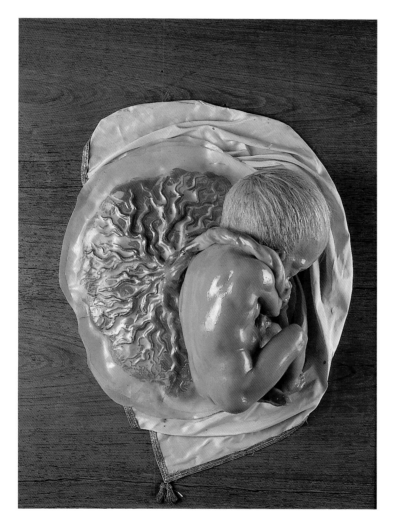

Newborn infant
with umbilical cord
and placenta

Präparat des Mut-
terkuchens mit
Nabelschnur und
Neugeborenem

Nouveau-né,
cordon ombilical,
placenta

Placenta, Fetus

Specimen to show
the blood supply
and circulation of a
fetus

Präparat zur Dar-
stellung der Blut-
versorung und des
Kreislaufes des
Föten

Fœtus : circulation
sanguine, artères et
veines ombilicales,
vascularisation du
placenta

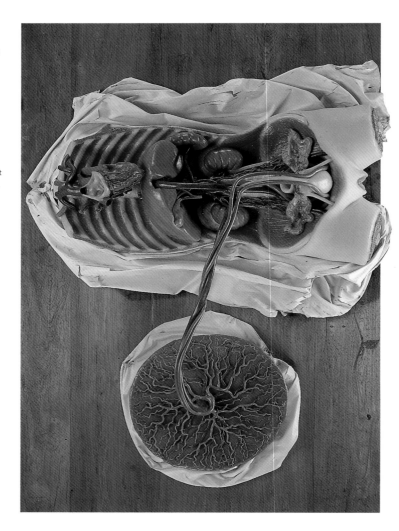

Placenta and
umbilical cord

Präparat des Mut-
terkuchens und der
Nabelschnur

Placenta et cordon
ombilical : artères
et veines

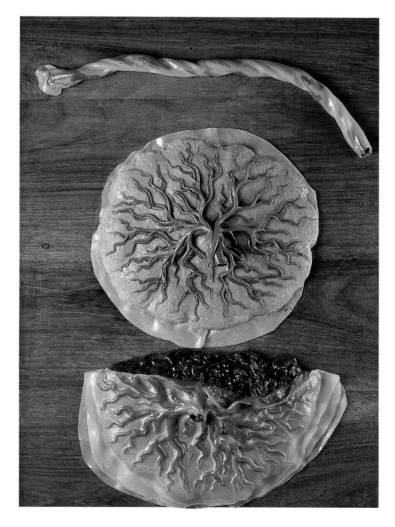

Funiculus umbilicalis, Urachus

Fetus with abdom-
inal cavity laid open
to display the
umbilical arteries
and vein

Präparat eines
Föten mit eröffne-
tem Bauchraum
zur Darstellung der
Nabelarterien und
der Nabelvene

Fœtus : artères et
veines ombilicales

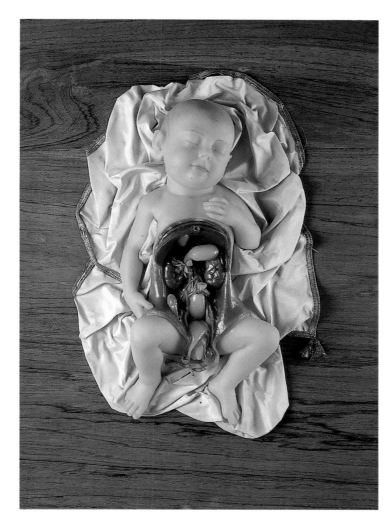

Fetus with abdominal cavity laid open and abdominal organs removed to display the urogenital system. The left testis has descended into the scrotum, the right testis is in the abdominal cavity.

Präparat eines Föten mit eröffnetem Bauchraum. Zur Darstellung der Urogenitalorgane sind die Bauchorgane entfernt. Der linke Hoden ist in den Hodensack abgestiegen, der rechte Hoden befindet sich im Bauchraum.

Fœtus : appareils urinaire et génital ; testicule gauche descendu dans les bourses, testicule droit encore dans la cavité abdominale

Fetus with thoracic
and abdominal cav-
ities laid open

Präparat eines
Föten mit eröffne-
tem Brust- und
Bauchraum

Fœtus : viscères du
thorax et de l'abdo-
men

Fetus with thoracic
and abdominal cav-
ities laid open. The
gastrointestinal
tract has been
removed to display
the kidneys.

Präparat eines
Föten mit eröffne-
tem Brust- und
Bauchraum. Der
Magendarmtrakt
ist entfernt zur
Darstellung der
Nieren.

Fœtus : viscères du
thorax et de l'abdo-
men : appareil uri-
naire

Specimen showing
the implantation of
the fertilized ovum
in the uterus and
the early develop-
mental stages of
the embryonic
membranes

Präparate zur Dar-
stellung der Einni-
stung der befruch-
teten Eizelle in die
Gebärmutter und
der frühen Entwick-
lungsstadien der
Eihüllen

Nidation de l'oeuf
fécondé dans l'uté-
rus, stades pré-
coces du dévelop-
pement des enve-
loppes de l'œuf

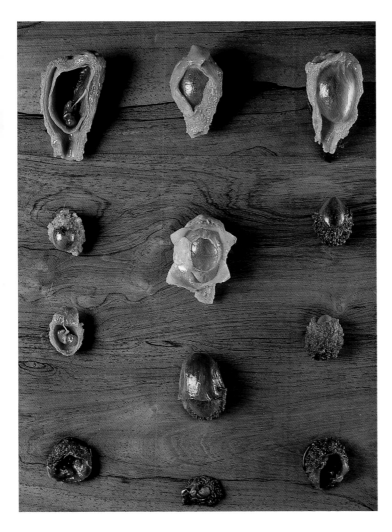

Display showing
the various devel-
opmental stages of
the embryonic
membranes and
embryo

Darstellungen ver-
schiedener Ent-
wicklungsstadien
der Eihüllen und
des Keimlings

Embryon et ses
enveloppes : stades
du développement

Uterus and fetus at
various stages of
development

Darstellung von
Gebärmutter und
Föten in verschie-
denen Entwick-
lungsstadien

Fœtus et utérus à
différents stades
du développement

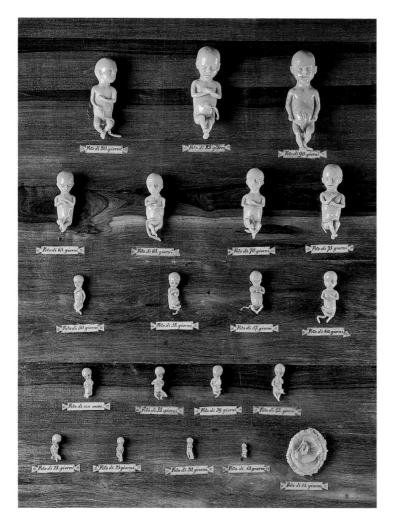

Display showing the various developmental stages of the embryo up to the third month of pregnancy

Darstellung verschiedener Stadien der Keimesentwicklung bis zum dritten Schwangerschaftsmonat

Embryons et fœtus : stades du développement jusqu'au troisième mois

Fetus, fourth
month of preg-
nancy

Darstellung von
Föten im vierten
Schwangerschafts-
monat

Fœtus au cours du
quatrième mois de
la grossesse

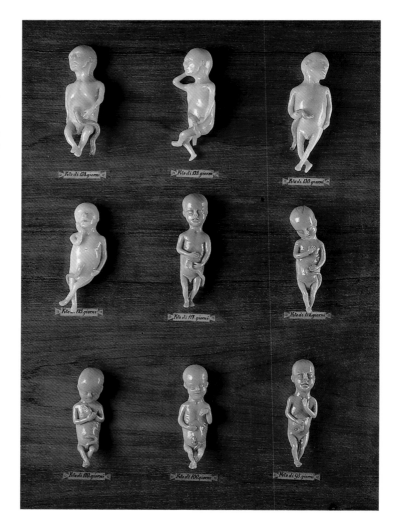

Fetus, fifth month
of pregnancy

Darstellung von
Föten im fünften
Schwangerschafts-
monat

Fœtus au cours du
cinquième mois de
la grossesse

Fetus, sixth month
of pregnancy

Darstellung von
Föten im sechsten
Schwangerschafts-
monat

Fœtus au cours du
sixième mois de la
grossesse

Fetuses, seventh
and eighth months
of pregnancy

Darstellung von
Föten im siebten
und achten
Schwangerschafts-
monat

Fœtus au septième
et au huitième
mois de la gros-
sesse

Fetus, ninth month
of pregnancy

Darstellung eines
Föten im neunten
Schwangerschafts-
monat

Fœtus au neuviè-
me mois de la
grossesse

Front view of specimen from page | Frontalansicht des Präparates von Seite |
Vue frontale de la préparation page **497**

699

"Dying cannot be experienced by anyone, it can only be observed in others."

» Das Sterben kann kein Mensch an sich selbst erfahren, sondern nur an anderen wahrnehmen.«

« Personne ne peut faire l'expérience de la Mort par soi-même mais seulement sur d'autres personnes. »

Immanuel Kant

Bibliography
Bibliographie
Bibliographie

G. D'Agostino (ed.), *Arte popolare in Sicilia*, Palermo 1991.

Aristotle /Aristoteles, *De memoria et reminiscentia*, 450a–b.

Id., *De anima*, 424a.

M. Armaroli (ed.), *Le cere anatomiche bolognesi del Settecento*, Bologna, 1981. *Atti del I Congresso Internazionale sulla Ceroplastica nella Scienza e nell'Arte. Firenze, 3–7 giugno 1975.* Biblioteca della Rivista di Storia delle Scienze Mediche e Naturali, Florence, 1977.

B. Bearzi, "Considerazioni di tecnica sul San Ludovico e la Giuditta di Donatello" (1950), *Donatello e il restauro della Giuditta*, ed. L. Dolcini, Florence, 1988, pp. 64–66.

R. Büll, *Das große Buch vom Wachs. Geschichte, Kultur, Technik*, Munich, 1977.

F. Cabrol, "Cierges", *Dictionnaire d'archéologie chrétienne et de liturgie*, III-2, Paris, 1914, col. 1613–1622.

F. Cagnetta, "Gaetano Giulio Zumbo (Siracusa 1656–Parigi 1701)", *Kunst des Barock in der Toskana. Studien zur Kunst unter den letzten Medici*, Munich, 1976, pp. 213–224.

L. Carolus-Barré, "Trois études sur le thème de la piété populaire au Moyen Age", *Actes du 99ᵉ Congrès national des sociétés savantes, I. La piété populaire au Moyen Age*, Paris, 1977, pp. 209–233.

L. Cattaneo, A. Riva, *Le cere anatomiche di Clemente Susini dell'Università di Cagliari*, Cagliari, 1993.

M. Cazort, M. Kornell, and K. B. Roberts, *The Ingenious Machine of Nature: Four Centuries of Art and Anatomy*, Ottawa, 1996.

R. Cedrini, "Il sapere vissuto", *Arte popolare in Sicilia*, ed. D. D'Agostino, op. cit., pp. 178–180.

G. Didi-Huberman, *La Peinture incarnée*, Paris, 1985.

Id., "The Portrait, the Individual and the Singular: Remarks on the Legacy of Aby Warburg", *The Image of the Individual: Portraits in the Renaissance*, eds. N. Mann and L. Syson, London, 1988, pp. 165–188.

Id., "Ressemblance mythifiée et ressemblance oubliée chez Vasari: la légende du portrait 'sur le vif'", *Mélanges de l'École française de Rome – Italie et Méditerranée*, CVI, 1994, 2, pp. 383–432.

Id., *La ressemblance informe, ou le gai savoir visuel selon Georges Bataille*, Paris, 1995.

Id., "L'image-matière: Poussière, ordure, saleté", sculpture au XVIᵉ siècle", *L'Inactuel*, no. 5, 1996, pp. 63–81.

Id., "L'image-matrice. Généalogie et vérité de la ressemblance selon 'Pline l'Ancien, Histoire naturelle, XXXV, 1–7'", *L'Inactuel*, no. 6, 1996, p. 109–125.

Id., "Image, organe, temps: Approche de l'ex-voto", *Le Fait de l'analyse*, 5, 1998, pp. 245–260.

Id., "Viscosités et survivances: L'histoire de l'art à l'épreuve du matériau", *Critique*, LIV, 611, pp. 138–162.

P. Fédida, "Le souffle indistinct de l'image" (1993), *Le Site de l'étranger: La situation psychanalytique*, Paris, 1995, pp. 187–220.

S. Freud, "Notiz über den 'Wunderblock'" (1925), *Gesammelte Werke*, XIV, London, 1948 (reprint, Frankfurt/M., 1972), pp. 3–8. (English translation: "A Note upon the 'Mystic Writing Pad'", *The Standard Edition of the Complete Psychological Works of Sigmund Freud*, XIX, London, 1953–1974; traduction française: "Note sur le 'bloc-notes magique', Résultats, idées, problèmes, II. 1921–1938, Paris, 1985, pp. 119–124).

T. Gantner, *Geformtes Wachs*, Basel, 1980.

A Giannini and G. Zampi, *Le cere del Museo dell'Istituto Fiorentino di Anatomia patalogica*, Florence, 1980.

P. Giansiracusa (ed.), *Gaetano Giulio Zumbo*, Milan, 1988.

Id., *Vanitas Vanitatum: Studi sulla ceroplastica di Gaetano Giulio Zumbo*, Syracuse, 1991.

J. W. Goethe, "Diderots Versuch über die Malerei" (1799), *Sämtliche Werke, Band 18, Ästhetische Schriften 1771–1805*, Frankfurt/M., 1998, p. 574. (Traduction française: *Écrits sur l'art*, Paris, p. 205).

E. H. Gombrich, *Kunst und Illusion. Zur Psychologie der bildlichen Darstellung*, Cologne, 1967. (English translation: *Art and Illusion. A Study in the Psychology of Pictorial Representation*, London, 1959; traduction française: *L'Art et l'illusion: Psychologie de la représentation picturale*, Paris, 1971).

A. Harvey and R. Mortimer, *The Funeral Effigies of Westminster Abbey*, Woodbridge, 1994.

H. W. Janson, "Realism in Sculpture: Limits and Limitations", *The European Realist Tradition*, ed. G. P. Weisberg, Bloomington, 1982, pp. 290–301.

E. H. Kantorowicz, *The King's Two Bodies: A Study in Medieval Political Theology*, Princeton, 1957, pp. 419–437 (French translation: *Les Deux*

Corps du roi. Essai sur la théologie politique au Moyen Age, Paris, 1989, pp. 303–315).

H. Kleindienst, Ästhetische Anatomie aus Wachs: Ursprung, Genese, Intergration, Ph.D. diss., University of Marburg, 1989.

P. Klossowski, Nietzsche et le cercle vicieux, Paris, 1991.

H. König and E. Ortenau, Panoptikum. Vom Zauberbild zum Gaukelspiel der Wachsfiguren, Munich, 1962.

L. Kriss-Rettenbeck, Ex Voto. Zeichen, Bild und Abbild im christlichen Votivbrauchtum, Zurich – Freiburg i.B., 1972.

J. Lacan, Le Séminiare, II: Le moi dans la théorie de Freud et dans la technique de la psychanalyse (1954–1955), Paris, 1978, pp. 177–203 (Deutsche Übersetzung: Das Seminar, Buch II. Das Ich in der Theorie Freuds und in der Technik der Psychoanalyse (1954–1955), Olten–Freiburg i.B., 1980, pp. 189–219).

B. Lanza, M. L. Azzaroli, M. Poggesi, A. Martelli, Le Cere Anatomiche della Specola, Florence, 1979.

B. Lanza and M. L. Azzaroli (eds.), La ceroplastica nella scienza e nell'arte: Atti del I Convegno internazionale, Florence, 1997.

Id., Le cere anatomiche della Specola, Florence, 1979.

M. Lemire, Artistes et mortels, Paris, 1990.

F. Lexa, La Magie dans l'Égypte antique, de l'ancien Empire jusqu'à l'époque copte, Paris, 1925, no. I, pp. 75–79, and no. II, pp. 87–98, 105–117, 185–206.

R. W. Lightbown, "Le cere artistiche del Cinquecento", Arte illustrata, III, 1970, nos. 30–33, pp. 46–55, and nos. 34–36, pp. 30–39.

Id., "Gaetano Giulio Zumbo, I: the Florentine Period", The Burlington Magazine, CVI, 1964, 740, pp. 486–496.

E. Mangenot, "Agnus Dei", Dictionnaire de théologie catholique, I–1, Paris,1930, col. 605–613.

G. Masi, "La ceroplastica a Firenze nei secoli XV e XVI e la famiglia Benintendi", Rivista d'arte, IX, 1916, pp. 126–136.

G. Mazzoni, I bòti della SS. Annunziata a Firenze. Curiosità storica, Florence, 1923.

E. Panofsky, "Artist, Scientist, Genius: Notes on the Renaissance-Dämmerung", The Renaissance, A Symposium, New York, 1952, pp. 77–93 (Traduction française: L'Œuvre d'art et ses significations, Paris, 1969).

U. Pfistermeister, Wachs: Volkskunst und Brauch, Nuremberg, 1982.

Pliny the Elder / Plinius der Ältere / Pline l'Ancien, Natural History, VIII, 215; XXI, 83–85; XXXV, 1–14; XXXV, 1–7.

J. Pope-Hennessy and R. W. Lightbown, Catalogue of Italian Sculpture in the Victoria and Albert Museum, London, 1964, II, pp. 417–32, 465–74.

M. Praz, "Le pesti dello Zumbo" (1960), Il giardino dei sensi. Studi sul manierismo e il barocco, Milan, 1975, p. 401–408.

M. Raven, "Wax in Egyptian Magic and Symbolism", Oudheidkundige Mededelingen uit het Rijksmuseum van Oudheden te Leiden, LXIV, 1983, pp. 7–47.

D. A. F. de Sade, Voyage d'Italie, ou dissertations critiques, historiques, politiques et philosophiques sur les villes de Florence, Rome – Naples (1775–1776), Œuvres complètes, Paris, 1973, XVI.

Id., Histoire de Juliette, ou les prospérités du vice (1797), ibid.

J. von Schlosser, Geschichte der Porträtbildnerei in Wachs. Ein Versuch. Jahrbuch der Kunsthistorischen Sammlungen des Allerhöchsten Kaiserhauses, vol. 29, Vienna – Leipzig 1910/11, pp. 171–258 (reprint ed. T. Medicus, Berlin, 1993). (Traduction française: Histoire du portrait en cire, Paris, 1997).

B. Schultz, Art and Anatomy in Renaissance Italy, Ann Arbor, 1985.

S. Waldmann, Die lebensgrosse Wachsfigur: Eine Studie zu Funktion und Bedeutung der keroplastischen Poträtfigur vom Spätmittelalter bis zum 18. Jahrhundert, Munich, 1990.

A. Warburg, "Italienische Kunst und internationale Astrologie im Palazzo Schifanoja zu Ferrara" (1912), Ausgewählte Schriften und Würdigungen, ed. D. Wuttke, Baden-Baden, 1992 (Traduction française: Essais florentins, Paris, 1990).

Id., "Bildniskunst und Florentinisches Bürgertum: Domenico Ghirlandajo in Santa Trinità, Die Bildnisse des Lorenzo de'Medici und seiner Angehörigen, ibid., pp. 65–102.

Front cover:
Anterior view of the right eyeball in the orbital cavity and the course of the
cutaneous nerves of the first branch of the trigeminal nerve (cf. p. 506)

Spine:
Anterior aspect of the heart seen from the left (cf. p. 342)

Back cover:
Whole body specimen showing the vessels and lymph nodes within the
abdominal cavity (cf. pp. 426–427)

The figures in square brackets in the running headers give information about
the location of the works shown here from the La Specola Museum. The Roman
numerals indicate the room, the Arabic numerals the display cabinet.

In den Kolumnentiteln geben die Angaben in eckigen Klammern Auskunft über
den Standort der abgebildeten Werke im Museum La Specola: Die römischen
Ziffern bezeichnen den Saal, die arabischen die Vitrine.

Les chiffres entre crochets apparaissant dans les titres courants désignent
l'emplacement des œuvres au musée La Specola : les chiffres romains indiquent les salles, les chiffres arabes les vitrines.

© 1999 Benedikt Taschen Verlag GmbH
Hohenzollernring 53, D–50672 Köln

Concept by Volker Gebhardt, Cologne
Edited by Petra Lamers-Schütze, Yvonne Havertz, Cologne
Design by Claudia Frey, Cologne
Cover design by Angelika Taschen, Cologne
Production by Ute Wachendorf, Cologne

Anatomical texts by Monika v. Düring
Anatomical captions by Monika v. Düring,
Volker Gebhardt, Jürgen Goldschmidt
English translation by Fiona Elliott (Marta Poggesi), Brian Holmes (Georges
Didi-Huberman), Francis Steel and Britta Fricke (Monika v. Düring et al.)
German translation by Daniele dell'Agli (Marta Poggesi), Stefan Barmann
(Georges Didi-Huberman)
French translation by Thérèse Chatelain-Südkamp (Marta Poggesi),
Henri Sick and Jean-Marie Le Minor (Monika v. Düring et al.)

Printed in Germany
ISBN 3–8228–7613–5